ISLAM IN PERSPECTIVE:
A GUIDE TO ISLAMIC SOCIETY, POLITICS AND LAW

ISLAM IN PERSPECTIVE
A GUIDE TO ISLAMIC SOCIETY, POLITICS AND LAW

PATRICK BANNERMAN

ROUTLEDGE
London and New York
for
THE ROYAL INSTITUTE OF
INTERNATIONAL AFFAIRS
London

First published in 1988 by
Routledge
a division of Routledge, Chapman and Hall
11 New Fetter Lane, London EC4P 4EE

Published in the USA by
Routledge
a division of Routledge, Chapman and Hall, Inc.
29 West 35th Street, New York NY 10001

Printed and bound in Great Britain by
Biddles Ltd, Guildford and King's Lynn

Phototypeset in 10pt Baskerville by
Mews Photosetting, Beckenham, Kent

British Library Cataloguing in Publication Data

Bannerman, Patrick
Islam in perspective: a guide
to Islamic society, politics and law.
1. Islam — Revival — Political aspects
I. Title
297'.1977

ISBN 0-415-01015-2

Contents

Contents

Preface

Today we are all increasingly involved with Muslims: some of us work in the Muslim world; some have business dealings with Muslims; and some have Muslim friends and neighbours. However, while recognizing that Muslim beliefs and practices are central influences on individual Muslims and on Muslim society, we may have difficulty in understanding what Islam is and what it means to Muslims. That difficulty is often compounded by the diversity in beliefs and practices. There are, of course, many valuable academic studies of Islam, using that term in its widest sense. However, having spent most of my working life working with Muslims and studying the history, politics, culture, and society of the Muslim world, I have come to the conclusion that these studies are not wholly satisfactory for those who seek a broad understanding of Islam today and of its historical development, but who may have neither the time nor the inclination to embark upon a rigorous academic examination of Islam. It follows that I believe that a different approach is more practical.

This volume draws together my thinking and my conclusions about Islam. It is, admittedly, selective in that I have concentrated upon those aspects which are of most concern to my colleagues: my aim has been to provide a general background and a broadly based consideration of the Islamic revival rather than a detailed and comprehensive study. Many of the themes and ideas elaborated in what follows have been developed over a number of years: but the opportunity to clarify my thinking, test my ideas against the evidence, and set them down in connected form did not occur until I was granted a sabbatical year, which I spent as Diplomat-in-Residence in the Woodrow Wilson Department of Government and Foreign Affairs of the University of Virginia in Charlottesville.

I must stress, however, that the views, opinions, and interpretations set out in this study are my own: they do not necessarily represent those of the Foreign and Commonwealth Office (FCO).

There are a number of technical points which should be noted, mostly relating to transliteration, which is always problematic. In what follows I have generally omitted diacritical marks but have otherwise followed the transliteration system which I learned as a student. I have not, however, distinguished between an *'ayn* and a *hamza*, both of which are indicated by an apostrophe. To do so

vii

seemed to me to be otiose for Arabists and to clutter the text unnecessarily for others. Plurals of Arabic words have normally been formed by simply adding an 's' to the singular. For convenience, I have used the Arabic for theological, doctrinal, legal, and other technical terms, but in order to assist the reader I have appended a full glossary of such terms. I have also appended brief biographical notes on the major historical figures mentioned or cited in this study since I consider the alternative — parenthetical explanations — is distracting. I have nevertheless inserted a brief definition when a term is used for the first time. Finally, I have included suggestions for further reading, but these are both selective and subjective.

It is, of course, a privilege to appear under the imprimatur of the Royal Institute of International Affairs. I am accordingly grateful to the Institute for its ready agreement to a sponsorship which seems entirely appropriate in view of my employment. I am also grateful to both the FCO and the University of Virginia for making this study possible. My thanks are due to my temporary academic colleagues in Charlottesville for their support, interest and encouragement; to the many friends I made in Charlottesville, who helped to make my stay there an unforgettable experience; and to the students, who made intelligent and stimulating company. It is always invidious to single out individuals, but I must note in particular Robert Evans and Inis Claude among my academic colleagues; Cora and Grover Pitts and Nesta Ramazani among my friends; and a small but very lively group of disputatious students. I would also like to place on record my thanks to my long-suffering colleagues in the FCO Research Department.

Finally, there are two people who have greatly influenced both the shape and content of this study. Ruhi Ramazani gave me much help and encouragement during my year in Charlottesville and introduced me to the gentle art of, to use his own words, 'what is known in the jargon as conceptualization'. James Piscatori provided inspiration, severe but constructive criticism, and encouragement, all in generous measure. The virtues of this volume are as much his as my own.

J.P.B.
December 1987
London

Introduction

Since the mid-1970s, if not earlier, the Western world has experienced a surge of interest, almost to the point of obsession, in Islam, and in particular in its political manifestations and political significance. This surge has been fuelled primarily by a belated recognition of the phenomenon characterized as the 'Islamic revival' and by the problems of dealing with the results of the Iranian revolution, which has been erroneously described as an 'Islamic revolution' and as 'fundamentalist'. The emergence of 'Islamic fundamentalism', seen by many as an hitherto unknown concept (notwithstanding its impeccable antecedents), the activism and violence of Islamic groupings in Egypt (culminating in the assassination of President Sadat), President Zia ul-Haq's much publicized imposition of 'Islamic principles' in Pakistan, the seizure of the Grand Mosque in Mecca in 1979, President Nimeiri's drive for 'Islamization' in the Sudan, and the emergence of so-called 'fundamentalist' tendencies in many parts of the Muslim world have all given added impetus to that surge of interest as Western governments (and that of the USSR, for that matter) have attempted to assess the general implications, durability, and political significance of the 'revival'. Other possibly significant factors have been the accession to economic power (albeit probably transient) of the major oil-producing states, many of which are Muslim; the ascription to them of a degree of political clout which few actually have and which fewer have sought or welcomed; concern about the fiscal policies of such states and the potential effects on the international economic system; the increased acerbity in the superpower relationship; Arab and Muslim impatience at the continued failures of others to achieve a resolution of the Arab–Israeli dispute and of its extension into the Lebanese quagmire; and the emergence of the Organisation of the Islamic Conference as a significant and potentially extremely powerful grouping.

As a result there has been a spectacular increase in publications, conferences, and workshops all seeking to analyse and to explain Islam to the public, whether informed or otherwise. Commenting on Islam has been a growth industry, with the product ranging from often ill-informed, superficial and misleading newspaper articles through popular potboilers to more scholarly and thoughtful periodical articles and books.[1] However, much of the industry is

1

flawed: 'misunderstandings of Islam and its theories and practices are rife, fundamental errors concerning the history of Islam are continually repeated, and a very confusing picture of the historical and political perspectives which influence the views of Muslims is presented.'[2] There are five main reasons for this state of affairs as far as non-Muslim writers are concerned. There is first a tendency to address the subject on the simplistic assumption that Islam is monolithic and thus to ignore the real diversity found in the Muslim world. Second, many treat Islam, particularly in the context of the 'revival', as a matter of faith and ritual alone, although lip-service is paid to the wider context. Third, many perceive the 'revival' as a socio-economic phenomenon on which belief and doctrine are a transient, ill-defined, and indirect influence. Fourth, assessments are frequently based too much on what Muslims *say* and too little on what they *do*, and vice versa. Fifth, the historical, social, and cultural environment is too often ignored.

Nor are we better served by modern Muslim commentators, who tend to be either polemical or apologetic in tone. Generally, they seek to demonstrate the superiority of Islam compared with Western, and other, ideologies by comparing Muslim doctrine with *their* perception of existing Western practice; by asserting on less than justifiable grounds that the theories and practices underpinning Western ideological, executive, and administrative systems were first identified, defined, or enunciated in the *Qur'an* or by the first generation of Muslims (while, paradoxically, rejecting those systems as alien and un-Islamic); by attributing the Muslim world's lack of power, unity, and significance to a combination of past imperial and colonial exploitation, continued cultural and economic imperialism (never clearly defined), government deviation from 'correct' Muslim principles and practice (never explained in detail); and by frequent use of bald unsubstantiated statements in preference to rigorous thought and research. Some also seek to discard some fourteen centuries of history and development as apparently both deviant and irrelevant; but they do not seem to recognize that the logic of their argument that there has been no genuine Muslim community since the period of the *Rashidun* (the 'Rightly Guided', the first four successors to Muhammad as leader of the community) is that there are no genuine Muslims and therefore no one who can define what a genuine Muslim community is or who can interpret the *Qur'an* and the *Sunna* (the practice and sayings of the Prophet as recorded in the *hadith* — pl. *ahadith*, the Traditions) secure in the knowledge that the interpretation is accurate and correct.[3]

2

These broad conclusions pose a major problem for a proper appraisal of the 'revival' and its more violent and extreme extension, those generally called radicals or 'fundamentalists'. Such an assessment must logically rest upon a sound comprehension of what has been revived and of the historical development which has made Muslims what they are today; and in such a process, a sound understanding of doctrine and the way it has developed is an important factor. Accordingly, the work of earlier scholars of Islam, both Muslim and non-Muslim, was examined to see what light it might throw on today's problems. Here too, however, the general conclusion was that their views were in some respects unsatisfactory in any consideration of the significance of Islam today. That this should be so is, it may be argued, inevitable since not only has the world changed since they wrote but also additional information, new sources, and further studies have changed perceptions. Scholarship is, after all, dynamic rather than static. There are, however, additional reasons which are equally important. The emphasis tended to be on theory and doctrine, with little attention being paid to actual practice. Thus, the ideal rather than reality is the basis of much of the earlier work. In addition, there is a concentration on the classical formulations, little proper attention to developments since about the tenth century CE, and the perpetuation of a number of propositions which are at least dubious today: for example, acceptance that 'the gate of *ijtihad*' (independent reasoning) was closed for all time; or the somewhat uncritical acceptance of the classical doctrine on the sources of Muslim law; the failure to deal satisfactorily with the dichotomy between the concept of the universal *umma* (the community of believers) and the concept of the state; or the perpetuation of the myth that man is in some sense God's viceregent on Earth.[4]

However, these criticisms of both modern and earlier scholars should not be taken to imply a complete rejection of their thinking and of their work: for it will be clear in what follows that this volume could not have been produced had it not been for their work. In addition, it must be recognized that there are exceptions to the general rule. Among modern scholars, individuals such as John Voll, Hamid Enayat, John Esposito, Mohamed S. El-Awa, Albert Hourani, Noel Coulson, Majid Khadduri, and James Piscatori might be cited, and no modern observer can afford to ignore the contributions of scholars such as Goldziher, Gibb, Schacht, Rashid Ridha, and Muhammad Abduh.[5] However, the research and study which prompted this volume did suggest that there might be

3

another approach to the definition, identification, or perception of both the totality of Islam and particular aspects of it which might provide a more practical basis for analysis, therefore offering a different starting-point for an assessment of the resurgence of Islam and of its more violent manifestations. No startling new theory is offered, however: merely an examination of the evidence from a more practically oriented perspective.

Although for Muslims, matters of pure faith or religion are central — the belief in the unity and uniqueness of God, belief in the prophethood of Muhammad and in the finality of the revelation, and so on — these are of less significance to non-Muslims except as part of the background. More important is the manner in which God's will has been interpreted and how Muslims will react in given circumstances. This requires a sound understanding of doctrine and theory — but an understanding which is qualified by the manner in which they are put into practice: for the Muslim historical experience is, not surprisingly, one of pragmatic adaptation of the ideal to reality, a point which is often overlooked. Moreover, since history — or historical development — is a continuum rather than a series of self-contained episodes, a study of past developments is often valuable in considering the present, and a study of past intellectual influences is part of the study of past developments. This line of reasoning suggests a logical framework: an examination of general perceptions of Islam, followed by an examination of particular aspects of Islam, and then of intellectual influences on current thinking in the Muslim world. Only then can the revival be considered rationally.

Accordingly, the chapters that follow will examine perceptions of Islam generally and of particular — and selective — aspects of Islam, intellectual influences which have affected the development of the resurgence of Islam, and the 'revival' itself. In so doing, however, the concentration will be on Sunni Islam since, for the purposes of this volume, the differences between Sunni and Shi'a relate primarily to the law and to the question of authority and government. Where necessary, the differences will be noted. It is not, of course, the intention to provide a modern version of Gibb's *Mohammedanism* or of Guillaume's *Islam*:[6] some understanding is assumed and the thrust is on the broader picture. In addition, the selective treatment reflects the interests of those who have to deal with Islam and Muslims in a practical manner. The areas which will be examined are: Muslim law and the legal system; the political system, which will be approached in terms of concepts

4

of state, government, and authority; the economic system; and the conduct of international relations.

Before commencing that examination there are three questions which have been raised in a variety of forms and which need to be addressed:

(a) Why should a person directly involved in the process of formulating and implementing foreign policy find it interesting or necessary to study Islam; or what has, in other words, prompted the study which has resulted in this volume?

(b) Why are other people's treatments of Islam unsatisfactory from a practitioner's point of view?

(c) Why have secondary and translated sources been used in preference to sources in the original language?

The first question betrays an unfortunate and all too prevalent point of view which denies Islam any influence on or connection with many aspects of national activity and implicitly relegates it to a limited role as a faith, thus ignoring both the claims of devout Muslims and the evidence of at least the past decade or so. After all, it occasions no surprise that Western governments and those who do business with the Soviet Union should devote considerable resources to the study and analysis of communist ideology as a necessary precursor to judging Soviet intentions, objectives, and responses, nor that the Soviet Union similarly studies Western ideologies. Why, then, should it be seen as unusual or wasteful of resources to do likewise for a belief system which informs the attitudes and perceptions of some 900 million people in more than fifty states?

Some of the shortcomings of orthodox views of Islam have already been touched upon and will be further elaborated in what follows, but there are a number of underlying difficulties which are worth stressing. Most non-Muslim commentators are either theorists who are concerned with theory and not with practice or are persons who seek to categorize Islam within a sociological, anthropological, or socio-political framework which is neither helpful nor appropriate. They seek to identify Islam and its role or influence in terms which do not give full weight to its social, cultural, political, and historical significance, seeking to explain trends in the Muslim world in terms of material issues alone. Muslim commentators today generally seek to apply classical doctrine to the modern world in such a way as to highlight the apparent gap between practice and

5

theory and excoriate Muslims for failing to measure up to the ideal, but practically unattainable, Qur'anic standards. They also, of course, find it difficult to accept the concept of dynamic change and are often concerned to counter misconceptions: the result is often polemical or apologetic and, although valid in its own right, not particularly helpful in purely practical terms. In short, other treatments tend to be intellectual exercises which are more or less divorced from reality rather than offering up practical guidance, preferably laced with a healthy admixture of theory and doctrine, or are partisan in the sense that they are polemic or apologetic.

Finally, secondary sources and translations have been used extensively and quite deliberately. This is, I recognize, open to criticism but it has been done intentionally. First, there has been a considerable increase in the availability of translations from Arabic, Hindi, Urdu, and Persian which has made available to a much wider audience material hitherto restricted to those able to read the original. Second, this study is necessarily directed towards my colleagues and their counterparts elsewhere. It is, of course, hoped that it might also appeal to a wider general audience with an interest in the subject matter but little linguistic skills. On both counts, the use of translated material and secondary sources seems justified since this can only extend both knowledge and understanding of Islam, of Muslims, and of their attitudes, concepts, and preoccupations.

1
Ways of Looking at Islam

Introduction

Five main reasons were cited in the Introduction for the fact that 'misunderstandings of Islam and its theories and practices are rife, fundamental errors concerning the history of Islam are continually repeated, and a very confusing picture of the historical and political perspectives which influence the views of Muslims is presented'.[1] Of these, the most glaring is that non-Muslim commentators too often address the subject on the simplistic assumption that Islam is monolithic, thus ignoring the remarkable diversity to be found in reality. Admittedly, some Muslim writers also perpetuate the myth,[2] but it is a fundamental misconception which has been neatly summed up by one commentator, who asks:

> Why should Islam be any more one-dimensional than say Christianity or Marxism, to mention just two of its ideological counterparts? . . . But in their overwhelming preoccupation to explain the current Islamic revival, the modern Islamicists rarely ask themselves why Islamic praxis should be any less varied, any less multidimensional, any less divergent from its doctrinal ideal than other ideologically inspired and defined social behaviour.[3]

One answer is that many of the non-Muslim commentators perceive Islam — and in particular, the Islamic revival — as both alien and hostile, and that such a flawed interpretation is characteristic of those who perceive a particular ideological group as alien and hostile. Thus, American Russophobes attribute to Soviet leaders a devotion to Marxist ideology and principles far more rigorous than the devotion to capitalist and Christian principles which they require in their own leaders, while Soviet leaders attribute to the West generally and to the United States in particular a doctrinaire capitalist orthodoxy which is both false and unrealistic.

It is certainly the case that the exceptions to the general rule tend to a more sympathetic and perceptive view of Islam and stress the diversity. Thus, one leading authority comments that 'while there is a unity in Islamic belief, there is also a variety of understandings both as to its implications and its implementation', and refers to 'the divergence (*ikhtilaf*) of thought and action which has existed and continues to exist in the Muslim world'. Similarly, another notes that

> the only definite thing one can say about the term 'Islam' is that it is Protean and imprecise. Every Muslim can agree that the profession of faith, 'there is no God but God and Muhammad is his Prophet', is an article of faith and not susceptible to differing interpretations, but there is little agreement that many other principles and ideas mean the same to everyone and are beyond question and change.[4]

As for Muslim commentators, the answer may be that an unwillingness to address the state plurality to be found in the Muslim world and to reconcile it with the concept of the universal *umma* has caused them to concentrate upon the unity of Islam and upon theory and doctrine. A subsidiary reason might be an unconscious belief that only in this way will it be possible for the Muslim world to hold its own against competing ideologies. Again, however, there are exceptions. One scholar, for example, has pointed out that

> Muslims do not have a unified and monolithic perception of their faith any more than the followers of other great religions. However much the orthodox dislike it, different groups of Muslims interpret the various Quranic injunctions and Prophetic sayings differently — each according to its historical background, and the realities encircling it — and not always in terms conducive to a dictatorial conduct of individual and social affairs.[5]

These quotations serve to illustrate a number of problems about the approach of some commentators. There are widely divergent interpretations of even the most fundamental issues. Compare, for example, the different views on the nature, qualifications, and attributes of the *imam* as between Sunnis, Shi'a, Zaidis, and the Ibadhis; or differing views on the doctrine of *taqiyya* (prudential caution, often mistranslated as 'dissimulation').[6] Moreover, since differing interpretations and attitudes depend in part on the historical, geographical, cultural, and political context, it is unwise to attribute to the entire Muslim community the views and attitudes of one particular national group. It is even more misleading, if not positively dangerous, to extrapolate to the entire Muslim community the experiences, interpretations, and professed attitudes of that relatively small, though influential, group, the intellectuals, on the rare occasions when they exhibit some degree of unanimity: for the great majority of Muslims do not normally concern themselves overmuch with doctrine and theory, preferring to devote their energies to more mundane but necessary occupations such as making a living. This is not to suggest that they are not devout and sincere Muslims, that they neither think or care about Islam, or that they will be indifferent to the exhortations of the activists and theoreticians. Nor does it mean that they are uncultured, since

> a recent analysis of the contemporary Arab experience applies to the Muslim world in general. 'Whether one wishes it or not, the Arab masses, while sometimes illiterate or, more generally, under-educated, are, to repeat, profoundly cultivated. This subconscious heritage in which village civilization and desert civilization, Koranic heritage and poetic heritage are intermingled is not unimportant.'[7]

In addition, as has been seen particularly in Iran, the populace can be profoundly stirred by an appeal to particular elements in that heritage to lend active and enthusiastic support to the activist or ideologue without necessarily fully understanding or being fully committed to the message. Finally, observers are prone to a too ready acceptance of the idea that the interpretation of 'the Quranic injunctions and the Prophetic sayings' is as much a part of the divine revelation as the revelation itself.

Conventional ways of looking at Islam

More fundamentally, there is an essentially flawed perception of Islam. Commentators, Muslim and non-Muslim alike, are generally agreed that Islam is more than just a religion in the narrow Western sense of faith, ritual, and dogma, that 'it is a complete way of life, catering for all fields of human existence. Islam provides guidance for all walks of life — individual and social, material and moral, economic and political, legal and cultural, national and international'. A variant formula is that 'it comprehends and fulfils all the requirements of life past and future until the end of human existence on the earth whether these requirements are spiritual, material, political, economic, social, moral, intellectual or aesthetic'.[8] Although terminology may differ somewhat there is general agreement on the bases of these formulations in both traditional and more recent speculative literature on Islam. There is, however, an all too common tendency to pay lip-service to the concept and then to revert to usage which clearly indicates that Islam is seen primarily as a religion in the narrow sense of the word, albeit one which is deemed either to have overriding authority in political, cultural, social, economic, and legal matters, or to have at least considerable significance in those areas. Analysis, therefore, tends to identify Islam as a factor *in* politics, and so on, and in so doing to define it, by implication at least, as an extrinsic and holistic influence upon normal activity. However, this does not reflect reality and it is more accurate to talk' of *Muslim* political, legal, and economic systems, in the particular sense that there are political, legal, and economic structures which are consistent with the basic principles and precepts of Islam and a manner of conducting activity within these structures which is held to be equally consistent. However, this should not be taken to suggest that there is a single and distinctive structural model applicable throughout the Muslim world, since this would be to deny the effects of practice, a matter which will be treated in more detail later. Nor does it imply that Muslim political, legal, and economic systems are radically different from those of other ideologies, for the differences, such as they are, are primarily in inspiration, focus, and articulation, as will be demonstrated.

How, then, should Islam be defined or perceived? It has been suggested that 'in the last analysis, it does not matter what non-Muslims say about Islam, whether in interpreting its meaning or its political import'[9] — a view which has been echoed by many Muslims, some of whom go further and deny to the non-Muslim any *locus standi* to engage in debate about or examination of the proper definition of Islam and how it should be perceived. There is something in this argument, since in the last analysis Islam must be what Muslims believe it to be: but that is a partial answer only. Thus, for example, the standard, if somewhat ritual, definition of Islam is 'the complete submission of man before God', 'submission to the will of God', or 'total submission to the divine will'.[10] However, this is a remarkably passive and negative description of what is an essentially active and positive action.[11] A more acceptable general definition would be 'a willing and active commitment to compliance with the will of God', or, as one eminent Muslim put it, 'Islam invites man to commit himself exclusively to his Creator, to harmonise his will with the will of God and to recreate the world with this noble commitment.' He indicated how this might be achieved and placed his definition in a contemporary context by continuing that 'the mission towards which Islam invites man is to harness all material and human resources for the promotion of virtue, justice and peace'.[12]

However, although it is reasonable to argue that Islam is what Muslims believe it to be, it is not reasonable to restrict the expression of that belief to what they say: what they show by their actions is, in their view, incorporated into, or accepted as part of, the totality of Islam, is often rather different to what they say, but is certainly important. The relationship between theory and practice implied in this is therefore an important factor, although it has been largely ignored in the modern literature by both Muslim and non-Muslim authors. Inevitably, there are exceptions, and some do clearly perceive the relationship. One scholar has commented, for example, that religion provides 'a basic plan into which are integrated all the activities of the society, economic, social, intellectual'. Having defined what he chooses to call the 'Islamic vision', he points out that it

> informs the whole life of society and of individuals in the Islamic world. This does not mean that the vision or religious belief absolutely determines the whole way of life, for there are various aspects which have a relative autonomy, but it exercises a certain control or pressure on the whole.[13]

Modern schools of thought

There have been attempts to categorize schools of thought and trends, particularly those of the nineteenth and twentieth centuries. Although terminology varies considerably, there appears to be

11

general agreement that there were four main trends, which might be broadly defined as:

- (a)   orthodox conservatives;
- (b)   quasi-orthodox conservatives;
- (c)   modernizing reformers;
- (d)   conservative reformers.[14]

The 'orthodox conservatives' argue that Islam is a comprehensive, complete, and perfect system which neither needs nor is susceptible to change. The proper application of Muslim principles and Muslim law is sufficient to deal with all problems and difficulties facing humankind at all times. They are not necessarily against modernization and economic development, but are suspicious of both as possibly alien influences and possibly corrupting factors, because of their identification with the non-Muslim world. Ideas, however, are another matter, and they will have no truck with imported (usually Western) ideas and intellectualism. They are, in effect, dedicated to the principle of *taqlid* (imitation) or 'the unquestioning acceptance of established schools and authorities'.[15] The 'quasi-orthodox conservatives', normally associated with the establishment and the ruling elite, hold similar views; but they are under pressure and, in practice, find it necessary to deal pragmatically with intrusions of Western influence, both material and intellectual, and with the imposition of Western practices on Muslim countries. In so doing, they have recourse to the time-honoured Muslim practice of *hiyal* (legal casuistry), though they would not necessarily admit to it. *Hiyal* have been neatly summed up, incidentally, as

> 'legal devices', which were often legal fictions. They can be described in short as the use of legal means for achieving extra-legal ends, ends that could not be achieved directly with the means provided by the shari'a whether such ends might or might not be in themselves illegal.[16]

The 'modernizing reformers' seek to reinterpret the fundamentals of Islam in the light of existing and constantly changing circumstances. *Taqlid* is opposed root and branch and the use of *ijtihad* is seen not only as permissible but as obligatory. They favour a process of synthesis between the essentials of Islam and the 'best of the West', and argue that adaptation and assimilation into a genuinely Muslim format is possible. Their attitude might be best characterized as 'accommodationist' and pragmatic, and they would approve wholeheartedly of President Boumedienne's comment to the Lahore summit meeting of the Organisation of the Islamic Conference that

> human experience in many regions of the world has shown
> that spiritual bonds, be they Islamic or Christian, have not
> been able to resist the violent blows of poverty and ignorance,
> for the simple reason that men do not care to go to heaven
> with an empty belly.[17]

The 'conservative reformers' insist that *bida* (innovation and corrupt practice) must be ruthlessly extirpated, that *taqlid* is wrong, and that *ijtihad* is essential. However, they tend to set limits to the use of *ijtihad* and argue that the solution is not synthesis but a return to their concept of the ideals, practices, and principles of the 'Golden Age' of Islam.

However, this scheme clearly requires a fifth category to cover those (for example, Hassan al Banna, Qadhdhafi, Maududi, Sayyid Qutb, Ali Shariati, and Khomeini) who originally followed one of the trends outlined in the previous paragraph but whose thinking has developed to the point where they no longer fit comfortably into the mainstream: those sometimes described as 'non-conformist'.[18] All except Qadhdhafi have had a significant impact on attitudes in the Muslim world, while Qadhdhafi is significant because he has faced up to a number of difficult questions which others have either failed to perceive or have not wished to perceive. In so doing he has taken the argument to its logical conclusion, though that conclusion — that the bulk of the corpus of doctrine, dogma, and law is man-made and therefore can be ignored — is hardly palatable to more orthodox thinkers.[19]

The literature also identifies, at a less sophisticated and intellectual level, four broad strands in the way in which Muslims perceive Islam: 'establishment' Islam, 'popular' Islam, 'populist' Islam, and 'social' Islam.[20] 'Establishment' Islam is, as the term implies, essentially that of the state apparatus, including most ulama. It is normally subservient to the ruling elite and tends to be quasi-orthodox in outlook. 'Popular' Islam is the generalized perception of the ordinary person in the street and tends to be simple, traditional, conservative, and orthodox. 'Populist' Islam is the perception of 'the disoriented, the disaffected, the discontented and the dissatisfied'.[21] It is almost always highly politicized, active, extremist, intolerant, and prone to the use of violence, and its adherents are regularly described as 'radicals'.[22] 'Social' Islam is predominantly a rural phenomenon, though it is found in an urban environment, and is exemplified in the social welfare and cultural activities of the *tariqas* (Sufi confraternities) in the Sudan and Senegal, and similar activities elsewhere, such as those of the *Muhammadiyya* in Indonesia. It does not actively seek political power and authority, nor does it normally seek to compete with the ruling elite for the loyalty of the populace. Nevertheless, it is often perceived by the ruling elite as a potential threat to their authority because of its undoubted social and cultural significance. 'Popular' Islam is not in itself politically important, though the ordinary person can be manipulated for political reasons through an appeal to his or her general beliefs. 'Populist' Islam is, as already indicated, highly politicized and actively challenges both the authority and the legitimacy of governments and of 'establishment' Islam. However, its adherents are generally ill-informed about Muslim beliefs and practices and appear more interested in political power than in an Islamic order.

Notwithstanding the value of such analyses for some purposes, they are not wholly satisfactory and a more practical identification of the main strands of thought and behaviour is:

(a) the conventional;
(b) the synthesizer;
(c) the reaffirmer.[23]

The 'conventional' trend reflects the views of the orthodox conservatives who firmly believe that Islam is a perfect and comprehensive system for regulating human activities, but who pragmatically recognize reality and are content to leave matters to the ruling elite as long as the latter make at least a bow in the direction of the principles and practices of Islam. The 'synthesizers' seek to reinterpret and modify the precepts of Islam so as to make them — and therefore Islam itself — more relevant to a complex and constantly changing modern world. The 'reaffirmers' seek to return to their concept of the purity of the early community, admit no authority other than God, the *Qur'an*, and the *Sunna* (though they are often very selective about the *Sunna*), and accept no interpretation of that authority save their own. All three approaches are to some extent flawed: the first because it comes dangerously close to functional agnosticism and fails to address adequately the relationship between faith and power, the balance between tradition and modernity and the dynamics of change; the second because it implicitly sets to one side between ten and fourteen centuries of continual development and also fails to address the points enumerated above; and the third because it suffers the same flaws as the second, and it also denies the characteristic diversity of Islam.

Towards a different view of Islam

The discussion thus far has identified a number of problems inherent in conventional analyses of Islam, but it also implicitly reiterates the question: 'How else might one look at and define Islam?' As indicated in the Introduction, there is a different approach which may be of greater practical relevance. It rests initially on a number of simple propositions. Islam is what Muslims believe it to be and it does comprehend more than matters of faith, ritual, and dogma. However, what Muslims believe Islam to be is determined not only by theory and doctrine, but also by the collective practices of groups of Muslims in different places and at different times. In addition, the corpus of theory and doctrine developed over the centuries is of great importance and cannot be ignored or discarded. Moreover, the diversity that is Islam must be both recognized and accepted as the result of widely differing social, cultural, political, and historical experiences. However, that diversity should not obscure the underlying unity provided by common beliefs, duties, and practices. Hence, the relationships between doctrine and practice, and between unity and diversity, need to be taken into account. Diversity is to be understood as going far beyond the conventional sectarian differences between Sunni and Shi'a, between the four Sunni schools, between the various Shi'a sects, or between Ibadhism and other Muslims. It also comprehends the Sufi *tariqas*; the mysticism so characteristic of Iran and the Indian subcontinent; the diversity of political, social, and cultural heritage; and the manner in which non-Muslim beliefs and practices have been assimilated or incorporated into a particular expression of Islam without suffering accusations of heresy. The standard example of the last mentioned is the Indonesian *abangan* (nominal Muslim) community or the 'ethnic' Muslim communities of the USSR, but a particularly unusual and extreme example is to be found in the Miri Nuba of southern Kordofan.[24]

Islam, then, does provide guidance for all fields of human behaviour at both individual and collective levels: it is indeed 'the whole duty of man' — but it is not holistic. This is so not only because doctrine asserts it, but also because Muslims generally act, be it consciously or unconsciously, on the premiss that it is the case. All Muslims, however hazy their grasp of the finer points of doctrinal hair-splitting, will readily affirm their belief in the proposition and it is a constant and much stressed feature both of noted Muslim intellectuals and of more unlikely commentators. Thus, for example, Hassan al Banna (1906–49), the founder of the Muslim Brotherhood, commented that 'Islam is a faith and a ritual, a nation (*watan*) and a nationality, a religion and a state, spirit and deed, holy text and sword.' Muhammad Qutb, the brother of the major post-Second World War ideologue of the Muslim Brotherhood, and a scholar in his own right, has asserted that there are two important and distinctive features of Islam:

(a) it comprehends every aspect of the human soul because it is revealed for every single person living on this earth irrespective of his race, colour, language, location, environment, historical or geographical circumstances, intellectual or cultural heritage and his contribution to material civilisation;
(b) it comprehends and fulfils all the requirements of life, past and future, until the end of human existence on earth whether these requirements are spiritual, material, political, economic, social, moral, intellectual or aesthetic.

Abul Ala Maududi (1903–79), one of the most popular modern Pakistani writers, states that the directives contained in the code of behaviour 'touch such varied subjects as religious rituals, personal character, morals, habits, family relationships, rights and duties of citizens, judicial system, laws of war and peace and international relations'. Though such views are to be expected from the individuals quoted, it is at first sight somewhat surprising that they are echoed by an active — and relatively secular — politician such as Abdul Rahman al Bazzaz (1913–73), a former Prime Minister of Republican Iraq. 'Islam', he commented, 'in its precise sense, is a social order, a philosophy of life, a system of economic principles, a rule of government, in addition to its being a religious creed in the narrow Western sense.'[25]

However, these views go too far, for although Islam does provide

16

guidance, that guidance consists mainly of general principles and not of detailed rules and regulations. Furthermore, it does so in two very different, though interdependent, ways, for Islam provides both the general framework or environment within which Muslims act and also the principles regulating their activity in specific and separate, though interrelated, areas of behaviour. In addition, the manner in which the principles are interpreted and put into practice in those areas of behaviour is important. Islam is, if the metaphor is not too irreverent, like an orange: there are readily identifiable and separate segments or sub-systems, but all are interconnected — and in some ways inseparable — and the whole is considerably greater than the sum of the parts. The sub-systems are faith (or religion), a legal system, a code of ethics and morals, social values and principles for regulating society, economic principles (though of an imprecise nature), and a generalized political philosophy.

Theory and practice: a neglected relationship

Theory and doctrine are obviously important, both in their own right, since they provide the essential unity of Islam, and also as a standard against which actual practice can be measured. However, theory and doctrine must be more than a rigid and possibly out-of-date set of rules, since this implies both intellectual sterility and a divorce from reality. It is clear that the revelation and its subsequent development into a coherent doctrine represents an ideal which humanity will, almost by definition, fail to attain. Although certain elements of the doctrine are immutable, however, the human development is not and adjustments are regularly made and accepted as circumstances change. Moreover, there is no single, universally acceptable definition of that ideal. One version — or set of versions — will be found in the teaching of the theological schools; another version is that articulated by the intellectuals; yet another in the perception of the ordinary person; and finally a more pragmatic version as understood by governments. It is, of course, easy to argue that these are all flawed pictures and that there *is* a single and authoritative expression of that ideal, as many, including some of the individuals discussed in Chapters 6 and 7, have done. However, the expression of that ideal differs from commentator to commentator, and in any case how can anyone know with complete assurance which is the correct expression?

17

It is important, therefore, to look also at actual practice, for just as doctrine and theory mould and influence behaviour, so does actual practice serve to identify the limits of what is attainable. 'Politics', observed Bismarck, 'is the art of the possible.'[26] The same might justifiably be said about at least some aspects of Islam: for example, there is a considerable difference between the doctrinal position on the unity of the *umma* and the reality of state and sectarian plurality today, and between the doctrinal position on the leadership of the community and the reality of government apparatus, kings, and presidents. It may be possible to criticize the leadership of Muslim states for the manner in which they act in particular matters, but it is surely unrealistic to castigate them for a failure to attain a consonance with the doctrine which is patently unattainable and impractical. Actions by individual Muslims and by governments who can legitimately claim to be seeking to comply with God's will are therefore significant determinants of what particular groups of Muslims at particular times broadly accept as consistent with the revelation — but, in the case of governments, only when that acceptance is supported, or at least not opposed, by the majority of the group: consensus, if not unanimity, is necessary.

The notions of consensus and of particular groups of Muslims need to be treated with some care, because there are complex relationships to be taken into account. The diversity of perceptions and practices already referred to several times is not merely a matter of inter-state differences, but also comprehends differences within states. Every Muslim is a member of a number of different groupings, each influenced by different factors; and there is often a discontinuity or a cross-border linkage as between the different groupings. A male Egyptian Muslim, for example, will consider himself part of the universal *umma* because of certain common beliefs and practices; but he is also an Egyptian, and will share certain attitudes and practices in common with his compatriots. He might also be a member of the Muslim Brotherhood, which provides yet another set of values, perceptions, and practices, and he may feel a certain kinship with Sudanese and Syrian Brothers. Even educational levels and geographic factors may be significant definers of a particular group. Similarly, an Indonesian Muslim may be at one and the same time a member of the universal *umma*, a member of the community of Indonesian Muslims, an *abangan* or a *santri* (devout and practising Muslim), a voter for the PPP (*Partai Persatuan Pembangunang*), and a member of the modernist *Muhammadiyya*

18

movement which restricts its activities to non-political social welfare and educational work. All have differing perceptions, attitudes, and practices, which are not necessarily mutually compatible. However, in both examples, it will be found that the individual unconsciously makes the necessary accommodation to ensure apparently contradictory group cohesion. In addition, there is sufficient coherence to both national perceptions and attitudes and the wider notion of the universal *umma*, given the strength and influence of the social, cultural, moral, political, historical, and spiritual heritage of individual states and of Islam more generally. The heritage should not be underestimated, nor should the underlying unity of the basic beliefs of Islam — the oneness, uniqueness, and unity of God and the prophethood of Muhammad, to which the Shi'a would add the Imamate — and of the common duties and obligations, all of which inform and influence the diversity.

Islam re-defined: a general view

To return to the broader question, Islam is clearly a faith — that is, it defines and regulates the relationship between man and God. That relationship, together with man's duties to God, is clearly set out in the *Qur'an* and has been further elaborated and clarified in the *Sunna*, and, for the Shi'a, the *sunna* of the twelve Imams. However, Islam also defines and regulates man's relationship with his fellow men both individually and collectively. It must therefore also comprehend a legal system, an ethical system, and principles of social behaviour. However, there are also political connotations, although these are not always as clear-cut, since there is an 'inherent link between Islam as a comprehensive scheme for ordering life, and politics as an indispensable instrument to secure universal compliance with that scheme'. This must, however, be qualified since

> another misconception about the fusion of religion and politics in Islamic culture is to think that in historical reality too all political attitudes and institutions among Muslims have had religious sanctions, or have conformed to religious laws. Often the reverse was true.[27]

One observer has addressed this point in his identification of 'a very old and difficult problem — that of the relationship between power and religion, or temporal authority and the faith, or religion and state'. He commented that Islam had

> failed to provide a formula for a flexible political order which could cope with change. It never quite managed to establish an acceptable relation between religion and state, power and belief. It insisted on the possession of both power and a universal religious truth, that is, on the sanctity of power. Soon however — by the 9th century if not earlier — mundane history with its concrete events, separated society from the state as an organisation of power.[28]

There is some truth in these views, but as will be demonstrated later, they are not as valid in absolute terms as they may seem to be at first sight.

Returning now to the network of sub-systems identified earlier, it must be remembered that although principles and guidelines are provided in the revelation for most, if not all, of them, the first sub-system, the faith, is both simple and formulated with precision and that the broad guidelines and statements of principles governing the other sub-systems permit considerable diversity of interpretation. Nevertheless, any matter which is clearly and unambiguously regulated in detail in the revelation is so regulated *ad aeternitatem*. It follows that Islam is not an actor or a factor in particular fields of activity; it is, rather, the framework within which activity takes place and at the same time the provider of general principles to be further elaborated in the light of circumstances and the provider of a more detailed and authoritative set of rules and regulations in a few selected cases. It both guides and defines, and provides the environment.

Matters affecting the general view

Detailed guidance or general principles

There are a number of other factors to be taken into account in this approach to Islam, whether to the totality or to individual sub-systems, some of which have already been touched upon, though not in detail. First, there is no reason to accept the assertions of some, but by no means all, Muslim activists that Islam provides detailed guidance covering man's relationship with both God

and fellow men and that such detailed guidance is both divinely
ordained and immutable. This argument imputes a degree of divine
ordination which is not justified by the historical record.[29] Certainly, the revelation laid down detailed rules in a minority of matters, but, so runs the standard rebuttal, for the rest guidance consists of general principles which 'have no clear-cut definitions in
the Qur'an or the Sunna, except basic norms'.[30] This view holds
that successive generations of Muslims not only could, but had a
positive duty to, elaborate political, economic, social, moral, and
legal systems which would be appropriate to the stage of development, circumstances, and reality, while remaining consistent with
God's will. A variant approach argues that the *Qur'an*

> does not in fact give many general principles: for the most
> part it gives solutions to and rulings upon specific and con-
> crete historical issues; but, as I have said, it provides, either
> explicitly or implicitly, the rationales behind these solutions
> and rulings, from which one *can deduce general principles* (original
> emphasis).[31]

This version may be more factually accurate, but it does not
invalidate the basic argument that the *Qur'an* provides basic principles: it does not matter greatly whether they are explicit or implicit.
There is, however, a fundamental objection to this reasoning in
that it comes perilously close to arguing that Muhammad carefully
tailored the content of the revelation to suit his political and moral
objectives. Hence, it comes very close to denying the central facts
for Muslims that the *Qur'an* is the Word of God and that the revelation is genuine.

Turning to the question of divine ordination and immutability,
notwithstanding what the activists and intellectuals may say,
Muslims have demonstrated clearly over the years that Islam
can be and is intrinsically flexible, pragmatic, and dynamic, subject only to the immutability of certain fundamental precepts.
In practice, there has been a continuous history of adjustment,
modification, change, and reassessment, as successive generations
sought to bridge the gap between the ideal but unattainable
society epitomized by the early community and the practical
requirements of both a constantly changing environment and the
constantly changing practice of Muslims. Hence, the assertions
noted at the beginning of the preceding paragraph need to be
qualified by the manner in which Muslims have acted. Some, of

course, argue that the entire period since the Golden Age is a period of deviation; but it is, though easy and attractive, intellectually dishonest to discard centuries of development and experience as deviation. The argument also ignores two points of substance: the significance of actual practice, and the fact that Muslims today are the product of that historical experience and have shown that they regard it as being important. In addition, of course, it traduces the achievements of many generations of sincere and devout Muslims and is, as will be demonstrated, inconsistent with the fact. The inescapable conclusion is that the *Qur'an* provides general principles in most cases, with detailed and specific rules only occasionally, and that the detailed interpretation of those general principles, being the work of man, is not divinely ordained and thus not immutable. However, that interpretation may be justifiably regarded as authoritative unless and until a more appropriate interpretation emerges. Thus, change is possible, though it must be carefully managed to ensure consistency and continuity.

The relationships between Muslims and non-Muslims

Second, it is inherent in the concept of Islam as the last and best of a series of revelations that Muslims must believe that it is superior to and supercessory of the earlier revelations — and the argument is often deployed, particularly where there is a conflict of law. Even here, however, the influence of practice may be discerned, for a more pragmatic, realistic, and tolerant form of Islam — and in particular a more pragmatic, tolerant, and realistic attitude towards the relationship between Muslims and non-Muslims — is more a feature of states which have a pluralist society and have undergone the colonial experience than of states whose population is entirely or predominantly Muslim and which have avoided the colonial experience. Paradoxically, it is also true that speculative and often radical reinterpretations of Islam tend to occur in the first group of states. (Egypt and the Indo-Pakistani subcontinent are obvious examples.) But this rule of thumb is breaking down gradually, and there have inevitably been exceptions. Furthermore, even in states of the second category (Saudi Arabia is an obvious example), an apparently rigid and conservative attitude is frequently tempered by pragmatic and under-the-surface realism, particularly if the ruling elite has been astute enough to recognize that a clear distinction between *din* and *dawla* (religion and state, faith and power) needs to be drawn but that the distinction has to be blurred in public presentation.

Faith and power: or theory and practice

Third, the Muslim insistence that the separation of 'Church' and 'State', which they see as characteristic of the Christian world, did not and could not occur in the Muslim world has caused considerable problems. In practice, a degree of separation occurred early on, but the intellectuals never managed to bridge the gap between the ideal and reality in a completely satisfactory fashion. Although, therefore, an adequate and flexible institutional framework for the development of the relationship did evolve, and although the machinery for managing the relationship has been available for many centuries, neither framework nor machinery ever acquired intellectual and doctrinal legitimacy in sufficient measure. Certainly, the need for an institutional framework and for a system of political authority was understood from the beginning and successive generations managed their affairs in accordance with principles which would be familiar to students of politics and international relations. However, the absence of sufficient legitimacy has forced Muslims to devote considerable time and effort to the task of finding an explanation for political activity and political institutions which was both doctrinally and juridically acceptable. This does not, however, really justify the argument that Islam's greatest failure has been its inability to develop an acceptable and satisfactory institutional framework for political development: for the importance of the relationship between faith and power was recognized very early on and practical arrangements for managing it have always proved possible. The real problem has been how legitimacy might be satisfactorily accorded to institutional and administrative arrangements, a matter which will be discussed in more detail in Chapters 3 and 8.

Muslim self-perceptions and self-deceptions

Fourth, some understanding of the reasons for the characteristically negative approach to the complexities of the modern world is necessary. Whatever the definition of Islam, it does provide a standard against which debatable actions can be tested and appropriate machinery for carrying out the testing, although the matter is complicated by the still unresolved debate over the permissibility or otherwise of actions which are neither expressly permitted nor expressly prohibited. (For Hanbalis, of course, there is no debate, since they hold firmly to the view that things are permissible unless specifically prohibited.) Muslims are human, however, and it is not really surprising that they find it easier to define what they are against than to define what they are for. Furthermore, the *Qur'an*, like the Ten Commandments, contains more prohibitions than positive instructions. The natural tendency is aggravated by a genuine, though not wholly justifiable, perception of continued economic, cultural, and social imperialism exercised by the former colonial powers and by the superpowers (particularly the US), which is seen as eroding indigenous and traditional cultural, social, and moral value systems. This perception is more prevalent among Muslims and Muslim states than among non-Muslims and non-Muslim states of the Third World, despite a shared colonial experience and a shared classification as under- or less-developed nations.

Although both groups share a feeling of backwardness and inferiority as compared with the industrialized world and both resent continued Western domination of world affairs, their responses are very different. The Muslim response tends to ascribe these feelings and the reality of the relative positions to a continued deviation from *al sirat al mustaqim* (the straight path), to the adoption of alien, non-Muslim values and ideologies together with their material products, and to the immoral behaviour of those more fortunately placed; while the non-Muslim tends to identify the factors which underpin the superiority of the industrialized world and to seek to incorporate them into the indigenous system. It has been argued that the Muslim response stems from the fundamental belief that Islam is, and must be, superior to other ideologies, since 'you are the best *umma* brought forth for mankind' (*Qur'an*, Chapter 3, verse 110 — hereafter Q3:110): any failure to maintain a position of superiority must be rooted in the failure to obey God. This reasoning, though comfortable and easy, is fallacious, since it does not give due weight to the fact that the period of Islam's greatest glory occurred well after the process of deviation is deemed to have commenced. Furthermore, it does not explain why the generality of Muslims failed to oppose the deviation, other than by consigning successive generations of Muslims, most of whom can be assumed to have genuinely believed that they were complying with God's command, to the purgatory of lack of faith. Muslim history shows clearly that although voices were regularly raised against deviation, there was little popular support for such views. Once again, practicality and practice show their significance.

Western media misconceptions

Fifth, the unacceptable face of Islam presented in the media and a number of recent books (titles such as *The Dagger of Islam* and *The Haj* come readily to mind) needs qualification, since the picture presented is considerably different to that outlined above: rather, Islam is portrayed as militant and violent, intolerant, expansionist and hostile, rigidly conservative, archaic and anachronistic, and finally brutal. Events in Iran during the past few years, the manner in which Muslim law was imposed in the Sudan, the violence of Muslim extremists in Egypt which resulted in the assassination of President Sadat, the seizure of the Grand Mosque in Makka in 1979, the fanaticism of Shi'a militants in the Lebanon, and the acts of terrorism which they have perpetrated are all cited as evidence supporting the popular image; but just how accurate is that image? The short answer is that apart from the accusation of expansionism, Islam *qua* Islam is none of these things, though some Muslims certainly do exhibit these tendencies. In any case, these are simplistic characterizations which are too sharply defined and do not reflect the complexities of Islam — or indeed of human beings who happen to be Muslim — nor the reasons why some Muslims may show these characteristics. In addition, the popular image does not distinguish between Islam as an ideology and Islam as part of the historical experience of its adherents.

However, the short answer does require some qualification and comment. Thus, for example, motivations for militancy and violence are often complex, ranging from an innate compulsion found in some individuals in every society to a reaction against the perceived militancy and violence of other ideologies, and will often include some degree of defensiveness. Moreover, it is not a characteristic confined to the Muslim world, though that is often implied. Relations between the various Christian authorities in Jerusalem under the Ottomans and the Mandate, the American action in Grenada, the Soviet invasion of Afghanistan, the liberation theology of Latin America, Sikh extremism, and the activities of the Baader–Meinhoff group and similar organizations are hardly examples of quietism. Yet apart from occasional aberrations deviating from the norm, the superpowers are fundamentally supine except in their relations with their allies, the Church militant is a polite fiction, and most societies are not fundamentally militant or violent, though members may be. In addition, as already noted, it is dangerous to extrapolate to the entire society the attitudes and activities of a small minority. As for intolerance and fanaticism, they are directed, in the Muslim world, as much against fellow-Muslims as against others and are rarely national characteristics — and never universally applied attitudes. It must however be recognized that it is in the nature of ideologies to proclaim their universalism — and it is in the nature of some ideologues to be intolerant of competitors ('The truth shall prevail!'). Hence, what major faith, political philosophy, or ideology is not inherently expansionist? The only one which springs immediately to mind is Judaism, and in its political manifestation — Zionism — it is hardly a shrinking violet.

Punishments meted out under Muslim law are frequently cited as evidence of brutality and it would be foolish to deny that in Western eyes today, amputations, executions, stoning, and corporal punishment are brutal. However, it must be borne in mind that the specific punishments prescribed in the *Qur'an* were unexceptionable at the time of the revelation, that in some cases lesser punishments are prescribed as alternatives, and that the rules of evidence are strict to the point of absurdity. Moreover, it is generally held today that the more extreme punishments should not be applied if those rules are not fully met or if there is any doubt. Furthermore, the generality of opinion today is that the more extreme punishments should be reserved for recidivists and that more generally accepted punishments should be applied in the first instance. Underpinning this are two concepts. First, if an individual is forced by circumstance to steal, for example, it is as much an indictment of society as of the individual. Society must therefore be given an opportunity to redress the wrong done before the individual transgressor can be subjected to more condign punishment. Second, an opportunity must be given to the transgressor to repent and to demonstrate that repentance suitably. Finally, although there is statistical evidence of the deterrent effect of severe punishment, there is also abundant evidence that the more brutal punishments are as abhorrent to many Muslims as they are to others and that much ingenuity is expended on devising ways of avoiding their use.

26

Islam, modernization and economic development: a difficult balance

Sixth, great caution is needed in dealing with the conventional wisdom that Islam and the process of modernization and economic development are incompatible, and that secularization and the relegation of Islam and its tenets to the limited sphere of belief, ritual, and matters of personal status is a necessary prelude to development and modernization in the Muslim world. The argument is based on the premiss that 'since the eighteenth century Enlightenment it has been commonly supposed that history was progressive and described a path from magic through religion to scientific rationalism, and that there was an indissoluble link between secularism and modernity'.[32] The argument does not, however, explain the resurgence of Islam, nor the undoubted fact that many Muslim countries have embarked upon relatively successful modernization and development schemes without following the progression noted above. Furthermore, it is clear that the more militant of the so-called 'fundamentalists' are not in any way opposed to modernization and development as such: it is the identification of the processes with 'Westernization' and secularism which they oppose, and most, if not all, modern Muslim intellectuals hold firmly, and with some justification, to the proposition that modernization and development within a genuine and active Muslim environment is feasible. As a member of the Saudi Royal Family put it, 'Material progress, yes, but not for the sake of material progress, but for the creation of a noble and serene and just society and to seek man's salvation in this world and in the hereafter.'[33] Mistakes have, of course, been made and there is a body of opinion in the Muslim world which agrees with the conventional wisdom. On the other hand, it is clear from actual practice that Muslims generally, and Muslim rulers in particular, reject the conventional wisdom and have been able to demonstrate that it is not necessarily valid for the Muslim world.

The mystique of Islam

Finally, the mystique which surrounds Islam needs to be dispelled. Many Muslims, and not a few non-Muslims, have argued that only 'insiders' can really understand Islam, are qualified to discuss Islam and can sensibly analyse what motivates Muslims. However, they spoil their case by arrogating to themselves (the Muslims, that is) the unrestricted right as 'outsiders' to discourse eloquently on the failures and shortcomings of Christianity, Judaism, capitalism and communism. Furthermore, in much of the discussion Islam is represented as something different — and by implication both alien and hostile. Yet Muslims are normal people who differ from others only in the inspiration of their beliefs and the manner in which they seek to express them — and even here, there are parallels with both Christianity and Judaism, such as the value of pilgrimage, the requirement to attend communal worship at specific times, and the spiritual values of fasting. Moreover, it is misleading to suppose that there is a distinctively Muslim or Islamic set of basic premises governing human activities in the social, cultural, economic, legal, ethical, and political arenas which differs significantly from those of other ideologies. Certainly, there are differences in detail, in the manner of articulation, and in the symbolism. The source of inspiration may also be different, but, as Ibn Khaldun, Ibn Taymiyya, al Mawardi, and others clearly recognized, the imperatives of power in the political arena are not different; the practical application of the code of law is identical; the ethical and moral values informing the legal code are almost universal; and the basic rules for ordering society are not specific to a particular way of life. Indeed, the basic values of the Muslim ethic and morality are both unexceptionable and familiar to most inhabitants of the Western world: virtue, honesty, compassion, care of the needy and the deprived, justice, freedom, equality, moderation, respect for the interests of others, and so on. Furthermore, Muslims regularly insist that the principles, practices, and ethics of other ideologies were inherent in Islam from the beginning and were often first articulated, identified, or defined in the revelation or in Muslim praxis, while at the same time insisting upon the separateness and distinctiveness of Islam. However spurious or apologetic the arguments, however, they have served to fuel the notion that Islam is, as it were, an alien culture, distinct from and inimical to that familiar to the West. The reality is rather different, although the similarities that do exist and which have been listed above, should not be overstressed, particularly since Muslims do perceive, rightly or wrongly, a separateness and distinctiveness.

Conclusions

The concept of Islam outlined above may be simply summarized. Islam is more than just a question of faith, dogma, and ritual; it does offer guidelines for all areas of human behaviour; guidance is provided not only in matters directly related to the basic faith but also in social, moral, and cultural standards; there are in addition general principles which should inform the legal, political, and economic structures of the Muslim world; and on certain issues, detailed guidance is given in the shape of specific rules. The guidance has been elaborated over the years into a fairly comprehensive 'code of practice', parts of which are, because they form part of the revelation, immutable. The remainder, though elevated by some to the status of immutable divine ordination, is susceptible to change, though of an ordered kind. Furthermore, since the principles and rules set out in the revelation are ideals and since the totality of Islam is influenced by reality and practicality, the actual practice of individuals and of societies is an important modifier and an important factor in identifying what Muslims believe Islam to comprehend. These two broad and apparently inconsistent strands — doctrine and practice — ensure that Islam exhibits both an underlying unity and a superficial diversity which are, at first sight, incompatible. However, that apparent incompatibility is the result of a perception among many non-Muslims that Islam is certainly alien and possibly hostile: the concentration is upon the differences from, rather than on the similarities to, other ideologies. Once this perception is dismissed, as it should be, it becomes clear that Islam is structurally similar to other ideologies claiming universal validity, though there are differences in the manner of articulation, the source of inspiration, practical details, and so on. It is equally clear that the discontinuity between the ideal and praxis in the Muslim world is no more marked and no more unusual than is the case elsewhere, and that doctrinal diversity is also not unique to the Muslim world. In short, these are of little significance to a proper analysis of Islam in general and of particular aspects of it, which are susceptible to the same type of analysis as are, for example, communism and the various forms of capitalist-oriented Western democracies. There are, nevertheless, limiting factors arising from the nature of Islam as the last, most perfect, and most universally applicable divine revelation.

However, since non-Muslim writers have tended to concentrate on the ideal as set out in the doctrine and theory, and Muslim writers, though often accepting that there is a relationship between ideal and practice, are generally unwilling to explore the nature of the relationship in an effective manner, there is a deal of confusion in the analyses of both. Furthermore, the essential dynamism of Islam has been obscured and this has contributed largely to the popular Western image of Islam as out of date, rigid, and uncompromising. Regrettably, these popular misconceptions have been strengthened by the manner in which Muslims have presented their case and by their insistence on propositions which are not only unrealistic but also inconsistent with historical fact. Thus, many Muslim writers regularly ignore some fourteen centuries of continuous development and call for a return to an idealized (and historically inaccurate) concept of the practice of the Golden Age or, alternatively, cleave to the tenth-century codification. Nevertheless, since Muslims hold strongly to such views, some account must be taken of them.

Although Islam therefore provides a broad ideology for its adherents, the revelation is but a small part of that ideology, much of which is susceptible to modification and has been modified, as the historical evidence clearly demonstrates. The ideology is not monolithic, since the guidance provided is interpreted differently in different places, according to the historical experience and the widely differing social, cultural, political, and geographical contexts. It is neither alien nor necessarily hostile, though individual Muslims may be hostile towards non-Muslims, since many of the principles, practices, and ethical values are similar to, or identical with, those of other ideologies and faiths. Finally, the unity of Islam does not preclude the identification of particular sectors or sub-systems which can be examined separately.

2
The Law

Introduction

Whatever the definition of Islam, the 'whole duty of man' is to seek to divine God's will and to live individually and collectively in full and willing compliance with that will: 'we made for you a law, so follow it and not the fancies of those who have no knowledge' (Q45:18). Inevitably, therefore, the revealed law plays a crucial role in Muslim thinking, but there is, and has always been, considerable argument over what constituted the divinely revealed law and the extent to which it is possible to distinguish between that law and fallible man's interpretation of it. Indeed, the terms used, though precisely defined, are frequently used loosely and confusingly. All jurists are agreed that the *shari'a* (literally 'the path') comprises the entire corpus of divinely revealed law, but there is no agreement upon the precise contents of that corpus. The term *fiqh* (literally 'understanding'), variously defined as 'jurisprudence', 'jurisprudential interpretation', and 'precise and profound deducing of the Islamic regulations of actions from the relevant sources',[1] means the process by which the rules of law and conduct were elaborated by the jurists by rational deduction from the traditional sources and precedent. The terms are often used interchangeably, however, and there seems no clear-cut and agreed distinction between the two in Sunni doctrine. Somewhat confusingly, the sources of *fiqh* are identical to the sources of the law. With characteristic clarity, Coulson has summed up the distinction thus:

> Islamic law has been alternatively described as a divine law and as a jurists' law. These apparently contradictory descriptions reveal the basic tension that exists in the system between

divine revelation and the human reasoning of jurists . . . The comprehensive system of personal and public behaviour which constitutes the Islamic religious law is known as the Shari'a. The goal of Muslim jurisprudence was to reach an under-standing (*fiqh*) of the Shari'a.[2]

Furthermore, many authorities have not always identified with any degree of clarity the essential difference between the Western and Muslim concepts of law. Although the moral and ethical principles underlying the Western concept differ little from those of Islam, the relationship between ethics and the law has been overlaid and obscured by more secular ideas of right and wrong, and of social responsibility. This can be seen particularly in the detailed Western legal codes which are held to reflect the 'will of the people' and which define human rights and obligations as reciprocal and relating essentially to the needs of society. Transgressions are identified (and punished) as crimes against the social order. The traditional Muslim concept, *per contra*, rests on the proposition that the *shari'a* (however defined) is the law of God set down for all time in the divine revelation. Muslims, by virtue of being Muslims, have accepted a positive obligation to seek to implement God's will and to live in consonance with that law irrespective of the conduct of others, both at the individual and the collective level. The emphasis is upon obligations rather than upon rights, and upon the divine origin of the law. The *shari'a* is not, therefore, 'law' in the normally accepted sense of the term: 'it contains an infallible guide to ethics. It is fundamentally a doctrine of duties, a code of obligations. Legal considerations and individual rights have a secondary place in it.'[3]

Finally it is inherent in the Muslim concept that legislative authority and power rest with God alone and that the *umma* is, in some sense, merely His trustee. 'It is because of this principle that the *Ummah* enjoys a derivative rule-making power and not an absolute law-creating prerogative.'[4] It is also because of this principle, so runs the reasoning, that the function of the jurist is simply to identify or discover what God's command is in any given situation and to apply the appropriate rule accordingly. The reasoning is questionable, however, given the extent to which Muslims have found it necessary in all ages to 'make' law without always finding it necessary to justify their actions. The jurist's functions are con-siderably more extensive and both the quotation and the reasoning are an exercise in false logic. Furthermore, the reasoning obscures the fallacy of one commonly expressed view: that Islamic law differs fundamentally from Western law, not least because it does not rest upon a system of case law. Yet the process by which the jurist identifies the appropriate rule is exactly the same as that followed by any Western lawyer seeking to find an appropriate precedent for the case in question.

The sources of the law

Orthodox Sunni doctrine states that the sources of the law are the *Qur'an*, the *Sunna*, *ijma'* (consensus of opinion), and *qiyas* (analogy). To these some authorities add *ijtihad* (independent reasoning), and a variety of terms all equating generally to the concept of *maslaha* (public interest). The rationale for adding *ijtihad* is that although *qiyas* is a specific and limited form of *ijtihad*, the latter term has much wider connotations: thus, the limitations resulting from the arbitrary restriction to *qiyas* are overcome to a greater or lesser extent. The addition of *maslaha* and similar terms is an equally pragmatic attempt to extend the flexibility of the system by extending the basis of the theory. The *Qur'an* and the *Sunna* of the Prophet are deemed to be primary sources and the remainder secondary sources. The resulting corpus of law is variously named the *shari'a* or Muslim law, the two terms sometimes being synonymous and sometimes having quite distinct meanings — and frequently being used, somewhat confusingly, in both senses. Nevertheless, it is possible to identify four different definitions for the term *shari'a* in the sense of Muslim law in history:

(a) it comprises the entire corpus of law elaborated over the first four or five centuries of the Muslim era and contained in the legal compilations of the recognized schools of law;
(b) it comprises the rules and principles contained in the *Qur'an* and the *Sunna* (the latter in its entirety);
(c) it comprises the rules and principles contained in the *Qur'an* and that part of the *Sunna* which is both authentic and concerned with the elucidation and interpretation of the divine precepts; and
(d) it comprises only the rules and principles contained in the *Qur'an*.

The first has generally prevailed and is widely held today, although

33

the second and the third are generally the basis for the arguments of most nineteenth- and twentieth-century thinkers. The fourth is rare and is habitually opposed as verging on heresy, but it does have considerable attraction in that it provides the maximum degree of flexibility. Given this diversity, it therefore seems reasonable to examine briefly the nature of the classical sources and their relationship.

The *Qur'an* and the *Sunna*: primary sources of the law

What needs to be said about the *Qur'an* in this context can be said briefly. For Muslims, the *Qur'an* is the revealed word of God. It must, by definition, be divinely ordained, immutable, and valid for all time and all places. However, the *Qur'an* contains clear and unambiguous instructions in detail on very few matters, and these relate mainly to matters of personal status — marriage, divorce, inheritance, dietary requirements, and so on — and to particular transgressions of the law. It is generally held that the *Qur'an* contains no more than 500 verses concerning legal matters, of which only some 80 are legislative in the strict sense of the term. The remainder does, of course, contain much in the shape of general moral exhortations from which broad principles have been deduced, but much is couched in obscure language. As far as the legislative verses are concerned, 'these eighty texts have been construed, by a method of statutory interpretation which Anglo-American lawyers might well find congenial, so as to extract the utmost ounce of meaning from them.'[5] For the rest of the *Qur'an*, 'nonlegal texts in the *Qur'an*, moral exhortations, and even divine promises have been construed by analogy to afford legal rules'.[6]

The function of the *Sunna* appears to be based on the premise that the *Qur'an* concentrates on laying down broad principles and guidelines and the *Sunna*, because it comprises the Prophet's teaching, positive practice, and tacit approval of the practice of others, represents an exemplar of the manner in which the Qur'anic principles should be put into practice. The *Sunna* is in part interpretation and in part the elaboration of the detailed rules to be adduced from the revelation. Furthermore, since the Prophet was the Messenger of God, the *Sunna* is generally held to be at least divinely inspired, if not, as many aver, divinely ordained and part of the revelation, though not with the same authority as the *Qur'an*.

In reality, the entire life of the Holy Prophet (S.A.W.), whatever he did or said was according to the teaching of *Qur'an* and hence, if all the events of his life and his teachings are taken together with all the authentic *Ahadith*, we get a complete *Tafsir* [commentary or interpretation] of the *Qur'an* put into practice by the Messenger of Allah himself, the bearer of the Divine Revelations.[7]

However, proponents of this line of reasoning seem also to recognize some form of categorization of the *hadith* in that they distinguish between *ahadith qudsiyya* and other *ahadith*. *Ahadith qudsiyya* are held to contain direct divine instruction, but, as one authority argues, 'one can only say that the ahadith qudsiyya, if genuine, ought to have found a place in the *Qur'an* and the very fact that they have not is an argument against their authenticity'.[8] While the general argument that the *Sunna* provides a complete *tafsir* (interpretation and commentary) of the *Qur'an* where it is clearly interpretative or elucidatory is unexceptionable, the arbitrary extension of divine ordination to all acts and omissions of the Prophet does not seem justified. Sunni doctrine does, after all, emphasize the fact that Muhammad was a mortal and this central fact has been reiterated by such conservative writers as Maududi: 'The *Qur'an* leaves no doubt that the Prophet is but a human being and has no share whatever in Divinity. The Prophet is neither superhuman nor is he free of human weaknesses.'[9]

A more comprehensible line of reasoning starts with the generally accepted proposition that the contents of the *Qur'an* are not always articulated in a clear and unambiguous manner. During the Prophet's lifetime, therefore, the community, and particularly those described as the Companions, would naturally seek elucidation from the Prophet concerning the more obscure passages of the revelation. Such elucidation and explanation has the character of an authoritative explanation: one of the main functions of the prophetic office was to clarify the true meaning of the *Qur'an*. Such clarification was provided not only directly by what the Prophet said, but also indirectly by the manner in which he acted and by his unspoken approval or disapproval of the thoughts, words, and deeds of others. The *Sunna* is therefore authoritative *only* in respect of the interpretation of the *Qur'an*, whether in respect of specific injunctions or the more broadly articulated principles. Furthermore, the *Sunna* is subordinate to and governed by the *Qur'an*.

The implication is clear: the *Sunna* shows how God's will *could* (not *should*) be implemented and further adaptation and modification to cope with new situations is in accord with the *Sunna*. Until such time as this proves necessary, however, the *Sunna* remains the most authoritative interpretation of the *Qur'an*. Proponents of this line of reasoning[10] cite in support of their reasoning such Qur'anic verses as 'Say, I am only a mortal like you' (18:111 and 41:6), and the *hadith*:

> I am only a mortal like you. In matters revealed to me by God you must obey my instructions. But you know more about your own worldly affairs than I do. So my advice in these matters is not binding.[11]

This *hadith* is, incidentally, interesting in that it draws a clear distinction between spiritual and temporal affairs, a distinction which emerged in practice but which is in contradiction with the fundamental proposition that Islam is more than just a matter of faith and that it comprises all areas of human activity. Sadiq al Mahdi goes further, and cites Abu Ja'far al Naqib: 'The Companions of the Prophet recognised that the spiritual message of Islam is fixed. To that they were faithfully committed. The social message of Islam is, however, flexible. Their experience amply demonstrated that flexibility.'[12]

One final point about the *Sunna* has been emphasized by many scholars. It is generally agreed now that there was a considerable industry in the fabrication of *hadith* in order to provide prophetic, if spurious, legitimacy for points of law, argument, and practice. Not even the process of sifting and analysing the *hadith*, which eventually resulted in the six canonical collections of *hadith*, put an end to the process and it is almost always possible to find a *hadith* to support a particular argument. Indeed, one rather cynical modern definition states that 'the Hadith is the form in which we state our conclusions'.[13]

Ijma', qiyas, ijtihad, and *maslaha*: secondary sources of the law

The remaining, secondary sources of the law are normally discussed separately, but may be conveniently taken together since they are all, in one shape or another, a form of deductive reasoning. In assessing their validity and value, the standard texts show clear evidence of *post hoc*, logical deduction. There has also been the usual diversity of doctrinal views concerning them. As far as *ijma'* is concerned,

> it was a reasonable deduction from Qur'anic teaching, duly consecrated by a *hadith* that God would not permit His people universally to be in error. *Quod semper, quod ubique, quod ab omnibus fidelibus* is no less a Muslim than it is a Catholic doctrine.[14]

There has, however, been considerable argument concerning those who are qualified to participate in the consensus. For some jurists, only the ulama, the men of learning, were so qualified; for others it had to be, based on precedent, the entire community; and as a variation of the latter, 'the consensus of opinion of the companions of the Prophet . . . and the agreement reached by the learned "muftis" or the jurists on various Islamic matters'.[15] In the end, however, practicality and pragmatism evolved a workable and justifiable formula: *ijma'* was defined as

> the concordant doctrines and opinions of those who are in any given period . . . the men with the power 'to bind and to loose'; it is their office to interpret and deduce law and theological doctrine, and to decide whether law and doctrine are correctly applied.[16]

This does imply widespread agreement throughout the Muslim world and may be thought to imply a temporal spread beyond the period in which the consensus was achieved. In practice, however, any consensus was both temporally and spatially limited: there was rarely broad consensus throughout the Muslim world and even the spatially limited consensus tended to be temporary and constantly overtaken. Nevertheless, the unity implied in the formulation was doctrinally important and the discontinuity between doctrine and actual practice was conveniently overlooked: pragmatic adaptation does, after all, require a realistic understanding of when to be discreet.

Whatever the interpretation, however, 'the infallibility of the *consensus ecclesiae*' was implied:

> thus, all that is approved by the sense of the community of believers is correct and can lay claim to obligatory acknowledgement, and it is correct only in the form that the

sense of the community, the consensus, has given it.[17]

'My community', the *hadith* runs, 'will never agree on error.' This *hadith* can, of course, be construed in two ways: there is the standard view that it gives a degree of authority and legitimacy to any matter on which consensus, as defined above, has been reached; or Muhammad Asad's view, which implies that consensus must be equated with unanimity, for he argues that no false or erroneous premiss will ever be subscribed to by the entire community: some portion will always cleave to the truth.[18]

Similarly, *qiyas* has a rational basis. Since the *Qur'an*, the *Sunna*, and consensus did not necessarily cover all contingencies, administrators and jurists relied upon their own judgement. Clearly, however, the free and unrestricted use of personal judgement and opinion was not conducive to consistency and order; some control was deemed necessary. In due course, therefore, the principle was established that where there was no clear and direct precedent in the more authoritative sources, those sources must be searched for a case sufficiently similar in underlying principles to provide an analogy and hence by deduction the correct judgement. *Qiyas* is, in fact, a specific form of *ijtihad* used to extend and apply the principles and rules set out in the *Qur'an*, the *Sunna*, and *ijma'* to the solution of problems not previously regulated.

Ijtihad covers a much wider range of mental activity, ranging from textual interpretation, to assessing the authenticity of a *hadith*, and to systematic deductive reasoning from first principles. It therefore allows for logical reasoning to deduce a rule where no precedent exists. Thus, for example, 'if it becomes established that smoking tobacco definitely causes cancer, a *mujtahid* (i.e. one qualified to practise *ijtihad*), according to the judgement of reasoning will establish the law that smoking is forbidden according to the Divine Law'.[19] This is, admittedly, a modern Shi'a ruling based on the premise that one purpose of the Divine Law is to meet man's best interests and welfare, but it is a vivid example of the manner in which *ijtihad*, if properly used, bridges the apparent gap between doctrine and practice. Most authorities state that the use of *ijtihad* died out in the tenth century on the grounds that its creative force had become exhausted and that there was in any case no requirement for further interpretation. Thus the 'gate of *ijtihad*' was closed for all time and the era of *taqlid* set in.[20]

It is generally admitted that, ever since the codification of the doctrine of Islam by the four great orthodox imams, this door (of *ijtihad*) is closed and that Muslims must conform their opinions strictly to the opinions enumerated by these imams without seeking to arrive by means of their own reasoning at a personal opinion about the tenets of Islam.[21]

However, one observer has recently argued convincingly that the orthodox view is incorrect, that the concept has been misinterpreted, and that throughout the centuries, *mujtahids* (and others) have contributed to the further development of positive law and legal theory.[22] This is an important point, since most leaders of reformist or renewalist movements necessarily claim the right to practise *ijtihad*. However, since they do so on the basis of discarding or ignoring the developments he describes, they are unlikely to accept his argument. Nevertheless his argument does provide a continuity of practice and a possible means of according legitimacy to the claims irrespective of the time-scale. He implies that the stream of *fatwas* (legal opinions) issued over the centuries presents a more incorporated (into the state system, that is), and tacitly approved continuation of the use of, *ijtihad*. He is cautious about the long-term implications, but is in no doubt about the significance. He states that

> Legal activity, whether in theory or in practice, continued unceasingly. The vast bulk of *fatwas* (legal opinions) that appeared and continued to grow rapidly from the fourth/tenth century onwards is a telling example of the importance of *fatwas* as legal decisions and precedents. It is in this large body of material that one may look for positive legal developments.[23]

Maslaha, which is regarded by some as a source of the law, is predicated on the premise that one purpose of the law is to serve man's best interests, and to promote his well-being and welfare in this world and in the next. Although these serious purposes remain the basis, however, the manner of interpretation can accommodate some unusual rulings and the implications of unfettered recourse to *maslaha* have led to theoretical — and practical — limitations. Thus, although it may be argued that anything which was clearly in the public interest, which was conducive to maintaining or improving public welfare, and which was not specifically forbidden, could be construed as part of God's design, jurisprudents were cautious in their espousal of the proposition and only in the Hanbali doctrine was it fully accepted. The Hanbalis argue, subject to certain limitations, that anything which is not specifically forbidden is permissible. In practice, the role of *maslaha* was generally restricted to a choice between differing interpretations of the rules, other things being equal.

The early development of the law, jurisprudence, and the administration of justice

More recent scholarship, further developing the pioneering work of Ignaz Goldziher and Joseph Schacht (see Introduction, note 5) demonstrates conclusively that actual practice was rather different to the idealized picture presented in the classical Sunni doctrine, that Muslim law developed over a period of centuries and that the first 100 years after the death of Muhammad were particularly important in the development of the law. Schacht has argued that because the Prophet's authority was, in the eyes of his followers, religious rather than legal, he exercised that authority outside the existing legal system, and that, in any case, his function was not to create a new legal system but to instruct humankind on how to act. Nevertheless, it proved necessary in due course for the Prophet to apply religious and ethical principles to legal problems and relationships as they existed at the time.[24] Fazlur Rahman, an eminent modernist scholar of the speculative rationalist school, takes a similar line in his argument that the *Qur'an*

> does not in fact give many general principles; for the most part it gives solutions and rulings upon specific and concrete issues: but as I have said, it provides either explicitly or implicitly, the rationales behind these solutions and rulings, from which one can *deduce general principles*. (original emphasis)[25]

However, as has already been argued, the reasoning which leads these two eminent scholars to adduce their conclusions does seem to come perilously close to accusing Muhammad of manipulating the context of the 'revelation' in order to serve his political and moral (and, it may be inferred, temporal) objectives. Such reasoning, if taken to its logical conclusion, could lead to the conclusion that Muhammad was no more inspired than the next person, that the divine revelation was a successful confidence trick, and that the

Qur'an is not the word of God. This is not to suggest that either Schacht or Fazlur Rahman either intended or would accept this extension of their argument; but since the conclusion would be completely unacceptable to a Muslim, the proposition adduced on the basis of the reasoning must be at least suspect. Coulson's line appears more reasonable: he points out that 'the so-called legal matter of the *Qur'an* consists mainly of broad and general propositions as to what the aims and aspirations of Muslim society should be. It is essentially the bare formulation of the Islamic religious ethic'. He points out that most of the moral, social, and ethical standards of a civilized society are cited in the *Qur'an*:

> compassion for the weaker members of society, fairness and good faith in commercial dealings, incorruptibility in the administration of justice are all enjoined as desirable norms of behaviour without being translated into any legal structure of rights and duties.[26]

During the period of the *Rashidun*, the *khalifa* fulfilled the functions of political leader, administrator, interpreter of the law, and judge, although, as many authorities have demonstrated, Muslim law, in the precise technical meaning of the term, did not yet exist.[27] However, both he and his appointed provincial governors faced new administrative, juridical, and fiscal problems arising from the imperial expansion. These were dealt with in part by *ad hoc* decisions based upon the general and total teaching of the revelation and the example of the Prophet, taking into account local customs and practices, and in part by adopting and assimilating into the embryonic Muslim *praxis* the legal and administrative institutions of the conquered territories. The rule of thumb appears to have been that anything not specifically prohibited was permissible provided it was consistent with the general principles and unless and until sufficient evidence could be adduced against a particular practice. More importantly, the legal concepts, principles, and methodology of the newly acquired territories were, by a process of osmosis as it were, incorporated and fully assimilated into the nascent Muslim legal system. In the process, the *Rashidun* also enacted regulations and legislation for the proper governance of the empire and dispensed justice personally, as did the provincial governors, to whom full administrative, legislative, and judicial authority had been delegated. This process continued under the Umayyad *khalifas*, although they and their provincial governors took the important and, in the long term, significant step of appointing *qadis* (judges), thus providing the framework for the later separation of the judicial and juridical processes from the political authority.

The *qadis* were originally more in the nature of 'legal secretaries' to whom judicial authority was delegated; but the *khalifa* and the governor retained the personal right to review a particular decision and to deal personally with any case. However, the *qadi* faced the same lack of systematic codification as did the governor and the host of other quasi-judicial officials introduced to cope with the complexities of imperial administration. They had, perforce, to give judgement on the basis of their own discretion, based on Qur'anic injunctions and Muslim principles identified by early *ijma*', and taking into account the customary practice of the region, as necessary. They also, of course, took into account the practice and example of the Prophet on the grounds that he was the most authoritative interpreter of the revelation; but at this stage there was no suggestion that the Prophet was other than a fallible and mortal interpreter — that is, the *Sunna* of the Prophet had not yet been elevated to the status accorded it in al Shafi'i's schema and subsequently accepted by all Sunni juridical authorities.

The position under the *Rashidun* and more particularly under the Umayyads, was that an embryonic legal system, embracing both practice and theory, developed haphazardly, drawing upon customary law, the elaboration of Qur'anic rules, the corpus of administrative regulations and decisions, and both concepts and practices borrowed from other legal systems. Despite the appointment of *qadis* and a wide range of administrative officials, some of whom had quasi-judicial functions (for example, the police and the market inspector), both the administration of justice and the elaboration of the law remained firmly vested in the *khalifa* and his provincial governors. Nevertheless, the system of legal administration which evolved was, though haphazard, practical: it worked. Parallel with this development, however, the later Umayyad period also saw the emergence of a group of pious specialists and scholars, from whose ranks the *qadis* were drawn more and more regularly. They began to think about, and to voice their individual views on, the ideals and ethics which should properly inform Muslim society and institutions.

This process received added impetus under the early Abbasids, who had pledged themselves to build a truly Islamic form of state and society. The pious scholars, however, approached legal administration and doctrine from the standpoint of the religious idealist rather than that of the legal practitioner. They therefore examined existing practice and regulations primarily in order to establish whether there were valid objections from a religious, ethical, or ritualistic point of view, and then approved, modified, or rejected them.

> They impregnated the sphere of law with religious and ethical ideas, subjected it to Islamic norms and incorporated it into the body of duties incumbent on every Muslim . . . As a consequence, the popular and administrative practice of the late Umayyad period was transformed into Islamic law.[28]

However, there was no real uniformity: the 'ancient schools of law' represented little more than broad but very local agreement on doctrine and practice. More importantly, they were the real beginning of the separation of the juridical and judicial processes from the apparatus of state, and therefore of theory and practice. It was during this period also that the concept of the *sunna* as the established doctrine of the individual schools emerged, as did the practice of identifying the origins of the *sunna* in the first generation of Muslims. 'The doctrine was represented as having roots stretching back into the past, the authority of previous generations was claimed for its current expression.'[29] This inevitably led to the emergence of a group of scholars who argued that the *Sunna* of the Prophet represented the best authority, on the grounds that he was clearly best fitted to interpret the *Qur'an*, though they still saw him as 'a *primus inter pares* but nonetheless a human interpreter'.[30]

Al Shafi'i: the classical theory defined

It was al Shafi'i who took the final step and developed into a coherent and consistently argued form the proposition, already vaguely mooted before his time, that the Prophet's legal decisions were in fact divinely inspired. However, al Shafi'i pushed the reasoning further and argued compellingly that the Prophet's actions and decisions outwith the limited legal field were similarly divinely inspired. The *Sunna* of the Prophet, as recorded in authentic *hadith*, was thus a means of transmitting the divine command, and as such a source for that command which was complementary to, and interpretative of, the *Qur'an*: 'whatever the Apostle has decreed that is not based on any [textual] command from God, he has done so by God's command' and 'the sunna of the Apostle makes evident what God meant [in the text of His Book], indicating His general and particular [commands].[31] Al Shafi'i also redefined *ijma'* as being the consensus of the entire Muslim community, oversetting the existing definition that the consensus of scholars in a particular area was authoritative in that locality. Finally, he repudiated existing forms of reasoning, which had produced a remarkable diversity of doctrine, and insisted that only strictly regulated analogical reasoning was permissible. Al Shafi'i thus established in systematic form the sources of the law, their order of priority, and their interrelationship: he is rightly regarded as the architect of the classical doctrine. He also achieved his aim of imposing uniformity, of achieving a unification of the law in place of the existing diversity.

Theory and practice in the post-al Shafi'i period

Notwithstanding the importance and real value of al Shafi'i's accomplishments, the doctrine which flowed naturally from his schema had the effect of further separating the jurists and the apparatus of state, in that it limited the area of jurisdiction of the Muslim law courts and excluded from the Muslim legal system both public law and the regulatory activities of the political authority. To be sure the principle of *siyasa shar'iyya* (government in accordance with the revealed law) has, since the eleventh century at least, provided a doctrinally acceptable rationale for the additional legislative provisions enacted by the political authority as and when the public interest or necessity so required, subject always to the requirement that such supplementary legislation must be consistent with the principles of the *shari'a*. However, a sharp and clear distinction was always drawn between Muslim law proper and *siyasa shar'iyya*, despite the fact that

> the doctrine of *siyasa shar'iyya*, based on a realistic assessment of the nature of *Shari'a* law and the historical process by which it has been absorbed into the structure of the state, admitted the necessity for, and the validity of, extra-*shari'a* jurisdictions, which cannot, therefore, be regarded, in themselves, as deviations from any ideal standard.[32]

Notwithstanding this self-evident fact, doctrine continued to insist on the difference between authoritatively interpreting Muslim law on the basis of the classical sources — a function which was held to be restricted to the jurists — and the regulatory activities of the political authority, which came to be seen as purely temporal in nature and not part of Muslim law, however consistent the regulations might be with the ideals and norms of Islam. In fact it is on this very dubious distinction that activists today base their condemnation of national legislation.

This development in public law in the post-al Shafi'i period was accompanied by similar developments in other areas of the law. As Coulson points out, the development can be measured by the extent to which practice diverged from the theoretical ideal. The divergence was particularly marked in the field of family law, where

> the classical doctrine of the Arab authorities remained inviolate as expressing the only standards of conduct which were valid in the eyes of God; and such deviations from this norm, as legal practice in certain areas condoned, were never recognised as legitimate expressions of Islamic law.

However, the divergence was more blurred in other fields, where the doctrine of *siyasa shar'iyya* recognized the political need for supplementary jurisdictions, as in the field of public, and particularly criminal, law, or where social forces or sheer practicality modified the strict doctrine, as in the field of civil transactions. In both these fields, the activities of the *muftis* (those empowered to issue *fatwas*, whether government officials or private individuals) were the means of synthesizing doctrine and practice. Coulson concluded that although the classical texts were respected and recognized as the ideal, 'from a realistic stand-point the classical doctrine never formed a complete or exclusively authoritative expression of Islamic law'. Moreover, the respect accorded to the ideal was the reason why 'developments in the doctrine often assumed the aspect of reluctant concessions to the practice by way of *exceptio utilitatis*'.[33]

These general arrangements remained broadly applicable throughout the Muslim world thereafter, though some changes did occur as a result of the spread of the European imperial system, and remain the theoretical basis for legislative and judicial processes. In more modern times, the adoption or adaptation of western European legal codes has been a feature, and the process has regularly been characterized as contrary to God's will.[34] However, this process is consistent both with the practice of the early community and with the doctrine of *siyasa shar'iyya*. The same could be said for legislation enacted by Muslim governments, subject to the limitations imposed by the doctrine. Furthermore, such legislation is in direct succession to the process established under the later Umayyads and the Abbasids. The crux is the relationship between such legislation — for legislation it undoubtedly is — and Muslim law. In this connection it should be noted that the 1907 amendment to the 1906 Iranian Constitution explicitly recognized both the duality of legislated and revealed law and a valid relationship between them, as does the current constitution of the Islamic Republic of Iran. Within the Sunni world, most constitutions specify that the *shari'a* shall be at least one source, if not *the* source of legislation (though the *shari'a* is never formally defined), and that no law shall be enacted which is inconsistent with or repugnant to the *Qur'an* and the *Sunna*.

Shi'a legal theory

The development of Shi'a legal theory has followed a similar pattern to that of the Sunni theory in that it too represents 'a systematically idealised rather than a historically factual account of the sources of the law'.[35] Indeed, some observers suggest that there is little intrinsic difference between the two since the end result is, in practice, much the same. This is a facile observation, however, since there are significant differences arising in particular from the Shi'a doctrine on the Imamate (see Chapter 3, pp. 73–4), and it is more realistic to say that for much of the detail of the law, Sunni and Shi'a theory arrive at broadly the same position but that the routes are very different. Moreover, Shi'a theory on the sources of the law and on the nature of the law provides a more dynamic form of law. In particular, the Shi'a draw a clear distinction between the *shari'a*, which comprises the divinely ordained law, and *fiqh*, which is 'precise and profound deducing of the Islamic regulations of actions from the relevant sources' or 'the study of the secondary commands (i.e. not the principal matter of beliefs and moral perfection but the commands regulating actions) of the Shari'ah of Islam gained from the detailed resources and proofs':[36] that is, the law. Furthermore, by elevating *aql* (reason) to the status of a source of the law, they reject the Sunni disavowal of *ijtihad* and have given deductive reasoning a more important place than it occupies in Sunni theory.

For the Shi'a, the sources of the law are the *Qur'an*, the *Sunna*, *aql*, and *ijma'*. *Qiyas* is rejected as unreliable if not false. However, the Shi'a definition of the *Sunna* and of *ijma'* differ from the Sunni definition. In the case of the *Sunna*, the Shi'a accept only those *hadith* transmitted through one or more of the Imams, and some 'believe that traditions of the Holy Prophet should be accepted through the channel of narrations by the people of the Holy Prophet's Progeny'[37] — that is, only *hadith* transmitted through the line of Imams are acceptable. The modern view, however, adopts the first, more liberal definition and also holds that the *sunna* of the Imams is also binding on the rational grounds that the Imams are, like the Prophet, sinless and infallible. The Shi'a concept of *aql* is closely linked to *ijtihad*, since 'the Shi'i jurist uses *'aql*, usually supported by the other three sources of the law . . . to arrive at legal decisions and this process is called *ijtihad*'.[38] Although the Shi'a thus reject the Sunni closing of the gate of *ijtihad*, the requirement to avoid straying from the example of the Imams has in practice been a limiting influence on its unfettered use.

The rationale behind the concept of *aql* is that although God is the sole creator and provider of the law, He has furnished man with reason and the power of reasoning so that he may properly identify the terms of the law. This did, of course, raise a problem in that some rational explanation for the inevitable differences of opinion among the ulama was needed, once the doctrine of the ulama as *al na'ib al 'amm* (general representative; see Chapter 3, pp. 74–5 for details) was established, since that doctrine identified the ulama collectively as the valid and licit transmitter of the *Sunna* and the authoritative interpreter of the law. This problem

> was overcome by arguing that if the truth lay in only one of two opposing views and this could not be discerned through the techniques of *usul al fiqh* then it would be obligatory for the hidden Imam to manifest himself and give a decision. If he does not manifest himself, the truth must lie with both parties.[39]

Thus, the Shi'a community can be assured that no incorrect ruling has been given unless and until the Hidden Imam manifests himself. In other words, any ruling derived by the use of reason from the *Qur'an* and the *Sunna* cannot be in contradiction with any ruling reached through the application of rational principles. This line of argument leads effectively to the Shi'a definition of *ijma'*, which means the unanimous view of the ulama on a particular issue. However, for it to be binding, it must be the consensus of the ulama of the time of the Prophet, or of the Imams. Where there is a difference of opinion, the ulama are required to consider the variations and in due course arrive at a unanimous consensus. However, it is only binding if it reflects the opinion of the Prophet or of one of the Imams: 'a somewhat paradoxical situation whereby the validity of a unanimous agreement is based upon the participation of a single individual.'[40]

The theory set out briefly above is essentially that of the *usuli* school (a rationalist use of the sources) and was largely in place by the sixteenth century CE. However, an opposing school, the *akhbari* (traditionalist), rose to prominence and doctrinal development paused until the controversy between the two was finally resolved in favour of the *usulis* towards the end of the eighteenth century CE. In essence, *akhbari* theory rejected the rationalist basis of the *usuli* view in favour of heavy reliance upon the *Qur'an* and the *Sunna* as explained by the Imams and upon a much larger corpus of *hadith* than that accepted as valid by the *usulis*. It follows that the *akhbaris* rejected the *usuli* linkage between the sources of the law and rational principles and they equally reject *ijtihad* in favour of *taqlid* — but a restricted form of *taqlid* in which it is the Hidden Imam who must be emulated.

The *usuli* victory was followed by a resurgence of theoretical development, with the main contribution coming from Shaikh Murtaza Ansari (1799–1864) in his definition of the principles to be followed in reaching a decision in cases where there was doubt. In such cases, he argued, the principles to be applied were:

> *al-bara'a* (allowing the maximum possible freedom of action); *at-takhir* (freedom to select the opinions of other jurists or even other schools if these seem more suitable); *al-istishab* (the continuation of any state of affairs in existence or legal decisions already accepted unless the contrary can be proved); and *al-ihtiyat* (prudent caution whenever in doubt).[41]

One of the more significant effects of this development was the theoretical extension of the area of jurisdiction of the ulama to virtually any matter where there was no clear-cut ruling, thus providing doctrinal justification for participation in matters previously regarded as the province of the political authority. Equally significant, however, was his establishment of a centralized and coherent leadership for the ulama, which eventually resulted in the institution of a single *marja' al taqlid* (reference point for emulation) — the highest authority whose rulings and opinions should be accepted by all Shi'a.

The classical theory and pre-modern practice: a recapitulation

Let us now pause and summarize the position. Theoretically, Muslim law (that is, Sunni law) is divinely ordained and therefore immutable, comprehensive in scope, touching upon all aspects of human activity, valid, and necessarily applicable at all times and in all places. In practice and in reality, matters are very different. In the first place, the corpus of Muslim law is derived from four sources — the *Qur'an*, the *Sunna*, *ijma'*, and *qiyas*. That the *Qur'an* was divinely revealed is necessarily a given, but the same cannot be said for the other sources. Although it is reasonable to argue that the Prophet was, though not infallible, the person most likely to provide a correct interpretation, this is far from proving that he was always divinely inspired or that all his actions were divinely ordained. Moreover, it is clear that Qur'anic injunctions to 'obey the Prophet' notwithstanding, the community both during his lifetime and during the period of the *Rashidun* (not to mention the Umayyads) did not regard him as infallible or as divinely inspired, except in his capacity as transmitter of the revelation. The process by which his *Sunna* was extended from formal decisions to comprehend all that he said and did and then elevated to the status of an authoritative and divinely ordained expression of God's will took place over some centuries and was the product of human reasoning — albeit, in the case of al Shafi'i, human reasoning of a rigorously systematic and formidably intellectual nature. *Ijma'*, whether it be the consensus of the entire community or of those deemed qualified to participate, must similarly be seen as the result of human endeavour, while *qiyas* is the process by which established principles are extended and applied to the solution of problems not hitherto expressly regulated — and thus a product of human reasoning.

Shi'a doctrine, as already suggested, was rather different since they distinguish clearly between God's law and man's interpretation. The former is immutable, but the latter is not necessarily so. Further, they do not talk about the sources of the law but about *usul al fiqh* — sources of jurisprudence. Moreover, they believe in the sinlessness and infallibility of the Prophet and of the twelve Imams, not only out of theological belief but on rational grounds. However, it is the distinction between God's law and man's interpretation and the importance attached to reason and rationality, together with its application through *ijtihad*, which is of particular significance; for it is these which distinguish Shi'a theory from that of the Sunni schools, in that they represent a juridical and theoretical flexibility to adjust to changed circumstances and incorporate into the theory the legitimacy of dynamic and adaptative practice. There are, of course, certain limitations and the practical development of theory in Shi'a jurisprudence was similar to that of the Sunnis until recently, though the relationship between Muslim law and the enactments of political authorities could be much closer and was certainly more logically based.

The jurisdictional scope of what came to be seen as Islamic law proper was restricted by the rules of procedure and possibly also by the jurists' failure — or refusal — to incorporate within their terms of reference a wide range of issues; it is also possible that limitations on jurisdictional scope were imposed by the political authorities. The precise cause is not clear but the result was an arbitrary limit to the scope of a legal system which the jurists insisted was comprehensive and universal. Rulers, therefore, continued to 'make' law, as they had done since the death of the Prophet, but, because of the separation of the juridical process and political authority, they had to accept a lesser theoretical — though not practical — status for that law under the doctrine of *siyasa shar'iyya*. The theoretical distinction is still maintained today in Saudi Arabia where government enactments are formally defined as 'regulations' rather than as 'laws', but as 'regulations' which must be consistent with the principles, aims, and ideals of Islam.[42] Similarly, in Iran, both under the Shah and under the Republic, legislation by the political authority was tolerated, if not seen as legitimate, as long as it was consistent with Shi'a doctrine. Although the dual system was clearly open to abuse by unscrupulous rulers (and was indeed often abused), it did provide a doctrinally acceptable framework for the continued flexibility and dynamism of *al nizam al Islami* (the Islamic order) so characteristic of the early years of Islam. More importantly, as Muslim law became rigid both in theory and to some extent in practice, it allowed the political authority wide discretion to decide the manner in which judicial powers and jurisdictional competence should be distributed, thus providing a response to the limitations on the jurisdiction of jurists and in due course paving the way for further restricting the competence of Muslim law courts.

However, the distinction between the two complementary systems has been seen as a distinction between Muslim law and a purely secular law, with the former generally applicable only to matters of personal status and the latter covering everything else. The secular law (the corpus of state-enacted laws), so the argument runs, was given spurious legitimacy by characterizing it as based on the principles of Muslim jurisprudence, despite the fact that it was 'not referrable to any Islamic sources, was not derived from them, and was not subsumed under them. It was, in fact, secular law juxtaposed with the *Shari'a* law'.[43] This argument, of course, rejects the widely held view that state acts and regulatory enactments were acceptable provided there was no conflict with the provisions of the *Shari'a* in favour of a more rigid requirement for such enactments to be derived from the *Shari'a* before they could be deemed acceptable. Furthermore, it holds that conflict between the two systems was inevitable and that the progressive adoption of European codes necessarily resulted in the relegation of Muslim law to matters of personal status alone.

However, this line of reasoning seems, as already suggested, to be inconsistent with the early practice and the historical development, particularly since the reasons why the corpus of Islamic law was not subjected to periodic systematic assessment were sociological rather than theological.[44] Furthermore, the division of functions between the two systems seems to have occurred for reasons of administrative (and, let it be admitted, intellectual) convenience. The doctrinal justification was a *post hoc* occurrence. The reasoning also ignores the very real problems of coping with legislative and juridical requirements not explicitly covered in the revealed law, as long as the principle that that law was all-embracing and comprehensive remained a regularly voiced article of faith. Furthermore, it ignores the often very real sincerity of the 'secular' lawmakers. In this connection, one leading authority commented, in discussing the legislative activity of the Ottoman Sultans, that 'in perfect good faith they enacted *kanuns* or *kanun-names* which were real laws, convinced that in doing so they neither abrogated nor contradicted the Sacred Law but supplemented it by religiously indifferent regulations.' He also pointed out that such Ottoman enactments repeatedly referred to Muslim law and used its concepts liberally, though he admits that certain provisions seem to amount to superseding that law.[45] Moreover, despite the apparent rigidity, Muslim law itself continued to develop as society changed, through the provision of *fatwas* (legal pronouncements) on request by the ulama and through the voluminous writing of many scholars.[46]

In particular, considerable latitude was permitted as far as criminal law was concerned. Muslim law distinguishes clearly between those criminal offences for which punishment is prescribed in the *Qur'an* and those for which punishments are not prescribed in the *Qur'an*. Offences in the first category are generally defined as *hadd* (pl. *hudud*, literally limits) offences and punishments. The rationale is that *hadd* crimes and punishments, being clearly regulated in the revelation, are on the one hand offences against God and on the other punishments prescribed by God. The punishments are therefore fixed and may not be made lighter or heavier by the judge or by the political authority. Nor may the perpetrator be pardoned. Other offences attract *ta'zir* (discretionary) punishment: the judge has discretion to impose such punishment as is seen fit taking into account all relevant circumstances.

However, custom and precedent have led to particular offences customarily attracting particular punishments. Homicide is treated somewhat differently, despite the fact that it is mentioned in the *Qur'an*, since it has a dual nature: that of a crime (by implication against God, society, and the individual) for which a fixed punishment is imposed; and that of a tort, which makes the offender liable to pay compensation, which may be in cash or in kind.[47] The technical term for the punishment for homicide or physical injury is *qisas* (retaliation or just retribution) and may be equated with *lex talionis*. The principle is well known: the imposition of an exactly equivalent injury as punishment, or, more popularly, an eye for an eye and a tooth for a tooth. However, Muslim law also prescribes the payment of blood-money in certain circumstances, and it is deemed a meritorious act to accept blood-money in place of retributory punishment. In addition, since the *hadd* punishments are severe, and include execution, amputations, and corporal punishment, judges were enjoined not to apply them if there was any doubt or if the approved evidence was not forthcoming, but to apply some lesser discretionary punishment. More generally, the principle of *takhayyur* (literally, choice), which permits recourse to another recognized school of law, further extended the flexibility of the system, and the general principle that things are permissible unless specifically forbidden[48] is clearly a valuable extensor of flexibility and change — but has been sparingly used other than by the Hanbalis.

A modern definition of the *Shari'a*

The confusion touched upon at the beginning of this chapter can be reformulated as a fundamental question: what is the proper meaning and nature of the *shari'a*, what is the real scope of Muslim law, and what is the legislative competence, in Muslim terms, of the modern political authority? For some, the answer is simple: the *shari'a* is Muslim law; it is comprehensive, universal, eternal, and not susceptible to change; its contents are set out in the authoritative codices of the orthodox schools. Those who hold this view do accept that a ruler has the right to enact legislation but insist that that right is not absolute, and that legislation is only valid if it falls into one of two categories:

'1. Executive legislation intended to guarantee the implementation of the provisions of Shari'ah.

2. Organisational legislation, intended to organise the society, protect it and meet its needs in accordance with Shari'ah.'[49]

Such legislation must, of course, be consistent with the principles of Muslim law and, preferably, clearly derived from them or from accepted rules of Muslim law. Clearly, though the term 'legislation' is used regularly, the distinction between true legislation, which is God's prerogative, and the promulgation of 'regulations' or 'orders' by the political authorities, which have a lesser status, is maintained.

Others, however, have concluded that this approach is no longer sufficient, and have resorted to a variety of ingenious (and sometimes extraordinary) theses to square the circle. It has been argued, for example, that *fiqh*, in the sense of jurisprudential rulings, are not part of the *shari'a*. All such rulings were originally

> intended by their authors to facilitate the application of *shar'i* principles to specific questions. In the course of time, however, these rulings acquired in the popular mind a kind of sacrosanct validity of their own and came to be regarded by many Muslims as an integral part of the *shari'ah*, the Canon Law, itself.

The argument used to justify this is that since the explicit injunctions of the *Qur'an* and the *Sunna* are not in themselves sufficient to cover all possible situations, amplification by means of deductive reasoning is necessary.

> However, quite apart from the fact that neither Quran nor Sunnah offers the slightest warrant for such an arbitrary enlargement of the *shari'ah*, one might with justice argue (as a number of Muslim scholars have argued through the centuries) that the limited scope of the explicit ordinances contained in Qur'an and Sunnah was not due to an oversight on the part of the Law-Giver but, on the contrary, was meant to provide a most essential, deliberate safeguard against legal and social rigidity.

Thus, the *shari'a*, in the sense of revealed law, comprises only those matters specifically and unmistakably ordained in the *Qur'an* and the *Sunna*; that is, 'what the Law-Giver has ordained in unmistakable terms as an obligation or put out of bounds as unlawful'. Consequently, it is argued, not only were Muslims intended to provide for such additional legislation as might be necessary through the use of *ijtihad* in consonance with the spirit of Islam, but also such legislation 'can amount to no more than a temporal, changeable law subject to the irrevocable, unchangeable *shari'ah*'.[50] Muslim Brotherhood activists share these views, and appear to argue that the *Qur'an* and the *Sunna* are the two fundamental sources of the *shari'a*, though they accord the *Sunna* a much less elevated place. However, they also subscribe to the distinction between the changeable and the unchangeable, though not to the reservation of the term *shari'a* to the explicit ordinances of the *Qur'an* and the *Sunna*, nor the conviction that legislative powers necessarily rest with mankind.[51]

Maududi, however, seems to confuse the *shari'a* as 'a complete scheme of life and an all-embracing social order where nothing is lacking'[52] and the more limited concept of the *shari'a* as a detailed legal code which requires the coercive power and authority of the state for its implementation. On the one hand, he distinguishes between

> the part of the *shari'ah* which has a permanent and unalterable character and is, as such, extremely beneficial for mankind, and that part which is flexible and has thus the potentialities of meeting the ever-increasing requirements of every time and age.[53]

On the other hand, in discussing the role of the *Sunna* he comments that

> this entire life-work of the Holy Prophet, which was completed in twenty-three years of his prophethood, is the *Sunnah* which in conjunction with *Qur'an* formulates and completes the Supreme Law of the real Sovereign and this Law constitutes what is called '*Shari'ah*' in Islamic terminology.[54]

Notwithstanding this confusion and the fact that Maududi does admit of human legislation within certain limits, he is much closer to the conventional or orthodox conservative view that the *shari'a* is indeed the law as set out in the codices of the schools of law — i.e. the classical doctrine — than appears at first sight.

Subhi Mahmasani (1909–), formerly a leading Sunni Lebanese politician, argues, on the basis of a frequently cited *hadith*,[55] that 'no relation exists between Islam and matters of daily living, unless these are concerned with a principle of religion'.[56] He defines religion as comprising matters of faith, the unity of God, acts of worship, ethical principles, and the basic rules for legal transactions, and holds that apart from such matters, Muslims are free to follow their own opinions (subject, no doubt, to the dictates of conscience).

Perhaps the most extraordinary line of thought, however, is that of Fazlur Rahman. He defines the *shari'a* as including

> all behaviour — spiritual, mental and physical. Thus it comprehends both faith and practice: assent to or belief in one God is part of the Shari'a just as are the religious duties of prayer and fasting, etc. Further all legal and social transactions as well as all personal behaviour is subsumed under the Shari'a as the comprehensive principle of the *total way of life*. (original emphasis)[57]

He distinguished this from *fiqh* which he sees as the process of understanding God's will and, later, as 'the earlier attempts at actual legislation by the representatives of the four schools of law'.[58] However, in discussing the sources of the law, he considers the *Qur'an* as not primarily a legal document, though it does contain some legislation. On the basis of specific examples, he concludes that the legislative provisions of the *Qur'an* had to take into account the attitudes and mores of the then existing society and argues that 'this clearly means that the actual legislation of the Qur'an *cannot have been meant to be literally eternal by the Qur'an itself*' (emphasis added).[59] He later notes that the Prophet's religious authority was binding:

> While he was alive, this authority was sufficient for and at any given point of time; . . . But after his death, that living authority was no longer available and had to be transformed formally into a doctrine of infallibility. *This means that whatever decisions or pronouncements of the Prophet were authoritative during his lifetime became infallible after his death.* (emphasis added)[60]

This is tantamount to saying that the legal injunctions of the *Qur'an* may be changed, but that those contained in 'the decisions or pronouncements of the Prophet [which] were authoritative during his lifetime' cannot! Mohammad Tawheedi, the translator of Mutahhari's *Jurisprudence and its Principles*, has an equally eccentric approach, though it must be remembered that this is a Shi'a view. He defines the *shari'a* as the divine legislation which was introduced and followed by the Prophet. However, the *shari'a*, he maintains, 'was not revealed for mankind as the Qur'an was revealed'.[61]

Conclusions

Clearly, Muslims must seek to identify God's will, His command, and the precise formulation of His law: they must seek to identify the *shari'a*, whatever the definition. However, the conventional approach (i.e. classical doctrine) seems inadequate since it denies the possibility that a particular legal ruling, formulated by a mere mortal, has failed to identify correctly God's command. (This is not in any way to impugn the sincerity of the framer or his genuine belief in the accuracy of his interpretation.) Muhammad Asad's approach, on the other hand, denies the possibility that human endeavour may, indeed, have identified God's will so accurately that it fulfils the requirement to be universally applicable in both time and space. Maududi seems to be in danger of denying both possibilities, as does Mahmasani while Fazlur Rahman seems close to heresy. In addition, all these approaches deny the value of some, if not all, of the development discussed earlier and, either explicitly or implicitly, arrogate to the ulama alone the task of identification which is incumbent upon all Muslims. They also perpetuate the arbitrary separation of the law and the judicial process from the political authority.

A more practical approach, and one more in keeping with both the letter and the spirit of the *Qur'an* and more consistent with the early practice, is to start from the premise that both jurists and the political authority are empowered to articulate, separately or together, detailed legislative provisions; that this articulation is, in both cases, part of the process of identifying God's will; but that the precise formulations of the *Qur'an* are inviolable and that the general principles articulated in the *Qur'an* should be observed. The authentic *Sunna* is certainly divinely inspired, though not divinely ordained, since the Prophet is mortal and fallible. It is, therefore, the most authoritative guidance available, but interpretation of it should be flexible. The detailed formulations of the schools of law which are the result of reasoning should, however, be regarded as authoritative only unless and until a more accurate, more correct, more appropriate, or more generally accepted ruling is formulated. Nor is there any doctrinal objection to the adoption or adaptation of foreign codes, within the framework of the broad principles already referred to: indeed, it might be argued that where such borrowing can be done without damage to the principles of Islam and without abrogating specific rulings in the *Qur'an*, Muslim economic theory would approve of it as an efficient use of resources.

Such an approach is less theoretical than might be supposed at first sight. The High Court of Lahore, in *Kurshid Jan* v. *Fazal Dad*, 1964, was asked to rule on the question: 'Can courts differ from the views of imams and other jurisconsults of Muslim Law [that is, the doctrine of the authoritative legal manuals] on grounds of public policy, justice, equity, and good conscience?' The judgement commented that this amounted to a survey of 'the vast subject of Muslim jurisprudence; by no means an easy task even for the most learned in this science, and undoubtedly the most difficult assignment undertaken by the members of the Bench'. Nevertheless, the full bench of the High Court found, with only one dissenter, that

> if there is no clear rule of decision in Qur'anic and traditional text [that is, the *sunna*] . . . a court may resort to private reasoning and, in that, will undoubtedly be guided by the rules of justice, equity, and good conscience . . . The views of the earlier jurists and imams are entitled to the utmost respect and cannot be lightly disturbed; but the right to differ from them must not be denied to the present-day courts.[62]

This line has also been propounded by others. It has been argued, albeit in a wider context than the law alone, that rulers may make decisions and promulgate rules and regulations where this helps to secure the interests of the people and to ensure justice. Furthermore, they may derive or borrow their enactments from any source, whether Muslim or non-Muslim. In the latter case, care must be taken to 'distinguish between accepting a practical solution to a problem and slipping into an attitude of inferiority toward the intellectual or ideological system upon which the solution is based. Thus, while the first is permissible, the second is not'. In other words, as long as what is taken or accepted from non-Muslims

> is limited to the solution rather than the doctrine and the solution is within the conceptual limits of Islam . . . and is not counter to a clear injunction of the *Shari'ah*, we are not violating the principles of the Islamic *Shari'ah*.[63]

The conclusions to be drawn from this survey are neither startling nor complex. It demonstrates a process of steady and pragmatic adaptation of the theory in order to accommodate the facts of life, however reluctant the adaptation might be. There is reinforcement for the view that the revealed law was not, in most cases, law as the term is normally understood, but was, as so many have argued, a set of general principles and exhortations which should inform man's relations with God, with his fellow man, and with his inner self. Since a system of law and order is necessary not only as in fulfilment of God's wish but also on logical grounds, people are duty bound to seek to draw from those principles and exhortations the detailed rules and regulations which comprise the law. However since the law is man's attempt to identify God's commands, the detailed rules and regulations are not necessarily immutable. On the other hand, legal formulations by past jurisprudents, though not necessarily immutable, are equally not to be ignored since they were best placed to offer authoritative interpretations consistent with the needs of their age. Implicit in this is another important strand. There is a continuity — a process of building on the past through modification, adjustment, assimilation, and incorporation — which opposes rigidity, stultification, and the abnegation of man's power of reasoning. The system can, and does, accommodate both the conservatism of precedent, which is characteristic of all systems of law, and the propensity for jurisprudents to 'make' new law when the relationship between doctrine and practice is skewed and doctrine overrides commonsense. When the law is an ass, it needs to be modified; but the attempts of some to jettison the entire corpus of legal development since the coming of Islam and to construct an entirely new legal system which owes nothing to the past is necessarily rejected.

3

Concepts of State Government and Authority

Introduction

One of the most hotly debated — and most confused — issues in Islam is the question of authority and sovereignty. This is normally dealt with under two broad headings, although the distinction between them is often blurred:

(a) the nature and form of the legal system; and
(b) the nature and form of authority, the state, and governmental institutions.

There are, however, and have been for many centuries, differing views about what constitutes a Muslim legal code, from what that code is derived, and its precise status. There has also been confusion resulting from a lack of consistency in terminology — for example, the blurring of the real distinction between *Shari'a* and *fiqh*, and the relative standing of the traditional sources of law. (See Chapter 2 for an explanation of these terms and for a more detailed treatment of the issues.) There is similar confusion over the concept of the true Muslim or Islamic state since the polity in the time of the Prophet and the first four *khalifas* (strictly, 'successors') was *not* territorially based, but comprised the entire *umma*. Nevertheless, that polity has remained the exemplar or paradigm for all time, despite the fact that 'neither the Qur'an nor the Prophet left any clear-cut guidance as to how succession to the state authority after the death of the Prophet would open up'.[1] The seeds of the tension so evident today between the unity and universality of the ideal and the territorial and political plurality of reality, between the rigid doctrinaire views of the 'radical' and 'conservative' thinkers, and

60

the flexibility of the political pragmatists were sown by this fact.

Further development and refinement of both concepts have been considerably hampered by the widely held view that the process of 'revival' or 'renewal' — the process of restoring 'the pure, original Islam purged from alien accretions'[2] — must oppose alleged innovations drawn from the practices and ideologies of non-Muslim cultures, in particular those of the West — modern, medieval, and classical — despite the fact that the political, social, cultural, economic, and to some extent legal structures of the West are rooted in precisely those broad principles to which good Muslims cleave. It should not, therefore, be a matter for surprise that there are many similarities both in theory and in practice between the two systems. Nor should it be a matter for surprise or condemnation that borrowing, as a form of short cut, has been widespread in both directions, although the borrowings by the Muslim system must always be metamorphosed, provided with suitable antecedents, and given legitimacy in the process of incorporation. For Muslims there is an added complexity in that the era of the *Rashidun*, the 'Golden Age' of Islam, has become an idealized state in which pristine and pure Islam sprang forth, like Aphrodite from the waves, completely furnished with all the impedimenta of a fully fledged state and society — law, philosophy, administrative machinery, economic principles, etc. Yet as many authorities, including Muslim authorities, have conclusively demonstrated, the evolution of the impedimenta of a fully fledged state and society took place over a period of some three centuries or more following the Golden Age. Furthermore, the period of the *Rashidun* was itself one of the most innovative in the history of Islam.

There is also a deal of confusion over the use of the terms *khalifa* and *imam* (leader) and the related terms *khilafa* and *imama* (the offices of *khalifa* and *imam* respectively). The two terms are largely inter-changeable, but to the extent that a distinction can be made, the former is applied primarily to the supreme leader of the *umma* exercising the temporal functions of the Prophet, while the latter is applied to him in his capacity as religious leader.[3] Since, however, the two functions are theoretically vested in a single individual and since Islam does not admit (in theory at least) a separation of religion and politics, of faith and authority, this seems inadequate. The jurists defined the structure of authority, both political and religious, in terms of the *imam* and the *imama*, but distinguished between the pure *imama* of the *Rashidun* and the less than perfect subsequent leadership, which was characterized by some degree of kingship or temporal authority. Juridically, the term *khalifa* was reserved for the *Rashidun* and for those subsequent leaders who matched up to their standards: by implication this was rarely if ever possible once the generation who had known the Prophet personally had died out.

In practice, however, the term *khalifa* continued to be used, but the term gradually changed meaning from 'successor to the Prophet' to 'vice-regent of God'. Authority was thus 'derived not from the community but directly from God, who as sole Head of the Community has alone the power to confer authority of any kind',[4] in violation of the generally accepted view that the consent and approval of the *umma* was necessary for a valid assumption of the office. The confusion and inconsistency noted above is well illustrated by the following quotation:

> The caliph is defender of the faith, the dispenser of justice, the leader in prayer and in war, all in one . . . According to Muslim tradition only the first four successors of Muhammad were caliphs in the strict sense; with Mu'awiya *mulk* (absolute monarchy) arose. Yet some of the Abbasid caliphs came up to the standard required of the *imam* as 'Commander of the Faithful', and although the distinction between *imama* and *mulk* is of great importance for political theory and practice alike we must not forget that the real meaning of the *khalifa* is God-centred rule in conformity with the *Shari'a*.[5]

The foregoing applies predominantly to Sunni Islam. There are, however, three issues which generally set the Shi'a apart from the Sunnis: the concept of the Shi'a community as *al khassa* (special, or the 'elect'), the Shi'a doctrine of the Imamate, and the doctrine of martyrdom. These three provide the justification for the discrimination against and the oppression of the Shi'a which has been a feature of their history; for the separate identity of the Shi'a community; and for the justification for the activist Shi'a response to discrimination and oppression. As to the first, the Shi'a recognize Sunnis as Muslims, but 'only Twelver Shi'ism confers true belief (*Iman*) and makes one a true believer (*Mu'min*)'.[6] They are thus a special group of the 'elect' among the generality of Muslims, set apart by their true belief. As to the second, since the Shi'a doctrine of the Imamate is covered in some detail later in this chapter, suffice it to say at this point that the doctrinal differences between Sunni and Shi'a are clear, deep-rooted and as great an obstacle to Muslim unity as is, for example, the doctrine of papal infallibility to Christian unity, but they need not and do not generally obtrude in purely political matters. As to the third, the Shi'a have certainly at the least suffered discrimination and more often persecution and oppression throughout much of their history, and fervently believe that all twelve Imams were martyred. However, it is the martyrdom of Husain, the Third Imam, which 'has given to Shi'i Islam a whole ethos of sanctification through martyrdom . . . a characteristic that recent events have demonstrated to be as strong as ever'.[7] However, as will emerge later, this distinction between Sunni and Shi'a is not of great significance for an understanding of Muslim politics generally, particularly in view of the manner in which Khomeini has sought to couch his appeal in non-sectarian language. It is, perhaps, best seen as yet another example of the combination of diversity and unity so characteristic of the Muslim world.

Sunni political theory

The classical Sunni theory of the Imamate, which underpins theories of sovereignty, authority, and government, has been summarized by many scholars. As one commented,

> Sovereignty belongs to God; authority is vested in the *khalifa* as the vice-regent of the prophet, the messenger of Allah. It is the duty of the caliph to implement the *Shari'a*, to defend the faith against heresy, and the faithful against attack, and to ensure their ability to live by the prescription of the *Shari'a* and thus to attain happiness in this world and in the hereafter.[8]

Another approach is equally succinct, and though the formulations are not identical, the essential elements are:

> The view which they [i.e., the Sunni jurists] put forward was that the Caliph or Imam is the representative or upholder of the Sacred Law; that his office is indispensable and of divine institution, although the holder is elected thereto by human agency; that as the Sacred Law is one and indivisible, so also is the Caliphate; and that as the Law is binding on all Muslims without question or qualification, so also is allegiance to the Caliph and obedience to his commands (except where these are contrary to the Law).[9]

There are three glosses on this theory which are of considerable significance but are frequently ignored, particularly by modern Muslim scholars, though it must be admitted that they have to grapple with the reality of the modern Muslim state. First, the social organization or polity was taken more or less for granted since it was implicit in the concept of the *umma*. Indeed, some jurists, particularly the early ones, did not admit the existence of the state as a legitimate institution in its own right. They were solely concerned with the exercise and location of the authority necessary for the common good of the community.

> Consequently, not only is all discussion of the institutions of government in Muslim political thought concentrated on the Caliph, who alone is considered to represent that authority, but also the state as such is regarded as a merely transient phenomenon, and, though possessed of temporal power, lacking any intrinsic authority of its own.[10]

Second, the so-called classical theory, habitually presented as the actual practice of the Prophet and the *Rashidun*, developed gradually over the centuries, almost always as 'an apologia for the *status quo nunc*';[11] in fact, the jurists' formulations were also intended to provide doctrinal legitimacy for the reality, which became more and more divorced from the early exemplar, as the empire expanded and the structure of authority became more defined. Third, one of the purposes of successive formulations was to refute the arguments of the sectarians who questioned not only the persona of the *imam* but the legitimacy of his authority, thus attacking the essential unity of the *umma*.

Central to the classical theory is the unity of the *umma* of which the *imama* was a symbol; but the underpinning of the theory was both complex and subtle. First, it is based on the proposition that 'the Law precedes the State, both logically and in terms of time; and the State exists for the sole purpose of maintaining and enforcing the Law'.[12] In addition, since ultimate authority and sovereignty rest with God alone, neither the Muslim state nor its leader exercise sovereignty as the term is commonly understood; the status is rather that of a vice-regency, but one in which delegated authority (and, by implication, limited sovereign powers) is vested not in an individual or a group but in the community as a whole, though the community must appoint one of its number to act as leader. Furthermore, the political unit is not territorially based, but comprises the entire community, though it has been argued that there is a Muslim concept of a territorial state which is not co-extensive with the whole community, subject always to certain limitations, and that this concept draws its legitimacy from the Madinan polity.[13] The leader of the community, as the 'means whereby the Law is translated from the sphere of potentiality into actuality and provided with temporal sanctions',[14] embodies both the organic fusion of religion and temporal authority and also the principle that that authority is legitimate only so long as it is exercised consonant with the principles of, and in compliance with, the laws of Islam.

Finally, the early community — that is, the community during the Prophet's lifetime and the period of the *Rashidun* — came to be regarded as the only truly Islamic polity and one which was an exemplar for all succeeding generations. The rationale was that the first generation of Muslims, the Companions, possesses a special quality of probity, an unparalleled understanding of Islam, and an unequalled ability to carry out its precepts, because of their personal knowledge of the Prophet and the zeal with which they embraced his teaching. Later generations are unable to achieve the standards set by the Companions and later leaders are deemed to have adopted secular and impious values and practices. In particular, the establishment of dynastic rule and the proliferation of administrative regulations and practices, which were very necessary but which were seen to be secular in inspiration, were cited as evidence of deviation, as was the establishment of semi-independent dynastic governorships in the provinces. Certainly change and adjustment occurred and a degree of corrupt and unjust practice may be reasonably inferred, but it seems unreasonable to imply that all political and constitutional arrangements and practices since 661 are illegitimate and un-Islamic by insisting that the *Rashidun* represent the only true Muslim polity, while at the same time averring that the *Qur'an* and the *Sunna* do little more than set out broad principles.

If it is for the community to decide upon the practical details in the light of those principles, if the absence of such details from the revelation is indeed evidence that it is God's will that this should be so, if 'my community will never agree in error' and if 'dissension among my *umma* is a blessing',[15] then later political structures and arrangements must be in accord with God's will, provided that the principles are taken into consideration and that rulers do try to implement the *Shari'a*. A more logical explanation, though one no doubt unacceptable to present-day theorists, is that, given the post-al Shafi'i opposition to change and the idealization of the Golden Age without much regard for reality, some means had to be found to explain in doctrinally acceptable terms the apparent deviation from *al sirat al mustaqim*. It might also be argued with considerable justice that the abandonment of the elective principle was in the public interest on two counts — the expansion of the *umma* made it impractical, and the establishment — and general acceptance — of the dynastic principle was conducive to stability and smooth succession: three of the *Rashidun* were assassinated and the election process caused dissension in almost every case.

Although the basic principles defining authority, constitutional practice, and governmental structure are therefore part of the corpus of general principles of Islam, it is

> a misconception to hold that the jurists meant to continue the application of the system which the Islamic state had known in the early stages of its history for choosing the ruler or for regulating the functioning of governmental institutions in the performance of their political and administrative roles.[16]

It should also be borne in mind, however, that Sunni political theory was effectively 'the *post eventum* justification of the precedents which have been ratified by *ijma*''.[17] It is also significant that the elaboration of political and constitutional theory post-dated the period of the early community and that the period of the *Rashidun* saw an explosive expansion of the Muslim domains — possibly the most explosive in the history of Islam. By the time of the Prophet's death in 632, Makka and Madina were under the community's sway, and the community was the dominant political power throughout the Arabian Peninsula (though not without regular challenge). The next twenty years saw the conquest of Egypt and parts of Libya, Syria, Iraq, Iran, and Khurasan. The exemplar was therefore a community possessed of an initially rudimentary constitutional structure; which was grappling with the problems of transforming what was, in effect, an autonomous local authority into an expanding imperial power on the basis of a revealed law which gave little practical guidance; whose political elements were in many respects obscure; and whose identifiable practice was inherently defective in relation to the task in hand. Not surprisingly, therefore, there was widespread adoption of existing administrative practices and structures and the assimilation of many useful ideas and institutions: the *Rashidun* were both practical and dynamic. They 'recognised that the spiritual message of Islam is fixed. To that they were faithfully committed. The social message of Islam is, however, flexible. Their experience amply demonstrated that flexibility'.[18]

Theory and practice: an uneasy relationship

The theoretical unity of the *umma* was never more than a pious fiction. It was riven with dissension and separatist movements from a very early stage: the *khawarij* (seceders) movement had its origins in the reign of Uthman, the third *khalifa*; the civil war between Ali, the fourth *khalifa* (though never universally recognized as such), and Mu'awiya, which culminated in the establishment of the Umayyad dynasty and the basic division between Sunni and Shi'a broke out in 656; the foundations of the short-lived Zubairid state (684–92 were laid in 680; and the emergence of semi-independent or independent dynasties was almost continuous. The latter process was an inevitable result of the need to carve up the expanding Muslim empire into provinces for administrative purposes and was, perhaps, accelerated by the practice of recognizing hereditary governorship of individual provinces, first established in Tunisia towards the end of the eighth century. It should, however, be noted that although this practice was forced upon the *khalifa* by circumstances and although the power of the dynastic 'war lords' was based upon military force alone, in most cases the latter continued to be formally appointed or recognized by the *khalifa*, thus maintaining the fiction of unity and providing legitimacy for their authority. However, there was, in fact, no ideational or ideological basis to their position. It was otherwise for the short-lived Zubairid state, for the Fatimids in Tunisia and, later, Egypt, for the Rustamids in Algeria, for the Zaidi Imamate in Yemen, for other Shi'a polities, and for the Ibadhi polity in Oman. Their leaders either claimed to be the rightful leaders of the entire community or adhered to deviant forms of Islam whose followers were content to live within their own belief system without bothering about the rest of the Muslim world.

The problems this process posed for the jurists and political theorists were exacerbated by the gradual dilution of the authority of the *khalifa* culminating in the effective abolition of the office following the Mongol successes in 1258: spiritual and temporal authority were formally separated and the unity of the *umma* in political terms could no longer be substantiated. Territorial plurality had become, as it was to remain, an accepted, if somewhat suspect, fact of life. Clearly, the theory had to be modified in order to give doctrinal legitimacy to reality, as well as to demolish the doctrinal position of the (mainly Shi'a) opposition. Successive jurists, therefore, sought to reformulate the doctrine first set out in cogent form by al Mawardi.[19] Of these, four are significant: Ibn Taymiyya (1263–1328), Ibn Khaldun (1332–1406), Dawani (1427–1501), and Fadhl Allah Khunji (1455–1521). Ibn Taymiyya's views, since he is generally held to be the inspiration of all significant reformist and renewalist movements in the late nineteenth and twentieth centuries, are still important. Ibn Khaldun described the political reality with a clarity rare among Muslim political observers, and offered a theoretical framework which still has validity — and not merely in the Muslim world.[20] Dawani and Fadhl Allah are similarly realistic in their formulations. These four collectively may be said to have squared a circle and resolved a problem which had bedevilled political thinking for some centuries, and their views therefore deserve some attention.

Ibn Taymiyya

Ibn Taymiyya was an adherent of the Hanbali school of law, and, as such, rejected all sources but the *Qur'an* and the *Sunna*, or precedent based solidly upon them: in particular, he rejected the alleged 'closure of the gate of *ijtihad*'. Although the Hanbalis have the reputation of being the most conservative (and, by implication, the most intolerant) of the Sunni schools of law, they have 'showed great flexibility in applying them [i.e., the principles of Islam] to the problems of social life'.[21] Like others before him, Ibn Taymiyya accepts that absolute sovereignty belongs only to God, but argues that authority (in practice a form of limited but delegated sovereignty akin to the early practice of delegating authority to provincial governors) devolved after the death of Muhammad upon all those who by virtue of their learning and probity were qualified to interpret God's command taking into account changing circumstances. He inevitably embarked upon a review of the historical experience in order to support his thesis.

His starting-point is that 'the administration of the affairs of men is one of the greatest obligations of religion; rather the fact is that religion cannot exist without it'.[22] His argument rests on two premises: first, the imperative nature of political authority, since the nature of religion is such that an organized social order is necessary for its proper functioning; and second, the institution of authority is a religious obligation since

> all that Allah has enjoined, like undertaking jihad (holy war), administering justice, performing pilgrimage or Friday prayer or prayer on feast days, as well as relieving the oppressed and execution of penalties, can only be accomplished by force and authority.[23]

He also cites a *hadith* in which the Prophet ordered that 'when three of them go on a journey they should appoint one of them as their leader' (a somewhat dubious but clever bit of casuistry). In short, Ibn Taymiyya sees the establishment of political authority as both a doctrinal and a practical necessity, but he also believes that it should be both dynamic and progressive. He also emphasizes the integrity and unity of the *umma*, though for him that unity is spiritual rather than physical, and is based on a common purpose which all must strive to realize. However, since the *umma* is, by definition, non-territorial and, in theory, encompasses the whole world, plurality of political units or states is inevitable until the whole world has become Muslim. The classical theory of the *imama* is given short shrift, although he accepts the premise that the *Rashidun* possess a *sui generis* character which cannot be recreated in history and which is a special dispensation from God. However, he fails to find a juridical basis for the classical thesis in the sources he considered valid — the *Qur'an*, the *Sunna*, and the practice of the *Rashidun*; and he therefore ignores it completely as invalid and concentrates on the task of finding juridical justification for the evident political diversity of the Muslim world. His standard sources are silent on this particular subject, but he does not consider them to have proved the standard line.

Furthermore, anything conducive of the public interest which is not specifically forbidden is not only permissible but, by implication, mandatory. Since political plurality might, depending upon the circumstances, be in the public interest, it could be legitimate. Thus, Ibn Taymiyya rejects the theory of political universalism so central to Muslim political thinking from the time of al Ash'ari onwards but which had become by his age a polite fiction — not to mention hypocritical and dangerous. In its place, he proposed a more realistic and practical theory based upon acceptance of the evident territorial and political plurality of the Muslim world which could neither be incorporated into the classical theory nor denied by appeals to that theory. Hence, Muslim unity can only be achieved through co-operation and co-ordination between political entities. 'There is no imperative, therefore, to press the world of Islam into a political unity or a federal state; it can better develop through the principle of cooperation, into a confederation of free sovereign states.'[24] Nevertheless, the essential link between religion and the law on the one hand and temporal authority on the other remained central to his thinking:

> The rulers are of two classes: the princes (of political authority) and the learned men (in the law) . . . It is the duty of each one of the members of these two classes to seek in all he says and does, obedience to Allah and His Messenger and conformity with (that which) the Book of Allah (enjoins).[25]

Although he rejected the unitary *imama* and the elective process inherent in it, he stressed the need for consultation:

> when (the ruler) takes counsel (with his companions) and one of them indicates to him what he should follow as prescribed by the Book of Allah, by the Sunna of His Messenger and by the consensus of the Muslims, he (the ruler) should comply with it.[26]

In case of disagreement the ruler should ascertain the opinions of all and then follow that advice which is more in conformity with the *Qur'an* and the *Sunna*. Finally, being a realist he recognized that this was a counsel of perfection to be followed only so far as is possible since 'Allah imposes not on any soul a duty beyond its scope.'[27]

For Ibn Taymiyya, the state is the result of neither divine commission nor the coercive power of military strength, but rather an organic unity based upon the co-operative efforts of the whole community in seeking to realize the ideals of Islam and to comply with God's commands and the precepts of Islam. However, that co-operation seems to be based on the precept: 'to each according to his need, and from each according to his capability.' Thus, the ruler is

> morally bound to take counsel of his subjects and work for their welfare, and the subjects are equally bound to offer

their good counsel to him. For religion is good counsel and everyone is a shepherd responsible for the good maintenance of his flock, the community, and everyone orders the good and forbids the evil and co-operates with others in acts of piety and God-fearing (*al-birr wa'l-taqwa*). The ideal of the social life is therefore not submission to the state but cooperation with the state.[28]

Ibn Khaldun

Ibn Khaldun's exposition has been well covered in the literature.[29] For the purposes of this study the crucial factor is that although he pays lip-service to the classical theory of the *imama* or *khilafa*, he accepts on the basis of historical evidence that it gradually metamorphosed into a form of temporal authority. Clearly, therefore, more than one polity may be found in the Muslim world and all such polities as base their rule upon compliance with the revealed law are both legitimate and doctrinally acceptable. He argues that human social organization is a self-evident necessity which requires the exercise of power and authority by a ruler on the basis of a rule of law. This may be either rational (i.e., secular in inspiration) or religious (i.e., based on the revealed law). The latter is, of course, preferable. The following extract from his *Muqaddima*, Book 3, Chapter 25, sums up his argument succinctly and convincingly:

In political associations it is imperative to have recourse to imposed laws, accepted and followed by the masses, as was the case amongst the Persians and other peoples, and no state can establish itself and consolidate its control without such laws. If these laws are laid down by men of intelligence and insight, the polity is founded on reason [and subserves the temporal well-being of the subjects]. But if they are laid down by God and promulgated by an inspired Lawgiver, the polity is founded on religion and is beneficial both for this world and the next. For men have not been created solely for this world since it is wholly vanity and futility, and its end is death and annihilation. Revealed laws have been sent to lead men to observe that conduct which will bring them to felicity in the future life, in all their affairs, whether of worship or

71

of mutual dealings, and even in matters of kingship — which is a phenomenon natural to human society — so that it should be conducted on the pattern of religion, in order that the whole body may be protected by the supervision of the Revealed Law.

That state, therefore, whose law is based on violence and coercion and gives full play to the irascible nature is tyranny and injustice and in the eyes of the Law blameworthy, a judgement in which political wisdom also concurs. Furthermore, that state whose law is based upon rational statecraft and its principles, *but lacks the supervision of the Revealed Law* [emphasis in Gibb's translation] is likewise blameworthy, since it is the product of speculation without the light of God. For the Lawgiver knows best the interests of men in all that relates to the other world, which is concealed from them. The principles of rational government aim solely at apparent and worldly interests, whereas the object of the Lawgiver is men's salvation in the hereafter. It is imperative, therefore, by the very nature of Revealed Laws, to bring the whole people to conform themselves to their ordinances in all matters of this world and the next. And this rule is the rule of the Lawgivers, that is to say, of the Prophets and of their successors, that is to say, the caliphs, and this is the true meaning of the caliphate.

Natural kingship, then, forces the people to conform to the private ambitions and uncontrolled desires of the ruler. Political government induces the people to conform to the dictates of reason for the promotion of worldly interests and the warding off of evils. The caliphate leads the people to conform to the insight of the Revealed Law in regard to their interests both in the world to come and those in this world which relate to it, since all the affairs of this world are assessed by the Lawgiver in the light of their relation to the interests of the future life. Thus it is truly an office of replacement (khilafa) of the promulgator of the Revealed Law in the guardianship of the Faith and the government of the world by its provisions.[30]

In fact, he believes that the caliphate or imamate 'existed to protect religion and exercise political leadership, and any kingdom which does this possesses the same type of authority'.[31]

Jalal al Din Dawani and Fadhl Allah Khunji

Matters were taken a step further by Jalal al Din Dawani, who argues that 'the governor is a person distinguished by divine support, that he may lead men to perfection and provide a corrective order for them'. He further argues that although government may be either righteous or unrighteous, righteous government (clearly the ideal) occurs when the governor rules with justice and in the interests of his subjects' material and spiritual welfare. The righteous governor must apply the *Shari'a*, although he is entitled to take into account temporal and spatial circumstances, subject to the proviso that in so doing he must act consistently with the general principles of the *Shari'a* and in the interests of the community. 'Such a person is in reality the Shadow of God, the *khalifa* of God and the Vicar of the Prophet.'[32]

Fadhl Allah bin Ruzbihan Khunji completed the process of effectively subordinating theory to practice, while maintaining the paramountcy of the theory which argued the converse.

> In *sharii* parlance (the Sultan) is he who exercises dominance over the Muslims by virtue of his power and military force. The *ulama'* have said that obedience to the imam/sultan is incumbent in whatever he commands and forbids as long as it is not contrary to the *shari'a* whether he is just or tyrannical. It is incumbent to give him counsel (*Nasihat*) as far as possible. It is permissible to call him *khalifa, imam, amir al mu'minin* or *khalifa* of the Prophet of God, but it is not permissible to call him *khalifat Allah*.[33]

> However, he too insisted that the ruler should maintain and observe the *shari'a* and should ensure that the community did so too.

Shi'a political theory

The Shi'a doctrine of the Imamate differs radically from the Sunni version, since they believe that it is necessary that there should always be an Imam whose functions are, broadly, to guide the community and to preserve and interpret God's law. The first Imam, Ali, was designated by the Prophet to be his successor, and successive Imams similarly designated their successors during their lifetime. Furthermore, since the designation was the result of divine inspiration, the Imams are effectively designated by God and are

charged by God to carry out all the spiritual and temporal functions of the Prophet, save that of prophesy. It follows that the
authority of the Imam in Shi'a doctrine is independent of circumstances: 'it makes no difference if human beings deny him or not,
help him or not, obey him or not or if he is absent from men's
sight.'[34] The Shi'a also hold that the Imams are sinless and
infallible and that it is incumbent upon all men to obey them, for
'their orders and prohibitions are Allah's orders and prohibitions'.[35] However, it is not merely a matter of belief, since Shi'a
ulama have generally set great store on the rational proofs of the
necessity for the Imamate and of the Imams' attributes. Thus, for
example, given that there are passages in the *Qur'an* which are not
clear and which therefore require elucidation, it is clear that God
could not have allowed such passages to be revealed without also
providing someone to explain them, in the person of the Imam.
Furthermore, since there are many possible interpretations, particularly in matters legal, the Imam is necessary in order to provide
authoritative guidance; for were it not so, fallible man is bound
to err, and it is inconceivable that a just and compassionate God
could hold a community responsible for failure to comply with His
command, unless proper and authoritative guidance had been
given.

The line of designated Imams came to an abrupt end in 874,
when the Twelfth Imam, Abu al Qasim Muhammad ibn Hasan,
disappeared. Shi'a doctrine holds that he went into occultation but
that he is still mysteriously present as *Imam al Zaman* (the Imam
of the day, often described as the Hidden Imam), thus fulfilling
the requirement for the permanent presence of the Imam. He will,
at the appointed time, return as the *mahdi* to bring salvation to the
earth.

This necessarily brief summary of Shi'a doctrine may not, at
first sight, appear to have much to do with concepts of state, government and authority; but this would be a facile conclusion, partly
because Shi'ism was originally 'a political legitimist movement,
which held that the headship of the community belonged to Ali and
his descendants',[36] and partly because this doctrine underpins, and
is modified in response to, later practical developments in much
the same manner as occurred in Sunni Islam. There is a difference,
however, in that the early Shi'a were normally a minority in
opposition to the Sunni holders of power. They therefore had no
real need to develop a fully articulated constitutional theory justi-
fying reality in acceptable doctrinal terms. Indeed, apart from the

short-lived Fatimid dynasty, the Shi'a held little power until the
establishment of the Safavid dynasty in Iran and its adoption of
Shi'ism in the sixteenth century, long after the occultation. 'By this
time, Shi'i doctrine had largely divested itself of political reality.'[37]
Theoretically, all political authority was vested, like spiritual
authority, in the Imam, but since he is in occultation, the exercise
of that authority is not strictly speaking possible. However rational
the argument, such an arrangement was clearly impractical, since
it left the Shi'a community without leadership, organization, or
structure. Hence, as early as the eleventh century a re-interpretation
of doctrine commenced which allowed the delegation of the judicial
functions of the Imam to the ulama. In exercising these functions
the ulama acted collectively as *al na'ib al 'amm* (general representative) of the Hidden Imam. Over the years their competence was
gradually extended to include most of the non-political functions
of the Imam.

It has been argued that the non-extension of the concept of *al
na'ib al 'amm* to the political arena results from a separation of
'Church' and 'state' whereby 'all political, administrative and
economic matters not directly concerned with the *Shari'a* and
therefore not under the control of the ulama were outside the concern of the sacred community [i.e. the Shi'a community]'. The Shi'a
lived, in effect, in two overlapping communities — 'the sacred community and the profane community' — between whose leaders there
was inevitably tension and rivalry.[38] However, a more reasonable
explanation is that the political authorities were generally powerful enough to prevent any attempt by the ulama to extend their
authority into political affairs.[39] That being the case, it was inevitable that the doctrine should evolve, that legitimacy could neither
be granted to nor withheld by the ulama from any government,
and that all governments were usurpatory of the prerogatives of
the Hidden Imam. Some authorities have taken this to mean that
all governments are illegitimate, but there has never been a clear
consensus on this point. Either way, however, no legitimate role
in political matters for the ulama as *al na'ib al 'amm* of the Hidden
Imam is implied.

As noted in Chapter 2, however, there was something of a hiatus
in the further development of theory pending the settlement of the
usuli-akhbari controversy, and the first major development thereafter
in political theory came, as in the case of jurisprudential theory,
from the enunciation of Shaikh Murtaza Ansari's four principles
(see Chapter 2, pp. 48–9). For by providing doctrinal legitimacy

for the extension of the jurisdictional competence of the ulama, he provided also doctrinal legitimacy for their intervention in political affairs and in the legislative and administrative processes of government — and, by a process of imaginative rational deduction, for the reconciliation of Khomeini's concept of *velayat-i-faqih* (government by the jurisconsult) with the concept of all government as usurpatory. For just as legitimacy could be neither granted to nor withheld from governments, so could legitimacy be neither granted to nor withheld from the legislative and administrative acts of the government. However, if the ulama can promulgate rulings over an extensive range of activities, secure in the knowledge that they are following the guidance of the Hidden Imam, it follows rationally that they cannot only legislate (though they would define their actions as identification, interpretation, and codification of the details of God's law) but also rule, pending the return of the Hidden Imam: for if they are *al na'ib al 'amm* of the Hidden Imam they have an obligation to exercise all the latter's functions, which include ruling or governing the community. Thus, the application of Shaikh Murtaza's four principles has resolved two major doctrinal problems, one peculiar to the Shi'a, and one common to all forms of Islam. For the Shi'a, the doctrine of usurpatory government can be set aside provided that the government is controlled by the ulama in their capacity as *al na'ib al 'amm* and the ulama can, by the act of participating in the government, accord it legitimacy. More importantly, the obvious need for governments to legislate, in the fullest sense of the word, can also be granted legitimacy, always provided that legislation is consistent with the principles and precepts of the *Qur'an* and the *Sunna*, and can, in the case of the Shi'a, be presented as identification, interpretation, clarification, or codification of the detailed provisions of God's law.

This line of reasoning has not, of course, gone unchallenged. There are generally three ways in which the ulama can relate to the authorities and activities of the state. They can co-operate with state authorities where the authorities enforce Shi'a law and where the ruler is just, and in so doing both derive their own authority and accord recognition to the state authorities as a rational consequence of their position as *al na'ib al 'amm*. Such co-operation is not permissible, however, if the ruler is not just and does not implement Shi'a law. The ulama may, *per contra*, remain aloof, leaving temporal government strictly to the temporal authorities, whether or not they apply Shi'a law and whether or not they act justly. In so doing, they neither grant nor withhold recognition and legitimacy; but they can also follow the line of reasoning set out earlier and seek actively to participate in and control the activities of the government, opposing where necessary and dominating where possible. This last is, of course, the dominant element in Iran today, though not without some opposition from those ulama who consider Khomeini to have extended the doctrine too far and who firmly believe that the ulama should not participate directly in government.

A variant approach to theory and practice

By the time of the nineteenth- and twentieth-century re-examination of Islam had commenced, the main thrust of Muslim intellectual thought concerning sovereignty and authority was towards developing a doctrinally acceptable formulation for state sovereignty and for the institutions and impedimenta of government. Sovereignty was simply dealt with: it necessarily rests with God, but man constitutes God's vice-regent on earth. An independent Muslim state, although a sovereign state in the normally accepted sense of the word, is in reality a vice-regency in which the sovereign powers are limited by God's overriding sovereignty. Furthermore, the sovereign powers inherent in the 'vice-regency' are vested in the entire Muslim community and may be termed a 'popular vice-regency'. This popular vice-regency therefore forms the basis of democracy in a Muslim state and as such underpins theories of representative government: a government can only be formed with the consent of at least the majority of the Muslim community and can continue in power only for as long as it enjoys its confidence and support. Furthermore, the absence of clear directions in the *Qur'an* and the *Sunna* is clear evidence that the detailed arrangements for government were deliberately left for man to devise in the light of circumstances.

However, Muslim states, particularly the modern states, function in practice in much the same manner as any other state and exhibit the same diversity of forms, ranging from absolutism to representative democracy, as do other states, leading Muslim activists to excoriate existing governments as illegal, illegitimate, un-Islamic, and a valid target for revolution. This fact, together with the continued tension between theory and practice, has also led some observers to conclude that there is a crisis of legitimacy of long standing in the Muslim world and that the greatest failure of Islam has been its failure to institutionalize itself — that is, a failure to develop an adequate, doctrinally acceptable, and generally accepted institutional link between faith and power, religion and politics. One such observer, for example, concludes that 'the Muslim state retained its essentially arbitrary character, *de facto* successor to a divinely instituted polity, but not a corporative entity embodied in the person of a monarch or a formalized assembly representing the "estates" of his realm'.[40] Another has argued that the Muslim jurist has not been able to study politics in isolation as a completely separate discipline. Issues such as the nature of the state, authority, power, government institutions, qualifications for rulership, limitations on a ruler's power, and individual rights and obligations could not be examined without reference to the law.[41] However, reality is once again rather different. As has already been suggested, the Muslim world has generally managed to ignore the theoretical problems inherent in the latter approach, and to develop practical and workable institutions and structures. The former approach seems to imply an external (and probably Western) standard against which Muslim practice should be measured, whereas the appropriate standard is the unattainable ideal. In this connection, it is surely wrong — and wrong-headed — to insist that familiar Western structures and institutions should be imposed upon the Muslim world and that only such structures and institutions are truly 'democratic'.

Thus, whatever form of government ultimately proves to be acceptable and successful in a Muslim state, the only certainty about it is that it will be an indigenous product. There may be borrowing from elsewhere, but that which is borrowed will have been incorporated and assimilated into Muslim terminology and practice and will have been given respectable Muslim antecedents and legitimacy. Moreover, the reasoning noted above suggests that the problem is peculiar to Islam and that the situation as defined is inevitable, given the basic concept of Islam as compliance with the will of God. Yet other faith-based ideologies (including communism) have had, and continue to have, problems over the relationship between the belief system and the institutions and instruments of power. Clearly, 'politics involves a set of active links, both positive and negative, between civil society and institutions of power. In this sense, there has been little separation, certainly none in our time, between religion and politics anywhere'.[42] Consideration of the position of the Established Church of England in British politics, Catholic influence in the Irish Republic, the activism of Pope John

Paul, communal troubles in India, and the status of the Emperor in Japan suggest that the relationship is as problematic for non-Muslims as it is for Muslims.

Furthermore, the concept of the nation-state, despite the appeal of the Greek paradigm, is a relatively recent development in Europe, as is the modern concept of sovereignty. The nation-state system is generally held to have been accepted in the provisions of the Treaty of Westphalia in 1648, while the concept of sovereignty was first systematically enunciated by Jean Bodin in 1576. There are striking similarities between the classical Muslim theory and Bodin's theory of 'the divine right of kings', which held that kings ruled by divine right as God's representative on earth, holding power directly from God. Any challenge to that power was tantamount to flouting God's will.[43] There are equally striking similarities between the 'popular vice-regency' briefly noted above and Althusius's reasoning. Althusius was, of course, concerned to oppose the inherent absolutism of the divine right of kings, and therefore argued that the power of a king was not, and necessarily could not be, absolute, since it was limited by the laws of God, the laws of nature, and the provisions of a mythical 'contract' between ruler and ruled.

Althusius's argument rested on the premise that the people were the original source of power and that the 'contract' entrusted to the ruler the exercise of that power, subject to certain conditions, which included the exercise of that power for the good of the people and subject to the limitations imposed by the laws of God and of nature.[44] This similarity does suggest that there is considerable validity in the argument that it is not capitalism or communism, neither is it Christianity, Judaism, Buddhism, nor Islam which provides the institutional framework for such political dynamism and political development as are generally accepted as legitimate. It is, rather, the practical application of the concept of the nation-state which has taken different forms in different places, according to the differing moral and ethical sentiments of the people, differing perceptions of the proper focus for national unity and identity, and differing practices.[45] There can be no doubt that the belief system remains a powerful influence even in the most avowedly secular nations. Islam's problem is not, therefore, that 'the transcendent referent for authority and political power remained partly divine and not purely secular';[46] rather, it is that the long-standing territorial pluralism of the Muslim world has not yet been formally incorporated into the theory and that the conflict between the universal *umma* and the reality of state plurality has therefore not been satisfactorily resolved at the theoretical level.

Furthermore, the apparent lack of indigenous and naturally developed institutional structures which have been accorded legitimacy seems to reinforce the conventional view that the nation-state has not yet come into being generally in the Muslim world; and that the Muslim world can boast of few identifiable nations. Indeed, some Muslim thinkers — as opposed to Muslim politicians — do not seem to have fully accepted the concept of the nation-state and have generally withheld doctrinal recognition and legitimation, while tacitly accepting the reality. However, the absence of legitimacy has caused many observers, both Muslim and non-Muslim, to conclude that the Muslim nation-state (whatever it may be) is somehow inferior, illegitimate, and unfaithful to Muslim principles.

This is sterile hair-splitting, however: Muslim nation-states do exist; they are not inferior, illegitimate, or necessarily unfaithful to Muslim principles; but they are most assuredly different to other nation-states. This might be explained in a number of ways. It may be argued, for example, that the nation-state cannot evolve without independence: nationalism can be, and normally is, a major force in the pursuit of independence, but the nation-state cannot fulfil this role. Few Muslim countries achieved independence before the end of the Second World War, and those that did were subject to considerable outside influence. In these circumstances energies are directed towards the achievement of independence and the reduction of external influence. It should not be a matter of surprise, therefore (so the argument runs), that the Muslim world boasts few, if any, nation-states. Yet an examination of practical perceptions within the Muslim world today suggests that the arguments are fallacious. No one with personal experience would accept that there is not a distinctive Egyptian, Iranian, Indonesian, Pakistani, or Algerian ethos; and that ethos is the nucleus of the nation-state — and may, incidentally, accept a surprisingly large element of internal plurality.[47] The nation-state does exist in the Muslim world, therefore, though it may be rather different in form and in inspiration from those of the rest of the world. Moreover, though the particular forms it may take today are relatively new, it is clear from the history of the Muslim world that 'nations' which were co-terminous with territorial units (states or polities) were common.

Conclusions

This raises an important point since it is conventional to argue that the development of the nation-state is part of the process of modernization and that modernization inevitably means secularization. In other words, one inevitable result of the development of the nation-state is that the political unit moves down the continuum between a purely divine and a purely secular referent for authority and political power to a point at which the linkage to the divine end of the continuum has become indirect. This has not yet happened in the Muslim World and it must remain an open question whether it is, indeed, either possible or desirable. Such evidence as there is, however, suggests that attempts to compress the process have not been successful and have been seen as artificial attempts to impose a secular non-Muslim and alien system. Indeed, it is instructive to consider the pattern in that most avowedly secular country, the United States. Recent years have seen the election of Presidents who are close to the born-again Christian tradition, religious leaders have been increasingly willing to endorse or oppose candidates for public office, television evangelism is on the increase and is no longer restricted to matters of faith alone: there has clearly been a reassertion of religion as a significant and overt political factor. This suggests that in the United States at least, and possibly elsewhere, the move down the continuum is generally felt to have gone too far and that the linkage between the belief system and the political system must, in order to respond to the national gut feeling, become more overt and more direct. In other words, we may be seeing a move back towards the Muslim doctrinal position, but it is a move which does not call into question the legitimacy of the political structure and the political system: what is being challenged is the legitimacy of the motivation in the particular sense that not only is the secularism of the ideology — and therefore the ideology itself — being challenged, but so also are the particular policies which flow from it being challenged.

A tentative conclusion might be that movement to the extreme of the purely secular end of the continuum is in the long run unacceptable to a society whose values are rooted, however indirectly, in a divinely inspired belief system. A further conclusion is that a state whose government claims Muslim credentials remains a state as long as the international community continues to accept it as such, and remains a Muslim state as long as its citizens regard it as such, a matter which will depend on practice and on the perceived proper relationship between theory and practice.

4

International Relations and International Law

Introduction

A reasonable working definition of the relationship between international law and international relations is that the law serves to regulate the relations between states. Although international law as an identifiable and coherent corpus of practice is a relative late-comer, the practice of regulating relations between political communities on the basis of identifiable and generally accepted rules and practices is considerably older:

> However primitive their institutions, however mingled their notions of law, religion and magic, political communities in the earliest recorded ages are found assuming some universally valid norms for their external relations and transacting their business with one another in forms attributed to immemorial use.[1]

For the followers of Islam, however, matters were, at least in theory, somewhat different. They were required, in pursuit of God's will, to seek to establish a universal community comprising all mankind in which public order was regulated by the revelation. The universal community was to be achieved either by proselytiza-tion and conversion or by force of arms, subject, at least in theory, to the injunction that 'there is no compulsion in religion' (Q2:256), although in practice that injunction was often violated: forcible con-version was not unknown, nor was the use of force to punish those who obstinately refused to see the light. The Muslim state was therefore necessarily imperial, expansionary, and co-terminous with the community. It sought to convert other peoples, who became part of the state by virtue of embracing Islam, though it permitted followers of certain specified faiths (*ahl al kitab*, the People of the Book — a term applied generically to Jews, Christians, and Sabians) to retain their beliefs, subject to certain conditions, even though the majority of the population of a particular area had become Muslim. The Muslim law of nations was necessarily concerned with the regulation of three relationships: that between the Muslim state and non-Muslim states; that between the Muslim state authorities and non-Muslims living within the Muslim state; and that between Muslims resident in a non-Muslim state and that state's authorities. The first necessarily implied confrontation in the absence of willing conversion or acceptance of Muslim suzerainty; the second was necessarily an unequal relationship; and the third was, in practical terms, a pious fiction, since no non-Muslim state was likely to take any more notice of Muslim doctrine or the views of Muslim governments in deciding its treatment of Muslim residents than Muslim governments would take of non-Muslim doctrine and views in deciding the appropriate treatment for non-Muslim residents. Moreover, the defence of the community was a duty, rather than a question of law.

However, what the classical Muslim law of nations did not deal with — and could not, in theory, deal with — was the relationship between Muslim states. Not surprisingly, therefore, the Muslim law of nations was essentially concerned with the conduct of war: war — or the absence of peace — was the normal relationship with non-Muslim states. Furthermore, it was not a separate system but was part of Muslim law: 'it is merely an extension of the sacred law, the Shari'a, designed to govern the relations of Muslims with non-Muslims, whether inside or outside the territory of Islam.'[2] However, since the Muslim expansion failed to subordinate the entire world to Muslim suzerainty or to convert all mankind to the true faith, the law was necessarily extended to cover the mechanics of peacemaking and the conduct of peaceful relations with other political entities, though this was, in theory at least, a temporary state of affairs. This extension resulted in the coining of the term *siyar* (literally, behaviour), a term which acquired a meaning equivalent to the Western concept of international law. *Jihad* (literally, exertion, though more often used for the narrower meaning of military activity — holy war) might still be the theoretical basis of the relationship between the Muslim polity and non-Muslim states, but the more neutral concept of *siyar* as comprising the rules governing a more or less peaceful relationship gradually superseded the more active concept of warfare — and did so for that most cogent of reasons: practicality and recognition of reality.

Given that the ultimate goal was necessarily the conversion or conquest of the entire world, the rules governing foreign relations did not, and could not, recognize an equal status for the other party (or parties), nor were they based in any way on those pillars of the international system, reciprocity, and mutual consent. In practice, of course, some element of reciprocity and mutual acceptance proved necessary in order to cover, for example, the exchange of prisoners, diplomatic immunity, the imposition of customs duty, commercial intercourse, and other facets of international relations and diplomacy. Even in areas such as these, however, reciprocity and mutual consent remained a secondary consideration. The *siyar* was, in fact, a self-imposed system binding upon all Muslims whether or not it served the interests of Muslims individually and collectively, and irrespective of its acceptance or rejection by others.

The Muslim theory of international relations

The theory was relatively simple. The world was divided into *dar al Islam* (the territory of Islam) and *dar al harb* (the territory of war: and, by extension, the territory of unbelievers). The former comprised the Muslim community and those members of the tolerated faiths, permanently resident in Muslim-controlled territory, who had accepted Muslim suzerainty and a subordinate position in return for protection and certain guaranteed rights (and, needless to say, obligations). *Dar al harb* comprised the rest of the world which Muslim rulers were duty-bound to bring under their authority. Although, therefore, the normal relationship was a state of war, it was not necessarily one in which military operations were being actively conducted. Rules were therefore needed to regulate not only the conduct of actual hostilities, but also the cessation of hostilities and the nature of the truce. However, such arrangements were held to be strictly temporary in nature and implied neither recognition (in the modern legal sense of the word) nor equality. They were no more than a device to accommodate the realities of peaceful co-existence imposed by the Muslim failure to achieve the universal community.

Jihad

Clearly, *dar al harb* must in due course be transformed into *dar al Islam* by one means or another. The doctrinally correct instrument is *jihad*, a term which is normally mistranslated as 'holy war'. The term does, of course, comprehend war but it does have much wider significance, and the concept of *jihad* is central to the Muslim law of nations. It is therefore sensible to examine both the theory and practice. Technically, *jihad* means exertion by Muslims individually and collectively *fi sabil Allah* — in the path of God — in fulfilment of the obligation to spread belief in Allah and to make His word supreme throughout the world. It was therefore

> not merely a duty to be fulfilled by each individual; it was
> also above all a political obligation imposed collectively upon
> the subjects of the state so as to achieve Islam's ultimate aim
> — the universalization of the faith and the establishment of
> God's sovereignty over the world. Thus the *jihad* was an
> individual duty, especially in the defense of Islam, as well as
> a collective duty upon the community as a whole and failure
> to fulfil it would constitute a gross error.[3]

The term was not restricted to military action, however, since exertion in God's path can take a variety of forms, peaceful as well as violent, and may be both internal and external. Jurists distinguished four ways in which the duty might be fulfilled: by the heart, by the tongue, by the hands, and by the sword. The first concerned the individual struggle against evil and the works of the devil: it was 'exertion' aimed at the willing and wholehearted compliance with God's will and at purifying both the soul and fallible man's actions and desires of all that was not in harmony with God and His commands. It was essentially an individual 'exertion' to become a better Muslim, although it could also cover collective exertion to make the community a better Muslim community. The second and third were concerned mainly with the obligation to 'enjoin what is right and forbid what is wrong' (Q3:110), and were therefore primarily concerned with morality and ethics, both individually and collectively, both within the community and in exhorting others to mend their ways. These three were often described as the 'greater *jihad*'. The fourth is 'precisely equivalent to the meaning of war, and is concerned with fighting the unbelievers and the enemies of the faith'.[4] The *jihad* in the sense of war was thus 'a permanent obligation upon the believers to be carried out by a continuous process of warfare, psychological and political, even if not strictly military'.[5]

Notwithstanding the wider connotations of the term *jihad* it came to be synonymous with 'Holy War', no doubt because Islam outlawed all forms of war other than the *jihad*. The grounds were rational: the only war which can be regarded as lawful must be not only *bellum justum* but also *bellum pium*. *Jihad*, as exertion with an ultimate and directly identifiable religious purpose, be it to impose God's law upon the unbelievers, to check transgressions against that law, or to defend the community, came to be understood as concerned with the external threat, and therefore as military, rather than psychological or political action; as dealing with the external and corporeal enemy rather than the internal spiritual enemy. There is naturally justification in the *Qur'an*: 'Believe in Allah and His Apostle and carry on warfare with your possessions and persons' (Q61:11); and 'To those against whom war is made, permission is given to fight, because they are wronged' (Q22:39). There are also many references to *jihad* in the *hadith*: 'And know that paradise is beneath the protection of the swords'; and 'I am the Prophet of mercy, I am the Prophet of fighting . . . I am the smiling warrior.'[6] It is important to remember, however, that although *jihad* includes the idea of holy war and is frequently retricted to that notion, it is not, and never has been, restricted solely to that definition.

Most jurists identify five types of *jihad* in the restricted sense of military action: against polytheists, apostates, dissenters, *ahl al kitab*, and in defence of the frontier. Some also add *jihad* against highway robbery. As to the first there is no compromise: they must either accept Islam or fight, since Muslims are under an obligation to 'fight the polytheists wherever ye may find them' (Q9:5). Apostasy was as harshly treated: apostates who remained in the Muslim domains were given a simple choice of returning to the faith or death, while those who left Muslim domains and formed a group sufficiently large to establish their own polity had the choice between returning to the faith or facing offensive war and eventual death. Once again there is Qur'anic justification, but the *Sunna* is more explicit: the Prophet is reported to have said: 'He who changes his religion must be killed' (by implication, a change from Islam). There is, however, a contrary view, namely that the *Qur'an* did not clearly prescribe specific punishment for apostasy and that the Prophet did not sentence anyone to death for it. Although a grave sin, therefore, apostasy was subject to discretionary punishment, although the usual limits for discretionary punishment do not apply in the case of apostasy. 'Thus, a court may either sentence an apostate to death, imprison him, or prescribe whatever other punishment it thinks appropriate.'[7] Dissenters, in the sense of holders of unorthodox views, were originally permitted to hold those views as long as they did not renounce the authority of the *khalifa*. Subsequently, dissent came to be regarded as a negation of the authority of the *khalifa* and of the unity of the *umma*, and as such had to be fought against. *Jihad* against the *ahl al kitab* was permissible only if they refused to acknowledge the suzerainty of the Muslims, to pay the poll-tax and to accept the status of second-class citizens.

Defensive *jihad* is self-explanatory. The rules for the conduct of war were elaborate, but only two are relevant here. First, the duty of calling the community to active service lay with the *khalifa* or with the provincial governors; and second, actual hostilities must be preceded by an invitation to embrace Islam (or, in the case of *ahl al kitab*, to accept suzerainty). The Shi'a doctrine of *jihad* does not differ materially from the Sunni doctrine outlined above as far as legal matters are concerned and similarly encompasses both the wider definition and the narrow concept of military operations. There was, however, a significant doctrinal difference concerning military operations. In the first place, since in Shi'a doctrine it is necessary for everyone to recognize and obey the Imam, it follows that *jihad* is justifiable not only against a non-Muslim for his non-belief but also against a Muslim who fails to obey the Imam. Second, only the Imam can judge whether or not *jihad* should be declared; but with the occultation or disappearance of the Twelfth Imam, the *jihad* entered a dormant phase — it is in a state of suspension until the return of the Imam. Later Shi'a doctrine resolved this dilemma in two ways. First, they developed the concept of the ulama as *al na'ib al amm* whose functions eventually included the declaration of defensive *jihad*, though not offensive *jihad*. Second, they instituted a different form of defensive warfare, known as *al harb al qudsi al difa'i* (literally, holy defensive war), which, if declared for a legitimate purpose, was itself legitimate — a considerable development of even Shi'a doctrine.

International law in Islam

In theory, the *siyar*, as an integral part of Islamic law, was derived from the traditional sources of that law. However, the classical theory of the *siyar* was not articulated in any clear fashion in either the *Qur'an* or the *Sunna*, although the underlying principles and assumptions were. Nor were analogy and consensus of particular value, and both the theory and the detailed rules derived more from political acts, custom, and reason: the terms of treaties and peace agreements; instructions issued by rulers and governors; the practical evolution of the concept of reciprocity; and direct experience in handling relations with other states. However, all these had to be incorporated into a Muslim framework and given the standard *post eventum* justification and legitimacy. Hence,

> the juristic writings of eminent Muslim jurists and judges provided a legal rationale of Islam's relations with other nations within the general framework of Islamic ethical principles and helped to formulate rules and principles on the basis of analogical reasoning (*qiyas*) and juristic preference (*istihsan*).[8]

As was the case with the domestic law of Islam, the theory of the *siyar* reached its first full and systematic exposition towards the end of the second Muslim century in the work of Muhammad bin al Hasan al Shaybani (750–804), and in particular through his *kitab al siyar al kabir*. The original text appears to have been lost and is known only through the elaborate commentary of Sarakhsi. Two points are of particular interest in this commentary. First, it contains a comprehensive definition of *siyar*:

> The siyar is the plural of sira, and this book is called after this term. It describes the conduct of the believers in their relations with the unbelievers of enemy territory as well as with the people with whom the believers had made treaties, who may have been temporarily (Musta'mins) or permanently (Dhimmis) resident in Islamic lands; with apostates, who were the worst of the unbelievers, since they abjured after they accepted [Islam]; and with rebels (baghis) who were not counted as unbelievers, though they were ignorant and their understanding [of Islam] was false.[9]

What this comprehended can be readily seen from the detailed list of contents in Majid Khadduri's translation of the *siyar*. The chapter headings alone are instructive: Traditions Relating to the Conduct of War; On the Conduct of the Army in Enemy Territory; On the

Spoil of War; On the Intercourse between the Territory of Islam and the Territory of War; On Peace Treaties; On Aman (Safe Conduct); On Apostasy; On Dissension and Highway Robbery.[10]

Second, apart from the general proposition that a state of war or hostility is the normal relationship, a number of principles emerge in Shaybani's *siyar*. Decisions should be based on custom, analogy, and territoriality: that is, the custom or analogy to be applied was that of the territory in which it was to be applied. Rulings by non-Muslims were binding on Muslims whenever they were resident in non-Muslim territory: that is, subject to the overriding authority of Muslim law upon Muslims everywhere, jurisdictional and other rulings made by the recognized authorities in any non-Muslim territory were binding upon Muslims resident therein. Reciprocity of treatment should be applied whether or not a temporary peace has been agreed. Subject to certain qualifications, the principle of *pacta sunt servanda* applies. Finally, though the principle is not explicit in the text, Shaybani and his colleagues recommended tolerance towards unbelievers and held that war — that is, organized fighting — should be embarked upon only when the inhabitants of *dar al harb* came into conflict with Muslims: it was essentially a doctrine of defensive *jihad*. Although this particular principle was later overturned by al Shafi'i, who held that it was a duty to wage war on the unbeliever simply because he was an unbeliever, whether or not there was any threat to the community, it was re-established later on by Ibn Taymiyya, and appears to be the view of the majority of today's jurists for whom reality clearly circumscribes the ideal. Al Shafi'i's reasoning is consistent with the obligation to establish the universal *umma* but is inappropriate in a world of nation-states.

There is one final point concerning the theory. Both the Muslim law of nations and the foreign relations of the Muslim state which it regulates are, as the above brief summary suggests, primarily concerned with the conduct of war and only secondarily with peaceful relations. This does, for many, reinforce the view that Islam is intrinsically expansionist, belligerent, and confrontational. We do well to remember, however, that the imperial powers were equally expansionary, belligerent, and confrontational. Furthermore, unless the order of words is purely accidental, the title of Grotius's monumental work on public international law, *De iure belli ac pacis*, suggests a similar preoccupation.

Pragmatic modification to the theory

Later developments concerned two major upsets to the classical doctrine: first, the breakup of the theoretical unity of *dar al Islam* and the emergence of distinct and independent Muslim political entities; and second, the practical requirement to modify the basis upon which relations with the non-Muslim world were conducted as the might and power of Muslim states declined and those of non-Muslim states increased. As to the former, some means had clearly to be devised to regulate relations between Muslim political entities. The first step was tacit agreement to set aside religio-political doctrines which were inconsistent with reality or which, if rigidly applied, would hinder rather than help the conduct of relations. External relations within *dar al Islam* were conducted on an essentially secular basis. This is turn fostered creeping pragmatism which ensured that concepts of equality and reciprocity, combined with systematic reasoning, custom, and practices borrowed from, or indistinguishable from, the European manual of diplomacy and international relations, became the normative principles. Practice was in fact indistinguishable from that of the rest of the world, although lip service continued to be paid to the theoretical unity of the *umma* and to the divine origin of the practice. Examples might include the arrangements between the Abbasid *mu'tamid* (governor) of Seville and his peers in Granada and Badajos for soliciting the assistance of the Almoravid powers in Morocco in the late eleventh century, the diplomatic and commercial relations between the Ottoman and Safavid Empires, the relations of the Zaidi Imamate in Yemen with its neighbours, and the tangled relationship between Sultanate and Imamate in Oman.

Similar rational considerations came to govern the conduct of relations with non-Muslim powers. This arose out of the practice of the jurists of re-interpreting the doctrine in the light of changing circumstances. Peace was no longer necessarily temporary and was not necessarily negotiated on Muslim terms. *Jihad* as a state of permanent war was no longer tenable and was no longer compatible with Muslim interests. The obligation remained but it went into a period of suspension — it became dormant although it might be returned to an active state at any time. Nevertheless, Muslims came to regard this absence of permanent war as the normal situation, although personal ambition often intruded; but warfare came to be more limited temporally. By the end of the sixteenth century there was general acceptance of the proposition that peaceful relations between states of different religious persuasions were not only possible but should be the norm, although in practice, this tended to be a counsel of perfection which was applied in a territorially and temporally limited manner. Nevertheless, a treaty between the Ottoman Sultan Sulaiman the Magnificent and King Francis I of France, concluded in 1535, set out clearly how far the implications of the change had been accepted — by the politicians at least — while absence of dissent and opposition from the theorists might indicate either tacit acceptance or a well-developed sense of self-preservation. The treaty included recognition of equality between the parties, a 'valid and certain peace' between them for the lifetime of the signatories, the grant of reciprocal rights, the grant of special privileges in the Ottoman Empire to French citizens, and clear acceptance of both consular and diplomatic missions on a basis of equality and reciprocity. More importantly, perhaps, it confirmed the incorporation of a measure of territoriality into the political and legal practices of Islam. It has been argued, in this connection, that the incorporation of territory as a basic element of the state in Islam was a relatively late development. However, the notion of territorial delimitation or definition as an element in the Muslim concept of state was not only accepted by some relatively early commentators on *siyar*, but also is necessarily inherent in the concept of *jihad* as defence of *dar al Islam*, and is explicitly recognized in the distinction between *dar al Islam* and *dar al harb*. It is equally explicit in domestic terms in al Mawardi's reference to a 'warden of the frontiers'.[11]

By the time Fadhl Allah had completed his part of the reconciliation between theory and practice (see Chapter 2), state pluralism — albeit state pluralism in as embryonic a form as occurred elsewhere at that time — had become the norm in the Muslim world, as had general acceptance that 'those in authority' who must be obeyed, were the temporal rulers, whether or not they sought or received legitimacy through the normative processes of Islam. In addition, the concept of defined territory as an attribute of the state was also at least implicitly accepted: indeed, one might legitimately argue that this concept became part of the apparatus of state institutions with the introduction of provinces and the imposition of a taxation system. Furthermore, the concept of territorial exclusivity — if not ownership — was inherent, albeit at lower than state level, in the disposition of cultivable land and in recognized tribal *diyar* (grazing areas), and, for that matter, in ownership of wells, which were a feature of pre-Islamic Arabia and which are still important there today.[12] The significant point, however, is that Muslims generally, despite periodic inveighing against alleged corrupt and un-Islamic practices on the part of the ruling elite both in capitals and in the provinces, accepted without much demur the embryo multi-state system, the attribution to the ruling elite of power and authority (with, in some cases, divine legitimation), some measure of sovereign powers on a delegated basis, and the right of the ruling elite to make such political and administrative dispositions as they saw fit. Moreover, the generality of Muslims did not appear to consider this as contrary to or inconsistent with Islam. The same appears to have applied in those parts of the Muslim world which came under the control of the European powers — India, North Africa, sub-Saharan Africa, Indonesia, and Malaysia. It is, of course, true that the majority of Muslims — the poorer uneducated masses — were hardly affected by the doctrinal hair-splitting and the intellectual disputation. There is no evidence, however, that they held different views to those outlined above and circumstantial evidence, in the absence of widespread, self-generated popular dissent, that they accepted the reality of life as it was as compatible with their belief system — that is, if they thought about it at all in these terms.

Indeed, one might well argue that the concept of territorial pluralism and all that this implies for concepts of authority and government has been articulated, if not accepted, since at least the tenth century. Thus, for example, the author of an anonymous Persian geography, *hudud al 'alam* (compiled in 983) comments that

> one country differs from another in four respects. First, by the difference of water, air, soil and temperature. Secondly, by the difference of religion, law and beliefs. Thirdly, by the difference of words and languages. Fourthly, by the differences of kingdoms. The frontiers of a country are separated from those of another country by three things: first, by mountains, great or small, stretching between them; secondly, by rivers, great or small, flowing between them; thirdly, by deserts, great or small, stretching between them.[13]

This quotation, of course, illustrates graphically the distinction in Muslim (and particularly Arab) minds between the frontier region and the frontier line, which has often bedevilled European frontier negotiations with Muslim states. Muslim/Arab tradition tends to think in terms of a frontier region where allegiance is likely to be fluid and which is not naturally susceptible to the drawing of precise lines of demarcation. This is, of course, to be expected in a system which is based on the concept of spheres of influence and personal loyalty as opposed to territoriality. Thus, the difference of opinion between the United Kingdom and the Imam of the Yemen over the interpretation of the *status quo* clauses in the 1934 Treaty of Taiz was inevitable: the UK government thought in terms of a frontier line, while the Imam thought in terms of less clearly defined frontier regions. It may be a truism to say that 'actions speak louder than words', but it is very appropriate: to dismiss the historical record as irrelevant is both foolish and dishonest. It is, after all, 'the record of what Muslims have done and this record is at least as reliable an indicator of what Islam is as what Muslims say it is'.[14] This line of reasoning, taken to its logical conclusion, would also reject — and rightly so — the conventional argument that actual practice is no more than deviation from the ideal and as such should be ignored as contrary to God's will. It does, after all, reflect man's fallible attempts to comply with that will.

Conclusions

By the time that the nineteenth- and twentieth-century re-examination of Islam had commenced, therefore, territorial pluralism within the theoretical unity of the *umma* was an accepted fact of life to the extent that Sir Sayyid Ahmad Khan could argue that the Ottoman Caliph 'is *not* our Caliph either according to Mohammedan law or Mohammedan religion. If he has the rights of a Caliph he has them only in the country and over the people that he is master of'.[15] It is true that Sir Sayyid Ahmad was concerned about the eventual unification and independence of all Indians irrespective of faith, but others too, for example, Jamal al Din al Afghani, Rashid Ridha, Muhammad Iqbal, and Maududi, accepted the facts of life (though some never accepted them intellectually). It is a moot point whether this should be seen as relevant only to the context of the fight against imperialism, as some have argued, or as the beginnings of a move towards the Muslim comity of nations advocated by Ibn Taymiyya and Muhammad Iqbal.

The conduct of foreign relations has, in sum, been based on secular concepts of national interest, and on acceptance of the normative rules and practices which were subsequently codified in manuals of international law and diplomatic practice. Muslim and non-Muslim practice and the contents of their respective manuals were virtually indistinguishable. Indeed, it is impossible to reach any firm conclusions about who were the first to articulate the practice. Although many modern Muslim commentators claim that the principles underlying the generally accepted rules and practices and some at least of the rules and practices governing international relations were first articulated in the *Qur'an* and the *Sunna*, history indicates clearly that they were at least known many centuries earlier and that Muslim rulers took over existing practice (and, for that matter, theory), except as instructed to the contrary in the revelation. Nevertheless, the first structured attempt to codify a law of nations — public international law — was made by Shaybani some eight centuries before Grotius.[16]

5

The Islamic Economic System

Introduction

The study of the economic principles and practices of Islam in any
disciplined and sustained fashion is a relatively modern phenomenon.
Although there had been some discussion of the economic principles
of Islam at an earlier stage, the real beginnings came in the third and
fourth decades of the twentieth century, with a substantial increase in
publications in the next two decades. This latter period also saw
'efforts at system formulations and discussions on specific issues relevant to modern life', but analytical studies of the economic injunctions
of Islam and analytical critiques of modern institutions are even more
recent.[1] A recent bibliography lists some 700 items, of which only
twenty-seven are dated before 1945 (some fifty items are undated).[2]
This is not to suggest that economic issues and principles were not
addressed in the classical literature: they were, but in a piecemeal
fashion and with the primary aim of setting out ground rules for economic activity, elucidating and elaborating the precepts of the *Qur'an*
and the *Sunna*, and so on.[3] There are, of course, some uncharacter-
istically clear passages in the *Qur'an* which prompted the comment
(albeit in a discussion of the compatibility of Islam and capitalism) that

> there are religions whose sacred texts discourage economic
> activity in general, counselling their followers to rely on God
> to provide them with their daily bread or, more particularly,
> looking askance at any striving for profit. This is certainly
> not the case with the Koran, which looks with favour upon
> commercial activity, confining itself to condemning fraudulent
> practices and requiring abstention from trade during certain
> religious festivals.[4]

96

However, the concept of Muslim economics is certainly confused, causing one undergraduate to open a discussion paper entitled 'An Islamic economic system — fact or fantasy' with the comment: 'If we identify the term fact with theory and the term fantasy with actual practice, it might be a little easier to proceed with the discussion.'[5] It is, nevertheless, clear than many devout Muslims who are also economists believe firmly in the existence of a distinctive Islamic economic system both in theory and in practice, and in one which differs markedly from both the capitalist and the socialist (or communist) systems. In their discussions of the theory and theoretical principles, however, they use standard economic terms: production, distribution, and consumption; capital investment and return on investment; choice and opportunity cost; and so on. As a result, the existence of a distinctive 'Islamic' economic system has been questioned. Since, however, Muslim economists — and, it may be added, some Muslim politicians — believe fervently in its existence and have striven to prove that existence by putting into practice the economic principles enunciated in the theoretical model, it is more pertinent to ask: 'In what way does the economic system of Islam differ, either in theory or in practice, from more familiar systems, if at all?'

Islamic economic theory

It has been argued that

the central feature of the proposed system is that individuals are guided in their economic decisions by a set of behaviour norms, ostensibly derived from the Qur'an and the Sunna. Two other features stand out: *zakat*, a tax considered the basis of Islamic fiscal policy, and the prohibition of interest, viewed as the centerpiece of Islamic monetary policy. Virtually all Islamic economists consider this trio — the norms, zakat, and zero interest — the pillars of the Islamic system.[6]

More generally, the key characteristics of the Islamic economic system are the right to private ownership of property, positive encouragement of the exploitation of resources, approval of material progress and prosperity, co-operation and mutual responsibility, acceptance of the rights of others, social justice, equitable distribution of wealth, prohibition of interest, and abstention from certain malpractices such as fraud, gambling, extortion, monopoly practices, hoarding, and the like. In addition, of course, there are specific Qur'anic injunctions concerning payment of *zakat* (alms, sometimes defined as an alms tax), inheritance, and so on. All commentators, without exception, emphasize that the general characteristics noted above, and man's detailed application of them in his daily life, are subject to certain ethical and moral limitations. Thus, the right to private ownership of property is subject to the proposition that 'the owner of the whole universe with its wealth and all good things is Allah, the Creator'.[7] Man's ownership is thus as a proxy or trustee, and is subject to two moral imperatives: good management on behalf of the real owner; and the requirement to apply surplus wealth productively in pursuit of social justice and the general good.

Similarly, although man is expected to exploit to the full all resources available, that exploitation must be the means, not the end: such activity must be undertaken *ad majorem Dei gloriam* and in the interests of the economic well-being of the whole community. Although, therefore, 'economic activity, the search for profit, trade, and consequently, production for the market, are looked upon with no less favour by Muslim tradition than by the Koran itself', there are ethical constraints since 'the Prophet heaps praise upon those who, far from being parasites, enrich themselves so as to be able to help the deprived'.[8] Individual or collective initiative and competition are certainly permissible, but always subject to the wider needs of the community, and so also for material progress and the pursuit of profit. Although equitable distribution of wealth is deemed necessary, it is not absolute: disparities in wealth distribution are acceptable, since men are not endowed with equal intelligence, ability, and skills, and the more fortunate are not expected to hide their greater wealth. However, conspicuous consumption, over-luxurious living standards, and the unproductive hoarding of surplus resources are discouraged or prohibited; and the wealthier are expected to contribute more to the social welfare of the poor and needy than those less well-off. Economic activity in Islam is subject to the same overall moral, ethical, and doctrinal constraints as are other human activities.

Specific obligations and prohibitions are relatively few in number. Payment of *zakat* is obligatory, though it may be distributed directly rather than paid to the state authority. The purposes for which it may be disbursed are strictly controlled and are set out in the *Qur'an*:

The alms are only for the poor and the needy, and those who collect them, and those whose hearts are to be reconciled, and to free the captives and the debtors, and for the cause of Allah, and the wayfarers. (Q9:60)

The rules of inheritance are mandatory in all their detail. *Riba* (interest or usury) is strictly prohibited. Proper care for the poor, the needy, the ill, and so on — that is, social welfare — is a duty incumbent on all Muslims both individually and collectively. Finally,

there must be respect for other people's property and abstention from unproductive malpractices, profiteering activities, and disruptive transgressions, such as robbery, extortion, deceiving, gambling, hoarding, 'cornering' the market, trading in harmful drugs and pornography and so forth. Furthermore, any earnings through expediency and manipulation of the law are not viewed as legitimate.[9]

Apart from these general rules, however, the basic principle seems to be that 'everything that is ethical is acceptable to the Islamic system, and anything unethical is thereby rejected'.[10] However, the practical application of these general rules and principles, which, zero interest and *zakat* apart, are familiar moral imperatives, requires a considerable degree of altruism, which is hardly characteristic of large and complex societies unless compliance is made attractive or failure to conform attracts coercive force. Islamic economists 'have simply assumed that in a society of pious Muslims, rational processes would not displace moral motives'.[11]

Taxation and interest

Zakat also poses problems, since there has been considerable argument about whether it is a voluntary or an obligatory payment, about whether the state has the right to insist upon payment to the central treasury, about the appropriate rate, about the categories of wealth (or possessions) on which it is payable, and about the precise meaning of the categories upon which it may be disbursed. Who, for example, determines who is poor and needy or what the cause of Allah really is, and who decides the allocation between the various beneficiaries? Over the years, however, *zakat* became in Sunni practice a form of mandatory tax collected by the state in cash rather than in kind. Shi'a doctrine held that the Imams were the legitimate recipient of *zakat* (and the *khums* — a further tax normally paid by the Shi'a, but not the Sunnis, and amounting to one-fifth levied on certain categories of income) after the death of the Prophet. Following on the occultation of the Twelfth Imam, responsibility for the distribution of *zakat* and *khums* was initially laid upon the individual, but the ulama gradually asserted their right to receive both in their capacity as *al na'ib al 'amm*. Although this theoretically gave them considerable financial independence from the government of the day, in practice payments were made or withheld as a means of signifying approval or disapproval of the policies of the ulama.

The extent to which the practice of treating *zakat* as a state-imposed mandatory tax on income and property is regarded as justified and legitimate is well illustrated by the Saudi decrees and regulations concerning income tax and *zakat* first issued in 1950. Under them, Saudi nationals and Saudi companies were obliged to pay *zakat* but were exempt from income tax (which was levied on non-Saudis). *Zakat* was assessed on 'all capitals and revenues resulting therefrom and all income profits and gainings obtained by the said individuals and companies' which were defined as

> those obtained by taxable Saudis from the carrying out of commercial transactions or industry or from personal business or from properties or monetary assets of whatever kind and description they may be, including monetary and commercial expenses and profits on shares and generally every income Islamic law has subjected to *zakat*.[12]

A *fatwa* issued by Shaikh Muhammad Ahmad Abu Zahrah is also instructive. He defines *zakat* as 'one of the regulations of the state; it rests upon a tax basis' and states that payment of *zakat* is evidence of submission and obedience to the authority of a ruler.[13] Thus, *zakat* has become a sort of property and income tax, and its disbursement on its proper purposes has become subsumed in normal state expenditure. Moreover, the state may raise additional taxes as necessary, provided the purposes for which revenue is required are legitimate and the rate of taxation does not amount to extortion.

Riba is a contentious issue, since, although the prohibition has clear Qur'anic sanction, the precise meaning of the term is hotly debated. Conservative theorists argue that *riba* means any form of interest, whatever the rate, on the grounds that it is a return on unproductive capital and imposes the risk entirely, and therefore unfairly, on one party alone, the borrower, and leaves the lender an assured gain. However morally sound the argument may be, the logic is dubious: for it may be argued that capital lent for a specific economic activity is hardly unproductive, and that a cursory examination of bankruptcy records anywhere demonstrates that the assured gain may be illusory. Lenders do take risks. The contrary argument is that *riba* is properly translated as usury, or excessive rates of interest, on the grounds that *riba* was a pre-Islamic practice under which failure to repay a debt in due time resulted in an extension of the time-period and a doubling of the amount repayable. Although this argument is also somewhat specious, it does suggest that some theorists recognize the inherent illogicality of banning fixed rate interest systems while espousing variable rate profit-sharing: for both are a return on capital.

Islamic banking

Whatever the proper definition of *riba*, the general insistence on the prohibition of interest has focused considerable attention on the vexed question of an Islamic banking system — the more so today, with the establishment of a number of 'Islamic' banks, operating particularly in the domestic banking systems. Can such a banking system work; does it work; and if so, how does it work? — these are the questions most frequently asked. The theoretical framework of Islamic banking has been defined by the International Association of Islamic Banks. According to them, the objectives of an Islamic bank are:

(a) Attracting and collecting funds and mobilising resources available in the Islamic nation together with consolidating such resources through the development of individuals' saving awareness.

(b) Directing funds to the investment activities that serve the objectives of the economic and social development in the Islamic nation.

(c) Carrying out banking activities and services in accordance with Islamic jurisprudence free from usury and exploitation, and in such a way as to solve the problem of short-term financing.[14]

As for deployment of resources, the International Association of Islamic Banks suggested the following:

1. Direct investment: in the establishment of organisations carrying out a specific economic, commercial, industrial, or agricultural activity (service).
2. Investment in partnership with others in projects in the following ways:
(a) Project capital — buying shares of other companies or participating in the capital of a specific project;
(b) Limited partnership (loan agreement) in limited deals. Part of the money or all of it is paid — (Mudaraba);
(c) Partnership leading to ownership — (Lease-purchase);
(d) Operations of 'resale with specification of gain' to enable individuals or bodies to procure the goods they need before the required price is available — (Murabaha).
3. Loans without interest in certain cases.[15]

On the basis of recent experience the answer to the first two questions must be a qualified affirmative. Islamic banks do

provide, on a fee basis, many of the services available at a Western bank, such as traveller's cheques, foreign exchange transactions, demand deposits, etc. Their peculiarity is that they neither pay nor charge interest; instead they share in the profits made by the bank, receiving a 'dividend'.[16]

Thus, investment deposits do not attract a fixed return, but an agreed share of the banks' profits (or losses) in the form of a 'dividend' (a term which was familiar in the Lower Gulf as early as the late 1950s). In discussing the use of available resources, one observer stresses that risk-sharing (or sharing of both profit and loss) is the fundamental principle for granting loans and advances:

For example, both the bank and the borrower may provide capital and share the profits. Or the bank provides all the capital to an agent-manager, who receives a share of the profits and may be authorised eventually to buy out the bank. The bank finances trade by actually buying the commodity, transporting it to the customer and selling it to him at a mark-up. The profit, not being interest, is legitimate. Or finally, in case of need, consumption loans may be made. For these an administrative fee may be charged, which again is not regarded as interest.[17]

However, as suggested earlier, some qualification is necessary: although Islamic banks can operate effectively in the domestic system and have shown this to be the case, and although experience suggests they can operate internationally, a number of problems have arisen. No means has yet been found, for example, to accommodate very short-term (i.e. overnight) investment requirements; effective participation in long-term investment such as major capital development schemes with long lead-times has not yet been fully brought into the system and the Islamic Development Bank's lending rate was 4 per cent at the end of 1984; interest-free multi-currency mutual credit arrangements have not been worked out; the problems of working on an interest-free basis in interaction with the international system in which interest is an integral part has not been solved; and in some non-Muslim countries, Islamic banks find it difficult or impossible to offer a complete range of services, because they are not deemed by the central banks to be banks in the normal technical use of the term (it is the inability to guarantee a deposit which is the major problem).

Partnership arrangements

The mechanisms referred to by the International Association of Islamic Banks in its suggested deployment of resources are uncontroversial and readily comprehensible to anyone, apart from *murabaha* and *mudaraba*, both of which are held to be a form of partnership. *Mudaraba* or *qirad* (an alternative term) has been a feature of Muslim economic activity since at least the eleventh century, when it was defined by Sarakhsi as follows:

> The word *Mudarabah* is derived from 'Darb on Earth'. It has been so named because the *Mudarib* (user of others' capital) qualifies to get a share of the profit on account of his endeavours and work. He thus participates in the profit as well as having the right to use capital, and strive according to his discretion. People of Madinah call this contract *Muqaradah* which is derived from the word *Qard*, meaning 'surrendering'. The owner of capital, thus, surrenders his own rights over that portion of capital, to the *Amil* (user of capital).

This is how it has been so named. We have, however, chosen the former name as it conforms to what occurs in the Book of Allah saying 'and others strive on earth seeking the gift of God . . .'

Averroes (Ibn Rushd) also referred to the concept:

there is no difference of opinion among the Muslims about the legality of *Qirad*. It was an institution in the pre-Islamic period and Islam confirmed it. They all agree that its form is that a person gives to another person some capital that he uses in business. The user gets, according to conditions, some specific proportion of the profit, i.e. any proportion they agree, one third, one fourth or even one half.[18]

Murabaha (literally, a means of making a profit) is a more complex mechanism. In the first place, classical doctrine requires that the subject matter of a sale must be actually owned by the seller or his agent. However, this condition does not apply to an offer, nor does it obtain during any period of negotiation prior to the making of a firm contract. The financing of trade therefore requires the bank to contract to purchase goods for delivery at some time in the future, but with immediate payment of the purchase price. The bank then contracts to sell the goods at an agreed price, which includes an agreed profit margin — hence the reference to mark-up. Payment may be immediate or deferred, in a single payment or by instalments, and the agreed mark-up or profit normally reflects the arrangements. In practice, the interval between the two transactions is likely to be short, and negotiations will be virtually simultaneous.

The various activities defined earlier as proper and legitimate use of resources may be more comprehensibly defined as 'trade-related' or 'investment-related'. The former category would typically include the financing of the sale and purchase of goods, the purchase of trade bills, the sale and purchase of property (with or without buy-back arrangements), leasing, rental, and hire-purchase arrangements (with repayments for the provision of capital to an enterprise to be inclusive of an agreed fee for administrative costs and the acquisition of property rights), and the financing of property development on the basis of development charges. The investment-related category would typically include various forms of partnership, participation term certificates (the Islamic banking equivalent of debentures), the provision of venture capital under *mudaraba* arrangements, and property development on a rent-sharing basis.

Justification of a separate Islamic economic system

An examination of the already voluminous and steadily growing literature shows clearly that the mechanisms and the accepted fundamental economic laws and principles do not differ markedly from those to be found in studies on capitalist and socialist economic systems, with the sole exception of the adjustments needed to deal with the prohibition of interest. However, even the mechanisms used to avoid the use of the term 'interest' are familiar: partnerships and lending. As already suggested, the only real difference between the dividend paid by an Islamic bank to depositors and the interest paid in the Western banking system is that the rate of return is variable and not fixed. Similarly, *murabaha*, as identified in the theory, disguises a fixed rate of interest as a mark-up or a profit; the use of agreed fees for administrative costs ensures a fixed return on capital; and *mudaraba* arrangements and arrangements to cover short-term lending are virtually indistinguishable from normal Western banking practice. Furthermore, 'like the mediaeval jurists before them, contemporary Islamic economists are apparently being pressured by practitioners to legitimize a variety of practices that amount to interest in disguise'.[19]

Great stress is laid upon the moral and ethical underpinning of the Islamic approach to economics. Although, therefore, economics is recognized as a value-oriented discipline, economic relationships must take into account ethical and moral considerations: self-interest alone is insufficient. Thus, man is bound to exploit economic resources, but must do so within a framework of socio-economic justice and for the ultimate benefit of all mankind. It follows that certain economic and other activities which are detrimental to these lofty aims must be eschewed. Furthermore, although inequality of income and wealth is not proscribed in Islam, the wealthier are expected to contribute more to the succour of the needy as a moral obligation, and the state authorities may enact measures to ensure that they do so. Even the concept of scarcity is defined in moral terms since scarcity is the result of man's immoderate material desires rather than of limited resources. The proper use of God's unlimited resources, which involves distributive justice, is the key.

In short, 'by emphasising cooperation and moderation in all human pursuits, whether profits or consumption, whether economic or non-economic, Islam views man to be more than a mere *homo-economicus*; he is a social being, whose aspirations transcend material needs'.[20]

In addition to stressing the moral and ethical values underpinning their vision of an economic system and emphasizing the need for proper obedience to and fulfilment of God's commands, 'Islamic economists' also argue that in these two ways their discipline and their economic system differ from those of capitalism and socialism, both of which they excoriate as essentially materialist and as having little or no concern for the spiritual needs of the individual or of the larger community. Furthermore, though capitalism does provide scope for individual effort, for the fulfilment of ambitions and for economic progress, it breeds selfishness, greed and corrupt practices because of the absence of moral and ethical principles. Western economic thinking and practice may have had their roots in Christian ideals, but these have been long abandoned in favour of pragmatic reasoning based upon the concept of *homo economicus*. Socialism is similarly flawed: it subordinates the individual's freedom of economic action to rigid state control, kills the incentive to work harder by removing the incentive of greater personal gain, is dehumanizing, and has also led to corruption and nepotism.

This line of reasoning is, of course, attractive to Muslims, but it is flawed. There are, after all, theological concepts basic to both capitalism and socialism and 'such concepts as utopianism, the future, liberty, discipline, fellowship, justice and a whole host of others have a strong theological base and are explicit in the literature'.[21] As far as capitalism is concerned, the argument goes too far and ignores the continued influence of the moral and ethical underpinning of the system most prominently exhibited by the plethora of major philanthropic institutions. Socialism, too, is unfairly pilloried and the moral idealism and altruism which are both inherent and explicit are brushed aside. Even more fundamentally, however, the comparison is between an *ideal* Islamic system and a Muslim perception of *existing practice* in the capitalist and socialist countries. The inconvenient discontinuity between their idealized system and the actual economic practices of Muslims and Muslim states is brushed aside as irrelevant or the practice is defined as deviation from *al sirat al mustaqim*: the same indulgence is not accorded to other systems. In this connection it is instructive to compare the situation in Egypt under Nasser and Iran under the present Islamic Republican regime. Nasser obtained a series of *fatwas* from al Azhar, and in particular from Shaikh Muhammad Shaltut (Rector of al Azhar from 1958 until his death in 1963–4) in order to provide doctrinal legitimacy for the principles and practices of his brand of Arab socialism.

In Iran, the Majles and the Council of Guardians are locked in a bitter struggle over the question of land reform and the sanctity of private property, with the Majles, whose members are drawn predominantly from the religious hierarchy,[22] pressing strongly for large-scale redistribution of land and the Council of Guardians opposing the proposed extent of redistribution on the grounds that it is contrary to Muslim law and doctrine. It is therefore as well to temper the Muslim ideal with reality, and to remember that the difference is of long standing to the Muslim world. Ibn Khaldun, for example, commented:

> It should be known that commerce means the attempt to make a profit by increasing capital, through buying goods at a low price and selling them at a high price, whether these goods consist of slaves, grain, animals, weapons, or clothing material. The accrued [amount] is called 'profit' [*ribh*]. The attempt to make such a profit may be undertaken by storing goods and holding them until the market has fluctuated from low prices to high prices. This will bring large profit. Or the merchant may transport his goods to another country where they are more in demand than in his own, where he brought them. This [again] will bring a large profit. Therefore, an old merchant said to a person who wanted to find out the truth about commerce: 'I shall give it to you in two words: Buy cheap and sell dear. There is commerce for you.' By this he meant, the same thing that we have just established.[23]

It has also been clearly demonstrated that the practices complained of in Muslim critiques were as prevalent in the Muslim world as elsewhere, and they remain just as prevalent today.[24]

Conclusion

The conclusion to be drawn from this necessarily summary analysis of Islamic economic theory and practice is neither spectacular nor surprising. In practical terms an Islamic economic system is unlikely to differ fundamentally from other economic systems as far as goals, institutions, and techniques are concerned. Indeed, it may be argued that the main difference from capitalist systems will be the absence of interest as a source of income and that the main difference from a socialist or centrally planned system will be Islam's acceptance of private property rights. 'Whether the Islamic economy will be nearer to a socialist or a capitalist economy will depend upon the value judgements of those who will prepare the blue-print of an Islamic economy.'[25] Despite the stress laid upon ethical and moral considerations, therefore, the only logical answer to the question, 'how to achieve utopian (and altruistically motivated) goals by pragmatic means?'[26] must be: in much the same manner as obtains in other economic systems seeking to achieve similar goals — but the labels and the explanations will be different.

6

Intellectual Influences, Part I —
The Indian Subcontinent

Introduction

Since about 1970 or earlier, as suggested at the beginning, the
Muslim world has exhibited an increased consciousness of Islam
and its values and a more active and assertive expression of that
consciousness in most parts of the Muslim world.[1] As part of the
process there has been a re-emergence of Islam as a political and
social force, particularly among the ruling elites: that is, to use the
terminology of Chapter 1, the political and social sub-systems have
been more prominent. It has been argued that the contemporary
revival may be explained as a natural consequence of the process
of modernization and that it differs from earlier revivals in that the
latter were elitist intellectual movements which had little or no
impact on the masses and had little or no participation by them,
while the current revival stems from 'the involvement of the masses
through modernization [which] is an unprecedented event in the
Islamic world. It does not occur before the 1920s', and that 'it was
modernization, most conspicuously in the form of urbanization,
which involved the masses and led to the formation of a reaction
different from those of the nineteenth- and early twentieth-century
elites'.[2]

This argument does not seem particularly convincing and will
be considered in more detail later. For the moment suffice it to say
that it does need considerable qualification, in that the leaders of
today's organizations are clearly — and in some cases by their own
admission — considerably influenced by the views of the intellectual elite discarded so summarily. However, the influence of
nineteenth- and early twentieth-century intellectuals was at the time
territorially limited for the most part and only in Egypt and in the

Indo-Pakistani subcontinent was there any real continuity. Major intellectual figures from these two areas have therefore been selected for analysis, in the full knowledge that both the limitation to these areas and the specific examples chosen are arbitrary, selective, and open to question. It should be noted that Hassan al Banna, Sayyid Qutb, and Abul A'la Maududi are included more for their popularity than for their intellectual qualities. Though this is not consistent with the broader thesis noted above, it is more consistent with the time-scale of the current revival: all three figures preceded the current wave. The selection of specific figures for examination is, of course, arbitrary and open to question, but Shah Wali Allah, Sayyid Ahmad Khan, Muhammad Iqbal, and Abul A'la Maududi seem to be the major subcontinental figures, and Muhammad Abduh, Rashid Ridha, Hassan al Banna, and Sayyid Qutb are likewise the major Egyptian figures.

Shah Wali Allah: orthodoxy, reconciliation, and reform

Shah Wali Allah (1703–62) was an orthodox conservative whose thinking and writing are generally held to have been a major influence on all subsequent Muslim intellectual thought in the subcontinent. His attitudes were, no doubt, influenced by the collapse of Muslim power in India following the death of Aurangzeb, the last of the great Mughal emperors, in 1707 and the subsequent disintegration of Indian Muslim society, and possibly by the teaching he imbibed in the Hijaz at about the same time as his peninsular contemporary, Muhammad ibn Abdul Wahhab. Like Muhammad ibn Abdul Wahhab, he laid great stress on *tawhid* — the oneness, unity, and uniqueness of God — and opposed any practice which smacked, however indirectly, of any association of man — or any other being — with God, or of any oblique reference to a relationship between man and the attributes of God. He appears to have accepted the concept of saints as well as prophets, who might in certain circumstances be regarded as intermediaries, but who could not in any circumstances be invoked or called upon for assistance: nor could they, in his view, be legitimate objects of worship, nor was it permissible to make cult figures of them. He was, inevitably, a staunch believer in a Muslim law which had as its primary sources the *Qur'an* and the *Sunna*, but he also believed that *ijtihad* was a legitimate tool in certain circumstances, provided that it was used with caution. He wrote:

> Ijtihad in every age is obligatory (on the Muslim scholars) and by Ijtihad I mean the full understanding of the Shari'ah values (Ahkam) based upon the fundamentals of Islam, the elucidation of their details and the compilation and codification of new laws, although it may be in conformity with the approach adopted by the founder of a particular school. The reason why I have spoken of Ijtihad as obligatory is that every age has its own countless peculiar problems and cognizance of the Divine injunctions with regard to them is essential. The material which has already been written and compiled is not only insufficient but also embodies many differences of opinion. The differences cannot be resolved without resort to the fundamentals of the Shari'ah, as also because the chain of authenticity leading back to the mujtahids is probably disrupted. Therefore the only way open is to review and reassess these differences against the principles of Ijtihad.[3]

This and other similar passages must be construed in the light of his concept of the *shari'a*. He held that 'the *shari'ah*, having arisen among the Arabs, is related to their customs, traditions and social institutions, and that the laws of the *shari'ah* change according to changing circumstances, and the needs of peoples and places'.[4] Furthermore, he regarded only the *Qur'an* and the *Sunna* as sources of the *shari'a* and refused to consider as obligatory those doctrines which are the result of reasoning alone and for which the *shari'a* offered no guidance. Many modernists have taken these collective views as support for the extensive use of *ijtihad* and as justification of extensive changes in Islamic law. Some have argued further that Shah Wali Allah tended to regard some of the laws of Islam articulated in the *Qur'an* and the *Sunna* as specific to the Arabs of Muhammad's age only; and some have claimed that he favoured an Indianized form of the *shari'a* and suggested that the universal and immutable elements in it should be separated from the local elements so that adaptation to the needs and circumstances of differing societies is possible. However, this view has been disputed on the grounds that Shah Wali Allah is no innovator, but remains firmly in line with classical doctrine, and that

> a thorough scrutiny of Shah Wali-Allah's writings show, however, that he is firmly opposed to such ideas and strongly

holds that the pristine Islamic *Shari'ah* in its Arabian form has been made obligatory on the peoples of all countries and all ages. He stresses its innate perfection to such an extent that he neither allows it to be abrogated, nor considers it appropriate to add anything or improve upon it.

Furthermore, Shah Wali Allah distinguished between the *shari'a* of earlier prophets, each of which was limited both territorially and temporally, and that revealed to Muhammad, which was, indeed, intended to be universally applicable and immutable for all time.[5]

It must remain an open question which of the two views is correct and whether the modernist scholars are justified in asserting that 'the emphasis on *ijtihad* is Shah Wali Allah's main contribution to modernist speculative thinking in Muslim India'.[6] The more conservative view seems the more plausible, though he was no rigid conservative. As one commentator suggests:

> That he appeals to the prophetic tradition (*hadith*) in preference to *taqlid* of the jurists of the past is certainly a sign that he wanted to restore the flexibility of Islamic jurisprudence in its formative period before the fourth century of the *Hijra* and thus re-establish that dynamism of Islam which plays such a great role in Iqbal.[7]

A proponent of *ijtihad* he certainly was, but he emphasized that it was to be used with caution and erudition. In addition, he recommended respect for the unanimity and consensus achieved by past scholars; and in so doing clearly opposed the school of thought which wishes to dismiss out of hand the entire corpus of intellectualism which happens to be inconsistent with their particular views.

Of much greater importance in terms of jurisprudential and theological reasoning is his firm espousal of the principle of *takhayyur*; he was one of the earliest so to do. The principle of *talfiq* had, of course, long been available to Muslims, allowing them to follow the precepts of a particular school of law which was not their own. This was, however, subject to the rule that the entire transaction must be completed in accordance with the rules of a single school. *Talfiq* is

> a traditionally recognized practice — according to which an individual might follow one School in marriage procedure, another in determining inheritance and still another in

establishing a *waqf* or in performing prayers. Usually, *talfiq* was not recognized as legitimate within what is essentially a single process: for example, in the case of marriage it would not be acceptable to follow Hanafi rules governing consent and Shafi'i rules on dowry.[8]

However, Shah Wali Allah does appear to have taken the process further than his predecessors and 'developed an inter-juristic eclecticism recommending that on any point of doctrine or ritual a Muslim could follow the rulings of any one of the four principal juristic schools'.[9] No doubt his reasoning owed something to his studies in the Hijaz where the Hanbali school was increasing in power as a result of the alliance between the Al Saud and Muhammad ibn Abdul Wahhab. Moreover, it is clear that he also favoured the harmonization of the views of the different schools as an eventual aim.

Shah Wali Allah also developed further the concept of the *khilafa* or *imama* in a manner which was a radical departure from the tradition of Indo-Muslim scholarship. He distinguished between two forms of successors to the Prophet, political and religious — the former being responsible for government and administration, and the latter for guiding the people in the discharge of their socio-religious obligations.

> Those who inherited his political functions are concerned with legislation, *jihad*, defence, taxation, administration of *waqf*, care for mosques and so on. The successors to his religious authority have the duty to teach and preach, to study *Qur'an*, *Hadith* and to instruct in them the community, whom they are to guide in their religious activities and to inspire towards spirituality and ethical behaviour.[10]

He did not however, advocate a separation of religion and politics, but rather of the functions within the religio-political framework of a universal caliphate. Thus, Shah Wali Allah

> has discussed in detail the nature, scope and responsibilities of the *khilafat par excellence* or *khilafat-i-khassah* as he calls it. It has external and internal aspects (*zahr wa batin*); the former is connected with government and administration, while the latter is linked up with the specific role of prophethood, which, according to him, is 'the fulfillment of God's intention to

reform humanity . . . suppress the evildoers and infidels . . . and enforce the *shari'ah*.'[11]

Interestingly, he accepts territorial plurality, subject to the overall authority of the *khalifa*, and argues that monarchy is necessary to maintain peace and order in individual states, which might have either an entirely Muslim or a mixed population. The duties of the *khalifa* were two-fold: the defence of *dar al Islam* and the supervision of Muslim rulers, on the basis that he had sufficient political and temporal power to ensure that the states were governed in accordance with the tenets of Islam.

Throughout his teaching, his writing and his political activities, Shah Wali Allah had, as one of his aims, a reconciliation between, if not a reunification of, the various schools of thought in the community: moderation and compromise were his natural preference.

Indeed most of his views were the result of his constant endeavour to shun extremism of every kind and to bring about compromise in place of conflict; he did enunciate principles with which 'all but extremists' would be inclined to agree.[12]

This is no doubt the basis of the respect paid to him by both orthodox conservatives and modernists and of his considerable influence on the thinking of both groups, an influence which is both clear and enduring. He was, notwithstanding the views of the modernists, an orthodox conservative or traditionalist, in that he rejected *bida'* and any alien accretions taken over by and incorporated into traditional Islam as a result of earlier contacts with other cultures and belief-systems. For him the *Qur'an* and the *Sunna* were supreme and infallible and his advocacy of *ijtihad* was not in support of its unfettered exercise. Indeed, he is often referred to as 'fundamentalist' before that term took on its current pejorative overtones.[13]

Sir Sayyid Ahman Khan: speculative rationalism

Sir Sayyid Ahman Khan (1817–98) is rightly regarded as the first significant Indian Muslim speculative modernist. He did not, however, establish a system of theology or a school of thought, though he did indicate a methodology and a series of principles which were refined by his successors and which are still a clear influence on the modern speculative rationalists. This may seem surprising in view of his early training in the school of Shah Wali Allah, who was, as we have seen, essentially an orthodox conservative; and indeed, Sayyid Ahmad Khan's first theological treatise, *Rah-i sunnat wa raddi-i bida'at*, published in 1850, was in this tradition. However, in his later work, 'he turned to Wali-Allahi fundamentalism again and again but only to transfer and reinterpret it in terms of his own revolutionary modernism'. He 'used it as the starting point for limitless and rationalist speculation'.[14]

His basic thesis was that 'the word of God (Qur'an) must be in harmony with the work of God (nature)'[15] — that is, that since the *Qur'an* is the word of God it could neither contradict nor violate the laws of nature, which are God's creation. He argued, therefore, that the *Qur'an* was the only essential element and that 'all else is subsidiary and of secondary importance'.[16] The classical distinction between 'clear' and 'ambiguous' verses in the *Qur'an* became in his hands 'essential' and 'symbolic' (the Qur'anic distinction between *muhkam* and *mutashabih*: see Q3:7). The former constituted the immutable fundamentals of Islam, while the latter were open to differing interpretations appropriate to different times and circumstances. He insisted, however, that the variable interpretations must nevertheless be consistent with the laws of nature and with reason. It follows that he rejected much of the contents of the canonical collections of *hadith* on the rational grounds that that which he rejected was repugnant to human reason and therefore also to the dignity of prophethood, or that it was contradictory to a Qur'anic injunction. The only acceptable *hadith* were those which were consistent with the *Qur'an* and repeated its injunctions; those which were explanatory or elucidatory of those injunctions; and those which dealt with basic legal formulations not covered in the *Qur'an*. Even when he accepted a *hadith*, however, Sayyid Ahmad Khan further limited its applicability by distinguishing between statements by Muhammad in his capacity as Prophet, and those which reflected his personal and fallible views and opinions. In the end he took the reasoning to its logical conclusion and rejected the *hadith* entirely except as 'a historical reflection of the ideas and attitudes of the first few generations of Muslims'.[17] He also insisted that *ijtihad* should be exercised freely and without limitation and that such exercise was a fundamental right for all Muslims, thus rejecting not only the traditional limitation of *ijtihad* to those qualified to exercise it, but also the rigidity of classical doctrine.

His long-term aim was the regeneration and revival of the Indian Muslim community, and in both this and in his critique of

115

traditional orthodox doctrine, his starting-point was his belief that the strength of the European powers was built on the capacity of their citizens for intellectual progress and development, particularly in the physical sciences, rather than on any inherent attributes of Christianity. It followed naturally that he believed that it was the lack of capacity for such progress which was at the root of the weakness of the Muslim world, thus rejecting the 'deviation' theory. He did not, nevertheless, hold that Muslims were incapable of such intellectual activity, merely that their education and training precluded it: the answer lay in modifying the educational system and through it the social and cultural framework. He therefore sought in his thinking and in his educational initiatives to integrate or synthesize Western and Muslim thought, on the grounds that Muslim acceptance of, and adjustment to, modern intellectual, and particularly scientific, realities were essential for the regeneration. He commented:

> If people do not shun blind adherence, if they do not seek that Light which can be found in the Qur'an and the indisputable Hadith, and do not adjust religion and the sciences of today, Islam will become extinct in India.[18]

In fact, Sayyid Ahmad Khan's views amount to a personal attempt at a reconstruction of Islam in such a way as to integrate a particular set of ideas into it, rather than an attempt at reformulation, and revolved around his views on the sciences. 'Today', he commented, 'we are as never before in need of a modern theology (*'ilm al kalam*), whereby we should either refute doctrines of modern sciences, or undermine their foundations or show that they are in conformity with Islam.' Since he also believed, in common with many before and since, that the true and original Islam had become overlaid with accretions that were not part of the original, he necessarily continued:

> If we are to propagate those sciences among the Muslims, about which I have just stated how much they disagree with the *present-day Islam*, then it is my duty to defend as much as I can of the religion of Islam, rightly or wrongly, and to reveal to the people the *original bright face of Islam*. (Emphasis in Rahman — see footnote 18)[19]

Politically, Sayyid Ahmad Khan was a realist, and he once

defined his political beliefs as 'radical republicanism tempered with a little economic socialism'.[20] He does not appear to have addressed seriously and systematically the nature of the state and the form of government, almost certainly because he had opted for gradual progress towards representative government in a British India and because he was a firm believer in the need for tolerance, co-operation, and good relations between the Muslim and Hindu communities. As with his theological views, in his later life he changed his political attitudes, after he recognized not only that his ideal arrangement required commitment from both parties but also that the Hindu community was not similarly motivated. Indeed, his views changed so much that he was able to comment, with remarkable prescience, to a British official:

> Now I am convinced that the two peoples will not be able to cooperate sincerely in any venture. This is only the beginning; later, because of the educated classes, this hostility will increase. Those who live long enough will see it grow.[21]

It has been argued that Sayyid Ahmad Khan's ideas did not in any way affect nine-tenths of the Indian Muslim population — the villages — and that there was considerable opposition to them even among the better educated and the intellectual elite. This implies that he was not a major influence on Indian Muslim intellectual thought.[22] Nevertheless, it is clear that Indian and Pakistani Muslim intellectuals do see him as a seminal figure, whether they agree with his reasoning or not. A more accurate assessment is that

> through his writings and life work he created the intellectual foundation for Islamic Modernism in India. He also helped to revive the communal morale of Muslims, and he resisted nationalist pressures to have Muslims join the emerging Hindu-dominated Indian-Nationalist movement. By helping to revive Muslim pride and by encouraging Muslim separatism, he opened the way for Muslim nationalism and the creation of the state of Pakistan.[23]

This view rightly believes that Sayyid Ahmad Khan's importance lay in the fact that he was responsible for the foundations upon which others built further rationalist development, but those who hold it are not blind to the opposition:

The position of Sayyid Ahmad Khan was not accepted by all the major Muslim teachers and the richness of Indian Muslim thought at the end of the nineteenth century and the breadth of the foundations provided by Shah Wali Allah are clearly visible in the variety of the more conservative positions that had emerged by the end of the century.[24]

Muhammad Iqbal: the reconstruction of the theory

Muhammad Iqbal (1875–1938) was unquestionably the most important of Sayyid Ahmad Khan's intellectual successors. As well as being a political and religious thinker, he was a poet, a philosopher, and a mystic in the tradition of Jalal al Din al Rumi, an important Sufi scholar of the thirteenth century. In addition, he had studied at Cambridge and at Munich and had an understanding of Western modes of thought and philosophy rarely seen among Muslim scholars of the twentieth century. He was thus able to combine Western and Muslim philosophic thought and apply the resultant amalgam to the reconstruction of religious thought in Islam, the title under which he published a series of lectures delivered in 1928 in which his philosophy and his ideas on the subject were set out. Notwithstanding the importance of Iqbal, it is important to bear in mind that he did not codify in any practical and coherent fashion his views on government, state, and politics. His importance lay more in the intellectual and philosophic framework he developed. His starting-point was that human knowledge and religious experience were not opposed to one another, that 'philosophic rationality and religious intuition were complementary ways of understanding the truth and that belief enabled him to combine a variety of perspectives'.[25]

The teaching of the *Qur'an* is, in his view, essentially dynamic:

The ultimate spiritual basis of all life, as conceived by Islam, is eternal and reveals itself in variety and change. A society based on such a conception of reality must reconcile, in its life, the categories of permanence and change. It must possess eternal principles to regulate its collective life, for the eternal gives us a foothold in the world of perpetual change. But eternal principles when they are understood to exclude all possibilities of change which, according to the Quran, is one

118

of the greatest 'signs' of God tend to immobilise what is essentially mobile in its nature.[26]

Following this assertion, he defined *ijtihad* as the principle of movement in Islam, and argued that 'the teaching of the Quran that life is a process of progressive creation necessitates that each generation, guided but unhampered by the work of its predecessor, should be permitted to solve its own problems'.[27] The qualification 'guided but unhampered' is significant, for he argued further that 'no people can afford to reject their past entirely; for it is their past that has made their personal identity'.[28] He thus demanded change, but not for its own sake, and not without due regard for the historical development. Perhaps his most significant line of reasoning relates to *ijma'* which he believed was possibly the most important legal principle in Islam. However, his concept of *ijma'* is a radical departure from orthodox formulations, for he saw it as a consensus achieved through the deliberations of a legislative assembly whose members collectively (and individually) exercised *ijtihad*. He also held that there should be some check on such deliberations since the members of the assembly were not necessarily fully conversant with the subtleties of Muslim dogma and of the principles of Islamic law. It was, therefore, inevitable that the *ulama* should participate fully in the activities of the assembly. This enlargement of the scope and authority of *ijma'* quickly became equated in the minds of the intellectuals with a combination of public opinion and democratic political institutions: thus, together with the principle of *shura*, it provided a doctrinal rationale for the later development of the detailed constitutional structures of a Muslim state.

His political philosophy starts with the premise that 'Islam does not bifurcate the unity of man into an irreconcilable duality of spirit and matter. In Islam God and the universe, spirit and matter, church and state are organic to each other.'[29] He thus accepted the classical concept of the universal *umma* in which the spiritual and the temporal are but different sides of the same coin. However, it was the classical concept with a difference. He concluded that not only was the ideal Muslim state unrealized, but also that the polity of the *Rashidun* did not represent that state: the ideal had never been realized historically and was perhaps unrealizable in the future. Possibly, therefore,

God is slowly bringing home to us the truth that Islam is

neither Nationalism nor Imperialism, but a League of Nations which recognises artificial boundaries and racial distinctions for facility of reference only, and not for restricting the social horizon of its members.

However, his idealism was tempered by the need, as he saw it, to provide for the future of the Muslim community in India and to deal with a Hindu-dominated nationalism. Although he saw nationalism as 'a subtle form of idolatry; a deification of a material object'; and concluded that 'what was to be demolished by Islam [i.e., Nationalism] could not be made the very principle of its structure as a political community', he recognized the strength of man's emotional attachment to his place of birth.

Nationalism in the sense of love of one's country and even readiness to die for its honour is a part of the Muslim's faith: it comes into conflict with Islam only when it begins to play the role of the political concept and claims to be a principle of human solidarity demanding that Islam should recede to the background of a mere private opinion and cease to be a living factor in national life.

The implication was clear: Islam and nationalism were to all intents and purposes identical in a state in which the majority of the population was Muslim; and thus 'Islam accommodates nationalism' in these circumstances. However, it is necessarily otherwise in countries where the Muslim community is not the majority: here, they are justified in seeking a separate cultural identity.[30]

Given the demographic characteristics of India, it is not surprising that Iqbal's solution to the problems of the Muslim community there began to crystallize around the 'two-nation' theory fully developed later on by Jinnah. His first major public pronouncement came in his Presidential Address to the Annual Session of the All-India Muslim League at Allahabad delivered on 29 December 1930, which reflected the conclusions summarized above and provided in broad outline his solution. He asked:

Is it possible to retain Islam as an ethical ideal and to reject it as a polity in favour of national polities in which the religious attitude is not permitted to play any part? This question becomes of special importance in India, where the Muslims happen to be in a minority.

His answer was clear and unequivocal. The religious experience of the Prophet, as disclosed in the *Qur'an* was, he argued, 'individual experience creative of a social order. Its immediate outcome is the fundamentals of a polity with implicit legal concepts whose civic significance cannot be belittled merely because their origin is revelational'. There was an organic relationship between the religious ideals of Islam and the social order created to provide for their implementation, and, he asserted,

> the rejection of the one will eventually involve the rejection of the other. Therefore the construction of a polity on Indian national lines, if it means a displacement of the Islamic principles of solidarity, is simply unthinkable to a Muslim.

Since India was a continent in which resided a disparate collection of communal groups, some ethnic in inspiration, some religious in inspiration and some a mixture, for whom collectively there was no common factor, the Muslim demand for the creation of a separate 'Muslim India' within an Indian state was fully justified. (This demand was implicit in the terms of a resolution passed at the All-India Muslim Conference held in Delhi in January 1929.) He went further than the resolution, however, saying that he 'would like to see the Punjab, North-West Frontier Province, Sind and Baluchistan amalgamated into a single state'. Such a north-west Indian Muslim state seemed to him the inevitable and ultimate destiny of the Muslims of that area at least. Although he was not necessarily advocating a separate independent Muslim state and partition of the Indian sub-continent, but rather a series of autonomous states united in some federal or confederal arrangement, it is clear that he could envisage separate independence.[31]

It can be argued that Muhammad Iqbal attacked his canvas with a very broad, and occasionally flamboyant, brush and that his contribution has been limited because of the lack of detail in his analysis and interpretation of Islam. It can also be argued that although his views were radical and very different, he gave the impression that he never fully believed in them and that 'he was a poet not a systematic thinker; and he did not hesitate to contradict himself'.[32] He has also been criticized for lack of originality in his thinking, which was little more than an Islamicized version of Western philosophic thinking. Notwithstanding such criticisms, there can be no doubt about the very real influence of his ideas, particularly in the subcontinent. Nor can the accusations of lack of originality stand up: his thinking was dynamic and his attempt to amalgamate Muslim and Western thinking was far from being an Islamic reflection of Western thought. Nor was he entirely the visionary idealist: his conclusion that mankind is, or must strive to become, God's vice-regent on earth was tempered with good-humoured reality in his instruction: 'Give up waiting for the *Mehdi* — the personification of power. Go and *create* him.'[33] A mind that has produced the comment: 'Sin has an educative value of its own. Virtuous people are very often stupid',[34] deserves, and has rightly been accorded, considerable respect for its originality.

Abdul A'la Maududi: conservative orthodoxy triumphant

Undoubtedly, despite the influence of individuals such as Muhammad Iqbal, the most famous (or notorious, depending upon the point of view) member of the Muslim intellectual movement of the twentieth century in the subcontinent was Abul A'la Maududi (1903–79). He is widely regarded as 'much the most systematic thinker of modern Islam', 'the best known, most controversial and most highly visible of all religious leaders of the country [Pakistan]', and 'possessed of extraordinary knowledge as well as keen and profound thought . . . not only possessed of challenging and provocative ideas, but also of a very powerful pen to express them'.[35] Yet despite such plaudits, Maududi is essentially a hard-line and rigid conservative, unoriginal and shallow in his thinking, conventional and prone to the belief that constant repetition is an adequate substitute for logical thought and presentation.

His starting-point is that God is One and Unique, the Creator and Lord of the Universe, the sole Authority, Sovereign and Legislator. The entire universe was created by God and obeys His law and command: the universe, therefore, 'literally follows the religion of Islam — for Islam signifies nothing but obedience and submission to Allah'.[36] The whole universe is 'Muslim', therefore, but

in the case of the inanimate world, and even in the case of that part of man's being which is beyond his control (e.g. the system operating in his physical organism, etc.) this submission (*Islam*) is involuntary and constitutes what might be termed as submission to the providential will of God.[37]

Man is, however, different, having been endowed with free will: he can thus choose to obey or not to obey, which is a voluntary act, but if the choice is, as it must be, to obey, the submission and obedience to God's will and His commands and directives must be complete and willing. The commands and directives are of course set out in the *Qur'an* and in the *Sunna*, which define the code of behaviour, and the *shari'a*, which sets out rules and regulations to be followed at both individual and collective levels. These cover all aspects of human behaviour and activity, including, at the personal level, religious ritual, personal behaviour, morality and family affairs; and at the collective level, social and economic affairs, government and administration, collective duties and obligations, the administration of justice, and the rules of international relations in peace and war. Moreover, these rules and regulations distinguish between good and evil, between virtue and vice, and set limits to the exercise of free will, while at the same time indicating how to establish the perfect Muslim society. In fact, Maududi argues, 'the *Shari'ah* is a complete scheme of life and an all-embracing social order where nothing is superfluous, and nothing is lacking'.[38]

Yet in discussing the scope for human legislation in an Islamic state, he, contradicting himself somewhat, states that 'there is yet another vast range of human affairs about which the *Shari'ah* is totally silent'.[39] Underlying Maududi's basic framework is his answer to the fundamental questions: how does man submit to God, and how can he learn or identify the commands and directives of God with which he is expected to comply? For Maududi, as for many before him, the answer lies in the doctrine of prophethood. Prophets were necessary to practise and to preach the basic truths revealed to them by God: they were required to seek to 'establish the Kingdom of God on the earth and to enforce the System of life received from him'.[40] Prophets were, therefore, concerned to achieve power in order to fulfil their ultimate objective. Some — Abraham, for example — got no further than preparing the ground; others — Jesus, for example — got as far as the beginnings of the 'revolutionary movement but their mission was terminated before they could establish the rule of God', while some, including Joseph, Moses, and Muhammad, were fully successful.[41] This did, of course, pose certain problems, for if the Kingdom of God had been established on earth fully and successfully, what happened to it and why was it not established in perpetuity? Maududi's answer is the infiltration of *jahiliyya* (ignorance) into

the Muslim social system as a result of the combination of new problems consequent on the rapid expansion of the Muslim state, and
of the fact that Uthman, the third *khalifa*, was less well-endowed
with the qualities needed for leadership than his predecessors.
Despite great efforts by Ali, the fourth *khalifa*, ignorance seized
power and 'began eating into the body of the community life like
cancer. Only Islam could check such an evil influence, but it had
already been thrown out of power.' Ignorance, he argued, subverted
the system of rule both overtly, in the shape of non-Muslim
philosophies, and covertly, as '"Ignorance" professed belief in the
Unity of God and Prophethood, performed pious acts of fasting and
praying and feigned eagerness to refer disputes to the Quran and
Sunnah.'[42] The constant struggle against Ignorance was a task for
all Muslims, but in particular for those he defined as *mujaddids*
(revivalists or renewers).[43]

Maududi's vision of the revival or renewal of Islam in its pristine
form, with particular reference to his own age, was rigid, uncompromising and authoritarian. His schema contained nine steps:

(a) diagnosis of the causes of the current state of 'Ignorance';
(b) a general scheme for reformation;
(c) a practical identification of available resources;
(d) the successful prosecution of an intellectual revolution;
(e) the institution of a practical programme of reform;
(f) the application of *ijtihad* throughout these steps;
(g) struggle against enemies of Islam;
(h) the revival of the Islamic order; and
(i) the prosecution of a universal revolution aimed at restor-
     ing Islam's rightful pre-eminent position.

Although, therefore, he concentrated on his own homeland, his
ultimate aim was always the establishment of a universal Islamic
order, supplanting all others; for if Islam is, indeed, the perfect and
total order he believes it to be, it cannot and should not be expected
to co-exist with any other system.

Maududi maintains his inconsistency in his concept of law.
Having defined the *shari'a* (see p. 54–5), he argues that in its entirety it 'stands as synonymous with "law" because the whole code
of life has been decreed by the All-Powerful Sovereign of the
Universe'.[44] For convenience, however, he distinguishes between
his concept of the *shari'a* and 'Islamic law', which he takes to be
those portions of the *shari'a* which depend upon the sanction of

state power for their enforcement. He continues that it is possible to 'distinguish between the part of the *Shari'ah* which has a permanent and unalterable character . . . and that part which if flexible and has thus the potentialities of meeting the ever increasing requirement of every time and age'. The unalterable elements are all contained in the *Qur'an* and the authentic *hadith*, and comprise:

(a) explicit and unambiguous legislative rules, for example the prohibition of alcohol, interest, and gambling, the *hadd* punishments, and the rules of inheritance;

(b) the principles governing man's behaviour, for example the general ban on intoxicants, the requirement for positive and unforced agreement by both parties to transactions, and (for Maududi at least) the proposition that man is both the protector of and in charge of woman;

(c) certain limitations on man's behaviour, for example the permissible number of wives and certain limitations on testamentary dispositions.[45]

The flexible part of Islamic law is the detailed interpretation contained in the standard works of jurisprudence. In this he follows many earlier authorities, but he fails to see the inconsistency between his concept of the *shari'a* as a detailed set of rules ordained by God and his legal system, which, though part of the divinely ordained *shari'a*, can be changed in certain respects. Although he appears to favour legislation as normally understood, it is clear that he is really concerned about identification of law rather than with lawmaking proper: the functions of his legislative assembly are therefore four-fold. First, there is interpretation. Although specific injunctions of the *shari'a* cannot be amended, there is a need for establishing the precise nature and extent of such injunctions, their precise meaning and intent, the conditions to which they should be applied, and the manner of such application; for the formulation of minor unstated details; and for deciding the extent to which the injunction should or should not be applied in exceptional circumstances. Second, where no clear and specific rulings have been ordained, analogical reasoning may be applied to identify the rule of law. Third, there may be cases in which the appropriate rule of law can be established only by inference from general principles. Fourth, *ijtihad* may be exercised subject to strict conditions. Despite his elaborate presentation, Maududi is really assigning to the legislative assembly the role of a *faqih*, a jurisprudent, and has not advanced the debate in any way. Moreover, he appears to advocate some degree of flexibility in the application of specific injunctions, while insisting that they are unalterable, universally applicable, and mandatory.

Similar criticism can be levelled at Maududi's concept of state and government. When shorn of all its repetitive accretions and Qur'anic justifications, his concept differs little from classical doctrine. Sovereignty rests with God alone; the Prophet is entitled, by virtue of his position as God's representative, to obedience; consultation is mandatory; the ruler is entitled to obedience only in so far as he rules justly and in a manner consistent with the *shari'a*; the status of the state is a vice-regency and that vice-regency is vested, as a 'popular vice-regency', in the entire Muslim community, which may for convenience delegate responsibility to a single individual or to a group. Even this last, the 'popular vice-regency' concept, according to which a government can only be formed with the consent of at least the majority of the Muslim community and can remain in power only so long as it retains general support and confidence, is clearly rooted in the classical concept of the 'double contract'.[46] It is also, of course, an attempt to assimilate the principles of Western democratic representative government which does little more than add a little flesh to the bones of earlier formulations.

Maududi is more consistent when he deals with the delicate issue of the non-Muslim citizen of the Muslim state, though he does lack a sense of realism. The non-Muslim is, of course, afforded such protection and rights as are afforded in the classical doctrine, but certain positions are not open to him and his position, whatever Maududi says, is that of a second-class citizen. To be fair, this is inevitable since Islam baldly states that there is a fundamental difference between Muslims and non-Muslims. Furthermore, there is positive discrimination in favour of Muslims, the benefits of which will be accorded the non-Muslim only when he sees the error of his ways. However, Maududi nevertheless continues to insist that Islam, particularly as he sees it, has a tolerance and a universality not found in other systems, despite the obvious discrimination.

Maududi's views are neatly and starkly encapsulated in his concept of an 'Islamic order' — indistinguishable for him from an Islamic state — and of the basic principles of state policy which would govern the state. These he finds explicitly or implicitly defined in the *Qur'an*, in verses 22–39 of *Sura* 17 — *Banu Isra'il*. They are:

(1) Allah alone is to be worshipped and unconditionally obeyed,

for He 'is the supreme Ruler, the Sovereign and the King and it is his *shari'a* which constitutes for man the code of conduct and for the state the law of the land'. (Verses 22–3 and 39)

(2) Parental rights are the most important of human relationships. Respect, obedience, and service must be given to one's parents and the state must 'so fashion its legal, educational and administrative policy that the institution of the family is upheld and strengthened and is provided with state protection.' (Verses 22–5)

(3) Man 'should not reserve his earning exclusively for his own needs' but should assist relatives, the needy, and the poor, for whom such assistance is a right and not mere charity. (Verses 26–8)

(4) Man should be neither extravagant nor miserly, for both are a misuse of God's bounty, and as such are evil; but disparities of wealth due to natural causes are not evil and no attempt should be made to eliminate them. (Verses 29–30)

(5) Birth control and family planning are forbidden. (Verse 31)

(6) Adultery and fornication are forbidden and society must eliminate the causes and incentives leading thereto through 'proper reconstruction of the social life through moral training, social education, legal measures and all other effective devices'. (Verse 32)

(7) The taking of human life (including suicide) is forbidden except for proper cause, of which there are five: retaliatory capital punishment for murder, killing enemies in a just war, capital punishment for those who attempt to overthrow the Islamic order, capital punishment for adultery, and capital punishment for apostasy, which is tantamount to high treason. (Verse 33)

(8) The rights of orphans and, by extension, those who are not capable of protecting their own interests must be protected by the state. (Verse 34)

(9) Contracts and compacts must be fulfilled. (Verse 34)

(10) Business transactions must be carried out with complete honesty and the state has a role to play in checking malpractice and exploitation. (Verse 35)

(11) An individual's actions as well as public policies, both domestic and foreign, must be based on solid evidence and not upon suspicions, doubts, and presumptions. (Verse 36)

(12) Arrogance and tyranny must be avoided in both individual and public life. (Verses 37–8)[47]

The opinions of Maududi set out at the beginning of this chapter are not universally held. For others, including myself, his thinking seems to be lacking in originality and depth, totally divorced from reality, inconsistent, and based on the precept that assertion, if repeated often enough, is a substitute for disciplined intellectual activity. There is also more than a hint of both apologetic rationalization and polemics in his writing. In discussing the revivalist movement, for example, he suggests that only four metaphysical doctrines are possible: atheism, asceticism, polytheism, and Islam. This last is superior not only because it must be but because Maududi demonstrates that the first three, or rather his concept of the first three, are defective; and the process of elimination confirms his view. Furthermore, although he makes sweeping generalizations and uses terms like *jahiliyya*, he rarely defines his terminology adequately and rarely supports his generalizations other than by reference to the *Qur'an* and the *Sunna*. While, therefore, his sincerity, his personal devoutness, his belief in his thesis, his popularity, and his influence cannot be denied, his real contribution is limited. In the first place his appeal is essentially to the intellectual; like many, he prefers to avoid grappling with the simple but powerful proposition that popular support requires more than fair words: it also requires full bellies. As Boumedienne put it:

> Human experience in many parts of the world, has shown that spiritual bonds, be they Islamic or Christian, have not been able to resist the violent blows of poverty and ignorance, for the simple reason that men do not care to go to heaven with an empty belly.[48]

Second, he has in most cases reformulated in modern language, and at inordinate length, doctrine which was frequently more cogently expressed in the past, or had been discarded as inadequate, unrealistic, or unsound. Third, he has invariably construed criticism of his reasoning as rejection of the principles of Islam. The 'man of destiny' can never admit to self-doubt or to the notion that others may have a legitimate point of view. Debate and dissent, which are essential to the dynamic development he sought, were literally unthinkable to him in relation to his views. Finally, idealism seems to be for Maududi an end in itself, in that devotion to the ideals of Islam will somehow cure all ills: he lacked Ibn Khaldun's clear-sighted realism and Ibn Taymiyya's practicality.

7

Intellectual Influences, Part II — Egypt

Introduction

Developments among the Egyptian intellectual elite were in some respects very similar to the Indian experience but in other important respects were very different. Speculative rationalism and orthodox conservatism were as evident in Egypt as in India; the ascription of current ills to a combination of corrupt practices, deviation from *al sirat al mustaqim*, and imperialist influences featured in the thinking of all major Egyptian thinkers; the secularist/orthodox conservative dichotomy is very clear; and the struggle for independence from imperial tutelage was as much a feature of Egyptian theological and political thought as it was in India. There is a distinct difference, however, which seems to derive from the nature of society and its self-perception. Indian society was diverse, disparate, and compartmentalized; nationalist feeling was, from an early stage, particularist, in the sense that it was rooted in a particular community — the Hindus; there was no common factor binding together and channelling the rational thought and emotions of the different communities; the Indian Muslim community, though large, was nonetheless a minority; and it is both significant and symptomatic that the common language both before and after independence was an imperial import — English. Egypt, on the other hand, though a pluralist society in the sense that there was ethnic and confessional diversity, displayed a degree of homogeneity missing in India.

Egypt as an identifiable polity dated back some four or five thousand years; it has had a common language, Arabic, for at least a millennium; there was a strong feeling, which transcended sectarian and confessional differences, not only of a common Arab identity,

129

but also, and possibly more deeply held, of a common and distinct
Egyptian identity; Muslims had been the majority and the dominant
community since shortly after the Muslim conquest; and, despite
occasional tensions, there was a universally, if tacitly, accepted sense
of tolerance. Muslim particularism in India was fundamentally
defensive, but in Egypt was a channel for the articulation of
nationalist and anti-imperialist sentiment. Egypt was thus a country
in which, to use Muhammad Iqbal's elegant phraseology, 'Islam
accommodates nationalism; for there [i.e., in a majority country]
Islam and nationalism are practically identical.' India was in Iqbal's
schema a minority country in which the Muslim community 'is
justified in seeking self-determination as a cultural unit'.[1] This
distinction and the consequent Egyptian nationalist strand in
the thinking of Egyptian Muslim intellectuals is both clear and
important. Although, therefore, many observers stress the importance of Jamal al Din al Afghani in Egyptian Muslim thought,
Muhammad Abduh is more representative and more important in
the purely Egyptian context and is, therefore, the starting-point.

Muhammad Abduh: the father of Egyptian modernism

Muhammad Abduh (1849–1905) was

> an Egyptian, deeply rooted in the traditions of his own
> country, and the nationalist element was important in his
> thought from the beginning . . . and he was always conscious
> that the common history and interests of those who lived in
> the same country created a deep bond between them in spite
> of differing faiths.[2]

Like Shah Wali Allah in the Indian setting, Abduh's thinking has
influenced and has given rise to two main trends of thought — the
speculative modernists who, in their more extreme form, are
outright secularists, and the conservative orthodox, though he was,
unlike Wali Allah, essentially a speculative modernist. His starting-
point was orthodox, though tinged with his Egyptianness. The *umma*
in general, and the Egyptian nation in particular, was in a state
of internal decay; but although he subscribed in part to the traditional and orthodox view that the cause of the decay lay in the failure
of Muslims to stick to *al sirat al mustaqim* and that the remedy was
to return to pure unadulterated Islam, he also recognized that

'as circumstances changed, society and its rulers inevitably found themselves faced with problems not foreseen in the prophetic message, and acting in ways which might even appear to contradict it'.[3] In particular, he perceived three major problem areas. First, there was the division of Islam into opposing sects, each believing that it alone held the true message. Second, he recognized the difficulty of acknowledging the true nature of Islam in view of the complexities and quiddities introduced into it by intellectuals through the ages. Finally, he saw a need to reconcile and re-unite the two main strands in Muslim and Egyptian thinking: the traditional, which offered stagnation, slavish imitation of Muslim tradition, and resistance to change; and the modernist/secularist, which offered uncritical acceptance of Western ideas and culture almost to the exclusion of the indigenous cultural and intellectual environment. The third and last was, in his view, the most important. He could see both the positive and negative aspects of both approaches and sought to bridge the intervening gulf and in so doing to strengthen the moral roots of Muslim and Egyptian society. The way forward, he believed, lay not in rigid adherence to either trend, but in recognizing the inevitability of changes. It was not, however, a question of change for change's own sake, but of changes linked indissolubly to the principles of Islam — changes which were 'not only permitted by Islam, but were indeed its necessary implications if it was rightly understood'.[4]

He aimed to convince the secularists that Islam was a valid guide to life and the conservatives that there was nothing in the trappings, values, and institutions of Western-inspired modernity and modernization which was inherently inconsistent with Islam. This complex may be conveniently reduced to a two-fold objective: first, to restate what Islam really is; and second, to reconcile Islam, so defined, and developing society. However, to Muhammad Abduh, the former was considerably more important than the latter. In his fragmentary autobiography, he commented that he had striven to rid Muslim intellectualism of blind imitation and to promote an understanding of Islam as the early community understood it. This involved a return to original sources, recourse to rational intellectual thought, and a reconciliation between Islam and the sciences which, collectively, would permit the attainment of the social order prescribed by God. He also sought to reform the relationship between ruler and ruled on the basis that the ruler,

although he must be obeyed, is only a human being, subject

to error and prey to his passions, and that he can be deterred from these errors and passions only by the counsel that the Community gives him in word and deed;[5]

there was for him a balance between the ruler's right to obedience and his obligation to provide justice to his people.

It was, perhaps, inevitable that Muhammad Abduh was driven to distinguish between the essential and unchanging elements of Islam and those elements which were not essential and could be changed and modified. 'The real Islam', he maintained, 'had a simple doctrinal structure: it consisted of certain beliefs about the greatest questions of human life and certain general principles of human conduct.'[6] However, the process of identifying those beliefs and principles required both revelation and reason which, he held,

are differing paths to truth and fulfill differing functions, but cannot contradict each other. 'The Muslims are agreed', says Abduh, 'that if religion can reveal certain things to us that exceed our comprehension, it cannot teach us anything that is in contradiction with our reason.' If there is a contradiction then one or the other has been incorrectly understood.[7]

He went further, however: since for him Islam is above all a religion of reason, he held that belief in the existence of God is based upon reason, that 'one must believe in the existence of God before he can believe in the possibility of prophecy',[8] and that reason will test both the content of prophetic messages and the credentials of those transmitting them in order to establish which are genuine. Having done so, however, reason must accept, and believe in, all that a true prophet came to reveal, that is, the entire content of the prophetic message.

In the case of Muhammad, he held that this was contained in the *Qur'an* and in the *Sunna*, as set out in the authentic *hadith*. These sources, together, contain

certain truths about the universe (both those which reason unaided can reach and those it cannot); the general principles of individual morality and social organisation; and the commandment to perform or abstain from certain acts (in particular acts of worship) which we could not otherwise have known to be right or wrong.[9]

In other matters, where there is no clear ruling, *ijtihad* is not only permissible, it is obligatory, subject to certain limitations concerning those who might validly exercise it. *Ijma'* was also given a fresh meaning, in that Muhammad Abduh saw it as the expression of a collective rational view. As such it was necessarily fallible.

> When the jurists are in voluntary agreement, says Abduh, with the interests of the Community in mind, they should be obeyed, 'for it can be said that they are free of error in their consensus'; but this is so not as a matter of dogma but only of reasonable expectation.[10]

Muhammad Abduh also picked up the distinction drawn since the days of Ibn Taymiyya, if not earlier, between acts of worship (*ibadat*, or obligations) and acts concerned with human relations and life (*mu'amalat*, or acts), and argued that there was a systemic difference between them in the teaching of the revelation: 'Quran and *hadith* laid down specific rules about worship; about relations with other men, they laid down for the most part only general principles leaving it to man to apply them to all the circumstances of life.'[11]

In fact, Muhammad Abduh's doctrinal position did not differ greatly from the classical approach, though he sought to give greater emphasis to the role of reason. He followed Ibn Taymiyya on *ijtihad*, but was prepared to define certain issues in a more rational and less orthodox manner whenever this suited his main aim of demonstrating the compatibility of Islam and the modern age. He displayed considerable intellectual caution, however, possibly because of an innate distaste for pure speculation, and a tendency to avoid difficult questions, as some aver. The more plausible reason, however, is that he was reluctant to devote energy to matters which were not directly relevant to the needs of the average Muslim and which had no direct bearing on the various reforms he advocated. He was thus generally supportive of the classical concept of the ideal society, with certain modifications. His ideal society was one which 'submits to God's commandments, interprets them rationally and in the light of general welfare, obeys them actively, and is united by respect for them';[12] but he believed that his ideal society had existed in the Golden Age of Islam — the early *umma*, the community of elders, or *salaf*. That society reaped the benefits of political success, economic prosperity, and an almost unparalleled intellectual development because it was an ideal society. In his schema this was only to be expected. Although individual good or bad behaviour was not necessarily rewarded or punished in this world, communities reap the rewards and punishments for their collective behaviour in the here and now.

Unlike others, however, he did not restrict his vision of the Golden Age of the *salaf* to the usual technical sense of the word as applying only to the first generation of Muslims. It is clear that he really means the central tradition of Sunni Islam during its period of more active development. In due course, however, the ideal society fell into decay, partly as a result of the introduction of alien elements and accretions, and partly as a result of a loss of a sense of proportion, and a consequent neglect of the distinction between the essential and the non-essential. As a natural consequence, the detailed social rules of the early Muslim society were accorded the status of articles of faith and revelation (and as such had to be accorded unchanging and unquestioning obedience). *Taqlid* had usurped the place of reason, and the function of the ulama became the preservation of knowledge, not the search for knowledge,

> because the property of knowledge, as a divine thing, is that it is complete and has been defined since the beginning, in the perfection of the Word which expresses itself to itself. Preservation . . . [of] and not search [for knowledge] because it is a property of knowledge as a human thing that it has been defined and completed over the course of the centuries, from the preaching of the prophets to the interpretation of the fathers of the Church. There is no progress, no revolution of ages, in the history of knowledge, but at most a continuous and sublime recapitulation.[13]

The process was of course encouraged by temporal rulers who saw it as a tool to be used in the constant struggle to maintain their own power and authority.

What, then, was Muhammad Abduh's solution? Obviously there had to be a return to the essentials of Islam, but this did not mean the ostracism of all foreign influences. Muhammad Abduh passionately believed in the necessity of acquiring the sciences of the Europeans before and as a precondition for the return of strength and prosperity as normal characteristics of Muslim nations. He was convinced, on the basis of his belief in the interrelationship of Islam and reason, that this was possible without abandoning or deviating from Islam; but it would require major reforms in Muslim institutions — in particular in the legal system, the educational system, and the forms and structures of government. His views on legal reform were an uneasy *mélange* of orthodoxy and modernity. As noted earlier, he distinguished between the essential and immutable part of Islam and that part which could be modified to meet changing circumstances, and he opposed the rigidity and infallibility of *ijma'* in the classical definition.

He therefore held that the law must be re-interpreted and that in the process two principles should apply: *maslaha* and *talfiq*, though with new definitions. Since the revelation contained only general principles governing social morality and relations, the specific rules to be applied had to be derived from those principles by the use of reason, bearing in mind the general welfare of mankind. Since the circumstances were constantly changing, however, so must the solutions and their manner of application. As for *talfiq*, Muhammad Abduh did not think in terms of 'borrowing' specific points of interpretation from another school of law, but aimed at a more systematic comparison between the schools and the development of a unified synthesis. On the other hand, he accepted not only that the *Qur'an* and the authentic *Sunna* were the final arbiters in legal matters, but also that the schools of law could not be dismissed out of hand, and 'throughout his career he never deviated from the established schools of law'.[14] The seeming contradiction can, however, be explained as a logical and reasonable reaction to the need, which he saw only too clearly, for a radical change in the traditional habits and ways of thinking of Egyptian society; and to his perception that such change could only be accomplished slowly.

Muhammad Abduh's views on political institutions and forms of government were less clear, partly because he found politics distasteful. His concept of the ideal government was similar to the classical jurists' concepts: there should be a just ruler who ruled in accordance with the law and in consultation with the people. However, he not only accepted temporal plurality but was also deeply influenced by his sense of being Egyptian, both matters which had to be reconciled with the universal *umma*. Accordingly, he defined the unity of the *umma* as a moral unity within which political plurality was accepted; but there should also be a restored *khilafa*, though he seems ambivalent about its proper functions. On the one hand, he has argued that it should have spiritual functions and spiritual authority only, even suggesting that there should be 'a chief of our Egyptian nation, acting under the religious sovereignty of the caliphate.'[15] On the other hand, he has argued that 'the traditional constitutional theory of the Caliphate in Islam, in its positive manifestations as distinct from its religious origins, is as much a system of civil law as the Western secular type' and that

> the Caliph was simply the political head of the community, he was not its Pope. He did not have the power or the position of the chief priest nor did he have the exclusive right of interpreting the Will of God.[16]

He rarely concerned himself with structures, although he did suggest, in response to a question posed in 1904, that some form of limited constitutional monarchy in which legislative authority rested with a representative assembly would be appropriate. This was clearly a long-term objective, however, the achievement of which could only come after suitable training. His political thought may be simply summed up. There is no doubt that he had a clearly defined ideal: 'a Muslim community bound together by a fraternal spirit and a sense of common fortunes, interests, and goals.' However, he developed no detailed scheme for achieving it and considered it could only be achieved after major social and educational reforms had been instituted. For him, the structure for an Islamic government 'did exist in the Golden Age of early Islam, and can exist again when Muslim society is again transformed, but it is this transformation and not the political system it will facilitate that is his real concern'.[17]

Rashid Ridha: pragmatic conservatism

Among Muhammad Abduh's disciples, Muhammad Rashid Ridha (1895–1935) stands out as the founder of the *salafiyya* movement, so called because of their adherence to the guidance of *al salaf al salih* (the pious elders or forefathers), though, unlike Muhammad Abduh, Ridha and his followers restricted the term to the first generation who had known the Prophet personally. Ridha's starting-point was a modification of the by now familiar attribution of the backwardness and weakness of the Muslim world to deviation and corrupt practices. However, he also rejects the argument of the 'secularists' that the main obstacle to progress was Islam itself. He commented:

> The Muslims say that it is religion that was the cause of

their sovereignty and well being and that turning away from it was what landed them in misery and caused misery to descend upon them . . . But most of them say this without understanding, imagining that there is an irrational secret in religion which enables believers to attain victory and power and gives them success by miracles and special blessings.[18]

He then outlined the contrary argument which concluded that 'the greatest obstacle in the path of Muslim progress is the Islamic religion itself and that if they [the Muslims] abandon it they can hope to follow in the footsteps of Europe and progress as she did'.[19] This was to him arrant nonsense, if not dangerous heresy, since

the teachings and moral precepts of Islam are such that, if they are properly understood and fully obeyed, they will lead to success in this world as well as the next — and to success in all the forms in which the world understands it, strength, respect, civilisation and happiness. If they are not understood and obeyed, weakness, decay, barbarism are the results.[20]

The real problem, he believed, lay in ignorance and neglect on the part of rulers and religious leaders, as a result of which corrupt practices and accretions had become the norm. The solution was simple, since basic beliefs, moral and ethical teachings, correct religious practice, and the general principles governing social and other relationships had been established during Muhammad's lifetime, as had the moral principles of legal and governmental practices and regulations. All that was needed, therefore, was a return to the practice

of the early days of the first four caliphs, whose Sunnah, together with his own Sunnah, the Prophet commanded Muslims to hold fast to and they should lay aside everything that has been introduced into Islam that is contrary to that Practice.[21]

It is not, however, an uncompromising and undiscriminating return, since Ridha distinguishes between the essentials of Islam and other matters. He rejects the simple distinction between *ibadat* and *mu'amalat* such as earlier thinkers had identified: that is, that *ibadat* are acts directed towards the worship of God and *mu'amalat* are acts directed towards other people and life in the world. Nor did he follow Muhammad Abduh precisely. Abduh had argued that

> there was a systematic difference between the teaching of revelation in regard to the one and the other. Quran and *hadith* laid down specific rules about worship; about relations with other men, they laid down for the most part only general principles, leaving it to men to apply them to all the circumstances of life.[22]

Ridha, however, regards certain matters and acts normally held to be *mu'amalat*, but which have religious significance, in a different light to other matters and acts.

This distinction is particularly clear in his consideration of legislation. In the course of a sharp criticism of those who hold that the principle of legislation by the *umma* or the state is contrary to Islam, he distinguishes clearly between the *shari'a*, which he deems to be a comprehensive legal structure for Muslim society and *tashri'* or *ishtira'* (legislative acts by the *umma* or the state). He points out that both *ibadat* and *mu'amalat* were ordained by God, the former to enable people to approach God and the latter to enable them to avoid evil and acts which are not approved of. Collectively, they were a means of purifying the soul and preparing for the life to come. He distinguishes between those *mu'amalat* which have a religious significance, such as respect for the person, honour, and property of others and the avoidance of sin, oppression, aggression, deceit, and treachery, and those *mu'amalat* which have no direct religious significance such as policy formulation, the conduct of government, organizational aspects of the administration of justice, taxation, and the rules of war. As far as the latter were concerned,

> the Prophet was a legislator (*mushtari'*) for his own time by his own *ijtihad*, being commanded by God to consult the Community in these matters, particularly those who are repositories of its confidence in its general interests and who represent its will from among the ulama, chiefs and leaders.[23]

Elsewhere, he extended this concept, arguing that 'beyond decreeing the elements of virtue, such as the necessity for justice in laws and equality in rights and forbidding rebelliousness, aggression, deceit, and treachery, and establishing penalties for certain crimes', legislative authority had been delegated to the leading ulama and the rulers, who were expected to consult together and to decide what would be most beneficial to the community in the light of prevailing circumstances.[24] Inherent in this argument was the further extension of the significance of public interest as a source of the law.

By thus elevating *maslaha* from its traditional role as a guide to the process of reasoning to being a positive principle for decision, and by drawing a distinction between two types of *mu'amalat*, Ridha was really confirming the right of the community to legislate. However, he was also arguing that there could be a corpus of positive law governing social relations and commercial transactions which was independent of the more narrowly defined *shari'a*, though subordinate to it, and which had a binding force deriving from the general principles of the *Qur'an* and the *Sunna*. It was, however, amenable to amendment, modification, and development in the public interest and taking into account changing circumstances. Nevertheless, he did not advocate a wholesale and unfettered use of *ijtihad* within this structure. Some control was necessary, he believed, and concluded that the political structure had to be reformed in such a way that the legislative process would be carried out by the modern equivalent of 'those who bind and loose' and those in authority acting in consultation. However, he had in mind a somewhat more formal and structured system than this might suggest, for he advocates the combination of these two elements together with the *mujtahids* into a single body to which the collective sovereign powers of the *umma* would be delegated, and which had both legislative and judicial functions. It was, in effect, a formalized structure for the exercise of a new form of *ijma'* since the collective agreement of the members of this body represented an authoritative statement of the law which was valid for its particular time and place. Combined with, and parallel to, this structural proposal, he also took Muhammad Abduh's concept of *talfiq* and further refined and clarified it. He repeatedly urged the ulama to collaborate in the preparation of a unified exposition of doctrine and of moral and ethical principles, drawing upon the major works of the four schools and concentrating on the immutable essentials; but he was content to leave certain practical details to the individual, who would follow the practice of the school of his choice.

Throughout his thinking, Ridha remained traditional and orthodox in many respects. Clear and unambiguous injunctions in the *Qur'an* were sacrosanct, as were those parts of the *Sunna* which were both authentic and unambiguous (though like others he did not define with any clarity how authenticity could be tested effectively). He also considered the consensus of the *salaf* to be similarly binding. However, he was able to reject the traditional rules in favour of a more pragmatic and flexible interpretation where the point in question did not fall into these categories. Thus, for example, he rejected the classical ruling that the punishment for apostasy is necessarily death, arguing that an apostate who openly revolts against Islam and is therefore a danger to the community is different from the apostate who quietly and privately abandons religious belief and thus involves no one else. Death is appropriate for the former but not for the latter. His reasoning is simple: not only is there no Qur'anic injunction that all apostates must be put to death, but there is also a clear and unambiguous Qur'anic condemnation of all compulsion in religion. The unanimous consensus of the jurists in favour of the death penalty for all apostates is therefore contrary to the principles of Islam and is accordingly invalid. Similar reasoning underlies his argument concerning *jihad* in the sense of military action or war. *Jihad* is always lawful in defence of Islam but is only lawful as a means of spreading Islam when the peaceful dissemination of Islam through missionary activity is forbidden or when Muslims are prevented from living in accordance with Muslim law. 'To use force to compel the ''people of the Book'' to become Muslims would infringe this same principle of freedom in the faith.'[25]

At the centre of Ridha's legal thinking was, therefore, his perception that a system of law could be both appropriate to the age and yet still truly Muslim. However, since a system of law implies the existence of an authority to enforce its provisions, he also turned his attention to political structure. His views were set out comprehensively in a long treatise originally published in serial form in *Al Manar* and later issued as *al khilafa aw al imama al udhma* (*The Caliphate or the Supreme Imamate*). The treatise was in part a reaction to the Turkish reduction of the Ottoman Caliphate to a purely ceremonial and spiritual office with no political authority; but Ridha's concern was to discuss 'the place of the Caliphate as a system of government among other systems and its history and what should be done in this day and age'.[26] Ridha was a staunch supporter of the classical doctrine, though with some adjustments to meet changing circumstances. It is important to bear in mind, however, that he was not a 'reformer' or a 'modernist' as those terms are generally construed: his aim was purification and he believed firmly in the necessity for the re-establishment of the *khilafa*. However, it had to be a different form of *khilafa* in as much as he recognized the practical impossibility of re-uniting the disparate and divided elements of the *umma* into a single polity.

The function of the *khalifa* had to be redefined, therefore, and this he proceeded to do, although he fails to deal adequately and consistently with the relationship between temporal and spiritual power and authority. On the one hand, he defines the powers of 'those who loose and bind' and 'those in authority' as comprising the powers of election and deposition of the *khalifa*, representation of the *umma* and its rights, participation through consultation in political decisions and administration, and authoritative determination of the law. The *khalifa* is, in effect, their nominee, with responsibility for directing the affairs of the community and for acting as chief interpreter of the law. Thus, he seeks to stress the temporal aspects of the *khalifa*'s role, arguing that his function is

> to protect the Faith and its adherents and to enforce the ordinances of the Shari'a. He is not empowered over the people in religious matters nor has he independent authority to determine the *shar'i* ordinances for them. His task is only to maintain order and enforce the law. Thus his power is civil and subject to consultation, not absolute or exclusive.[27]

On the other hand, in discussing the direction of religious and cultural matters in his revived *khilafa*, spiritual authority has a positive role, and he clearly sees it as the *fons origo* and ultimate controller of temporal authority. His argument seems to rest on the traditional position that the Prophet had no spiritual successor in the sense of one who enjoys infallibility in the interpretation of doctrine, who is absolute, and who can 'make' new doctrine. Nevertheless, the *khalifa* does in fact have spiritual authority in the sense of being the leader of the community, while his temporal authority is a prerequisite for a truly Muslim polity, having been 'established by God in the general interest in order to assure the application of the Shari'a.'[28]

It is clear that Ridha's political thought is, in essence, theoretical and idealist: he pays little attention to the practical structures of government. To some extent he seems to regard the institutional identity of 'those who bind and loose' and 'those in authority' as tantamount to the establishment of a form of representative power and authority, but he does not suggest in any way that they might be

141

elected or might be in any way responsive to the general public — only to the public interest, which is a very different thing. Nor does he address the political structure in existing Muslim polities. Notwithstanding these and other criticisms, he was and remains an important figure in Egyptian conservative intellectualism despite the fact that he and his followers, the 'Moderate Party', as he liked to call them, were small in number, no more than 'a little group of the first reformers and a few of the later generation'.[29]

Hassan al Banna and the Muslim Brotherhood

The importance of Hassan al Banna (1906–49) lies more in his activities than in his thinking — indeed, it is not always easy to distinguish his own thought from that of the organization he established as a practical first step towards the establishment of a genuine 'Islamic order' — the Society of the Muslim Brothers (*Jama'iyyat al Ikhwan al Muslimin*), commonly known as the Muslim Brotherhood or the *Ikhwan*. It is, nevertheless, right to regard Hassan al Banna, as many do, as Ridha's spiritual heir, in that both were relatively conservative in their thinking. However, Hassan al Banna differed in that he was not content with mere theorizing and he recognized the importance of practical economics: once the Muslim Brotherhood had been firmly established, considerable effort and resources were devoted to providing for the material needs of the membership as well as for their spiritual needs. In this Hassan al Banna differed from all others discussed as intellectual influences, not excluding Maududi, who founded a political party to further his aims. It should be remembered, in this context, that later incursions of the Muslim Brotherhood into political affairs stemmed from the realization that this was necessary if the Society's aims, both spiritual and material, were ever to be achieved. The Society clearly recognized the need to acquire political power in order to implement a manifesto — a proposition that visionaries and intellectuals often ignore.

Like many before them, Hassan al Banna and the Society believed that the decline of Islam commenced immediately after the period of the *Rashidun*, with the transformation of the *khilafa* into a temporal and purely political kingship and the consequent failure by the *umma* to live in accordance with God's revealed command. However, they were also concerned about the disunity of the Muslim world 'because it induced and perpetuated the subservience of Muslim

states and people to foreign ideas and controls'.[30] The chief blame
for this lamentable state of affairs lay with the 'men of religion'
for their failure to check and eradicate the corruption of Muslim
society; but they also argued that imperialism was, in the Egyptian
context, a further positive cause of decay. Imperialism took two
forms: there was the 'external' imperial power which had imposed
itself and its civilization of Egypt by force; and there were the
'internal' imperialist forces which served the interests of the external
power. Among the latter, they identified political parties and the
trappings of Western democratic and constitutional arrangements
which gave free rein to personal greed, ambition, and interests, and
which were tools of British and Western ideologies. Furthermore,
imperialism perpetuated the failure to apply principles of social
justice and the consequent gap between the haves and have-nots
and encouraged foreign economic exploitation.

Imperialism had also seriously corrupted society and morality:

> The introduction of the traditions and values of the West has
> corrupted society, bred immorality and destroyed the inherited
> and traditional values of Muslim society . . . Finally, the
> introduction of Western codes of law has corrupted and
> perverted the nation's thought, mind, and logic.[31]

More serious for the future, perhaps, was the concept of dual
imperialism, since there was inevitably an identification of the
Egyptian non-Muslim with the foreigner and therefore with the
forces of imperialism. In Hassan al Banna's view the ills which had
befallen Egypt — and indeed the entire Muslim world — were the
result of centuries of corrupt practices, innovations and deviations
combined with political, cultural, religious, legal, and economic
imperialism, which had an external and an internal form. However,
he identified not only the broad causes but also more precisely
formulated problems. In his view the most serious problems were
the disunity resulting from the political disputes between the Wafd
and the Liberal Constitutional Party; the drift away from Islam to
apostasy and nihilism; opposition to tradition and orthodoxy; the
current of secular thought in the newly organized Egyptian University; secular and libertarian societies; and the widespread circulation
of books, newspapers and magazines which were overtly anti-
religious or irreligious.[32]

In addition, he shared his followers' views on the pernicious and
evil influences of imperialism whose supporters, both foreigners and

those who had acquired Egyptian nationality, exploited Egypt's economic resources for their own benefit and that of their country, and openly despised the Egyptians.[33]

The solution was simple and echoed the views of all earlier activists: a return to true Islam and the sloughing off of the shackles of imperialism in all its forms. However, the Brotherhood's view of what that true Islam was, though cast along broadly the same lines as Ridha's ideas, was not identical with it. Hassan al Banna commented:

> We believe the provisions of Islam and its teachings are all-inclusive, encompassing the affairs of the people in this world and the hereafter. And those who think that these teachings are concerned only with the spiritual or ritualistic aspects are mistaken in this belief because Islam is a faith and a ritual, a nation (*watan*) and a nationality, a religion and a state, spirit and deed, holy text and sword.[34]

They argued further, however, that their concept of Islam did not mean a literal return to the seventh century, but a return to the true principles of Islam and the establishment of an 'Islamic order', which would be based on three principles:

> (a) Islam is a comprehensive, self-evolving (*mutakamil bi-dhatihi*) system; it is the ultimate path of life, in all its spheres;
> (b) Islam emanates from, and is based on, two fundamental sources, the Qur'an and the Prophetic tradition;
> (c) Islam is applicable to all times and places.[35]

They also averred that it was a duty 'to institute in this homeland [Egypt] a free Islamic government, practicing the principles of Islam, applying its social system, propounding its solid fundamentals and transmitting its wise call to the people'.[36]

Precisely what the Brotherhood intended, and more particularly what Hassan al Banna had in mind, has been the subject of some dispute. On the one hand, it has been argued forcibly that the Brotherhood 'could hardly be more explicit in their demand for an Islamic state',[37] while on the other hand a careful distinction has been drawn between a Muslim state (religious government) and an Islamic order (government inspired by religion), which is seen as a distinction between a return to the seventh and eighth centuries and the establishment of a genuinely Muslim society in the twentieth century.[38] It does not matter greatly which argument is accepted, however, since both approaches rightly indentify the ultimate objective of the Brotherhood as a state in which Muslims can live in accordance with God's command. The real distinction between the two approaches lies in the perception of the means to achieve that desirable objective — by evolution or revolution. The first argues that under Hassan al Banna's leadership, the Brotherhood tended to avoid any suggestion of a revolutionary rejection of the existing political system in Egypt as long as there was some hope of achieving power — and through power, their objectives — through peaceful and constitutional means.[39] However, it is implicit in this line of reasoning that accession to power through unconstitutional means was not ruled out if it proved to be necessary. The second rests on the premise that, given the gradualist approach and given his distinction between a Muslim state and an Islamic order, revolution was unnecessary.

The Brotherhood's concept of state and government was ill-defined, as far as practical details were concerned, though their starting-point was both clear and precise: it was necessary, both religiously and socially, to apply — and to live in accordance with — God's revealed law, the *shari'a*. Beyond that, three broad principles should inform the political structure and institutions:

(a) the *Qur'an* should be regarded as the basic constitutional document;

(b) there must be consultation (*shura*);

(c) the ruler is bound by the teachings of Islam and the will of the people from whom he receives his authority to rule and to whom he is responsible.

Detailed arangements would necessarily be left to be decided in the light of circumstances and the public interest, since there was no generally accepted theoretical or practical framework on which to draw. As far as the *shari'a* was concerned, the Brotherhood believed that its two sources were the *Qur'an* and the *Sunna*, but the former required a fresh and clearer interpretation, while the latter needed a careful re-examination in order to distinguish the true *Sunna* from false report. In addition, the relationship between the two sources was, in their eyes, different to the orthodox view. As one member of the Society put it, the *Sunna* is 'a kind of supplement to the legal injunctions of the Qur'an, but mostly it is a spiritual inspiration and guide to the whole Islamic system'.[40] In other words, the Brotherhood maintained the centrality of the law, as they were bound to do, but chose to define it in such a way as to give the maximum possible flexibility and adaptability to cope with changing circumstances.

However, the Brotherhood were not content, as noted above, with mere theorizing. In particular, once the realization dawned upon them that their broad aims could not be realized without direct participation in the national political system and the acquisition of political power, they developed, under Hassan al Banna's leadership, a series of programmes for the reform and development of the political system: a new Constitution, the abolition of political parties, new electoral procedures, an overhaul of the machinery of government, and so on. However, they also advocated educational, moral, and economic reforms, and sought, within their limited resources, to establish a number of practical Society-funded enterprises to provide for members' needs in these areas. These factors, together with their active opposition to imperialism and their concern not only with 'Muslim rebellion against the internal corruption of, and external encroachments on, the lands of Islam, but also [with] worldly considerations of bread and status',[41] may help to explain the undeniable mass appeal of the Society, despite the fact that the activists were predominantly urban and middle class. An additional, and possibly more significant, factor, however, is that the Brotherhood under Hassan al Banna's tutelage, did not deny the importance and influence of the historical experience. They 'not only sought to imbue the present with some sense of the past but also to redefine the past in terms meaningful for the present'.[42] They were thus able to appeal to both the traditional conservatives and those who, to varying degrees, had become Westernized. This, despite the latter-day image of violence and militancy which has distorted perceptions of the Muslim Brotherhood, is likely to be their, and Hassan al Banna's, most enduring legacy.

Sayyid Qutb: radical ideologue and the politics of despair

Sayyid Qutb (1906–66) had, until his middle years, more in common with the Westernized Egyptian intellectual elite than he did with Muslim conservatives, although his early traditional Qur'anic education remained a deep and abiding influence throughout his life. However, as a result of his distaste for British policy in the Middle East both during and immediately after the Second World War, and of his experiences during a protracted visit to the United States, he reverted to his early influences and joined the Muslim Brotherhood, though there is some confusion over the timing and sequence of events. One authority states that he joined the Society in 1945, shortly after his return from a two-year sojourn in the United States. Another, however, suggests that the visit to the United States took place in 1949 and that he joined the Society shortly thereafter.[43] A third provides more circumstantial evidence, arguing that Sayyid Qutb was originally a man of letters with some interest in political affairs, and that in addition to his work as an Inspector for the Department of Public Instruction he wrote both books and articles for the press, mainly on literary topics. In 1945, however, he turned his attention to national politics and social problems. By 1948, he had become a thorn in the establishment flesh and was accordingly sent to the United States for an indefinite period, ostensibly to study the American educational system. However, 'standing alone on the deck of the liner carrying him to New York, suddenly cut off from his entire world, Sayyid Qutb rediscovered Islam'. He returned to Egypt in mid-1951 and joined the Muslim Brotherhood towards the end of the same year.[44]

Whatever the true sequence, Sayyid Qutb shortly became one of the more prominent ideologues and propagandists of the Society, although 'in his writings on the nature, function and mission of Islam, Sayyid Qutb appears to have passed through several stages in which he became progressively radicalised'.[45] His early, relatively liberal, views are set out in *al idala al ijtima iyya fil islam* (*Social Justice in Islam*), first published in 1951, but his more mature and rigid views are set out most clearly in two volumes: *fi zilal al qur'an* (In the Shade of the *Qur'an*, a commentary on the *Qur'an*) and *ma'alim fi'l tariq* (*Milestones*), in which he attempts to demonstrate the natural superiority of Islam, to outline the perils facing it, and to prescribe a remedy. He is generally regarded, along with Maududi, as the most influential and widely read intellectual of the twentieth century, as a leading ideologue and as a man who provided, in *Milestones* 'the royal road to the ideology of the Islamicist movement of the seventies'.[46] However, these judgments seem, as will become clear, overdrawn and based on an assessment of quantity rather than of quality, at least as far as his socio-political views are concerned.

Sayyid Qutb follows the familiar argument that sovereignty rests with God alone, that humankind stands, in relation to God, as God's vice-regent on earth, that the only genuine Muslim polity was that of the *Rashidun*, that deviation, corruption, and deterioration set in with the Umayyad dynasty, and that a return to the purity of the early community was an absolute requirement. However, he took matters further in his elaboration of Maududi's concept of *jahiliyya*. 'Jahiliyyah', he observed, 'is after all Jahiliyyah, to whatever period it belongs. It is in fact deviation from the servitude of God and rebellion against the God-sent system of life.'[47] Society is therefore polarized: there is Islam and there is *jahiliyya*. The latter, which is perhaps best translated as barbarity or non-Islam in the sense in which he uses it,

> signifies the domination (*hakimiyya*) of man over man, or rather the subservience to man rather than to Allah. It denotes the rejection of the divinity of God and the adulation of mortals. In this sense, jahiliyya is not just a specific historical period (referring to the era preceding the advent of Islam), but a state of affairs. Such a state of human affairs existed in the past, exists today, and may exist in the future, taking the form of jahiliyya, that mirror-image and sworn enemy of Islam.[48]

However, Sayyid Qutb has no place for compromise, for sincere but not wholly successful attempts to live in accordance with God's command: any society is either a genuine Muslim society or is a *jahili* society, and all modern societies, including the so-called Muslim societies, are *jahili*.

> It so appears that our entire environment is seized in the clutches of Jahiliyyah. The spirit of Jahiliyyah has permeated in our beliefs and ideas, our habits and manners, our culture and its sources, literature and art, and current rules and laws, to the extent that what we consider Islamic culture, Islamic sources, Islamic philosophy and Islamic thought are all products of Jahiliyyah. This is why the Islamic values do not enter our hearts; our minds and hearts are not enlightened by the clean and bright concept of Islam, and no immaculate and ideal organization of people arises from among us as Islam had set up in the first generation.[49]

It appears that some 900 million people are wrong and that the greater part of fourteen centuries of continuous history and development are irrelevant.

Notwithstanding this comprehensive denial of the existence of a genuine Muslim society, Sayyid Qutb seems to believe that such a society can be brought into being again, by a 'return to the source of guidance from which the matchless society of Islam drank deep' — that is, the *Qur'an*.[50] However, he conveniently overlooks the fact that there is in his schema no individual who is in a position to interpret the contents of the *Qur'an* correctly. Later in *Milestones*, Sayyid Qutb argues that the renewed Muslim society cannot come into existence as a result of mere human endeavour: a revelation of divine message will be accorded to a single individual, who will then in the manner of the Prophet, propagate the true faith. A genuine Islamic society comes into being when the number of believers reaches three, but it is necessarily a society which is separate from the society in which they live: for

> it is important that anyone who wants to be a Muslim needs to know: he cannot practice his Islam except in a Muslim milieu, where Islam is sovereign. Otherwise he is misguided in thinking that he is able to realize Islam while he is a lost or persecuted individual in *jahili* society.[51]

Whether, however, he intends a physical and actual withdrawal or a figurative and symbolic withdrawal is not clear, though some of the extremists who have taken his philosophy to logical, if absurd, lengths have no doubts.

The new Muslim society, consisting initially of three individuals, will be the nucleus or the vanguard of the renewed universal Islamic society whose members are committed positively to an unceasing struggle against *jahiliyya* using all available means. *Jihad* is thus a necessary component of Sayyid Qutb's credo, but it is a *jihad* which is both internal and external and which is essentially positive and offensive rather than purely defensive. He comments:

> One has to keep in mind, that the establishment of God's domain in the world, the elimination of human kingship, the reversion of authority from the hands of the usurpers towards God, the faithful enforcement of the Divine Laws and the annulment and revocation of the human laws — all these campaigns cannot be realized merely by the help of persuasion and propagation of the message. Those who are ruling over

the people by usurping the authority of God cannot be made
to abdicate their authority by mere persuasion and appeal.

Furthermore, since the prophetic message was 'positive, practical
and dynamic', and since the mission was important,

> it was inevitable that this announcement should not remain
> confined to mere propagation of the message but should side
> by side also take the form of a movement [which] removes
> from the path other material obstacles on top of which is the
> political power which is established on intricate and complex
> but interrelated ideological, racial, class, social and economic
> foundations.[52]

The *umma* — that is, the genuine Muslim society — has thus the
duty to act as necessary to regain its proper position as 'the best
umma brought forth for humanity commanding the good and
forbidding evil' (Q3:110). However, this can only be achieved by
the assumption of political power and authority, and since the *umma*
must avoid contamination, that assumption of power can only be
achieved by a revolutionary rejection of the *status quo*, and not, as
in Maududi's scheme, by the gradual transformation of society.

When it comes to the structure of the state and governmental
institutions, Sayyid Qutb argues that circumstances dictate
structures, subject always to the overriding divine imperatives.

> The Islamic civilization can adopt for its material and
> extraneous organization multifarious and varied shapes but
> the principles and values on which this civilization rests are
> undoubtedly eternal and solid for they are the real pillars and
> embankments of this civilization. They are Servitude to God
> only, human assembly on the conceptual foundation of unity
> of God; dominance of humanity over materialism, promotion
> of human values and by dint of it subjugation of the animal
> within human being and its use in the bringing up humanity,
> respect for family organization, establishment of the vice-
> regency of God on earth according to the instructions and
> advice, convenant and terms set by God and the sole
> hegemony of the Divine code and Divine system of life over
> all the affairs of the vice-regency.[53]

However, he also firmly believes that it is 'indispensable that constant changes take place in these forms and sketches' and that this flexibility and capacity for change is inherent in Islam.[54]

The *shari'a*, which is as central to Sayyid Qutb's world view as it is to that of others, is defined in terms which are very reminiscent of Maududi (see p. 54–5): it comprises 'the entire scheme which God has devised for regulating the human life'.[55] However, he rejects Maududi's distinction between the mutable and the immutable.

> A Muslim has not the authority to seek guidance and light from any other source and well-head except the Divine one in any matter which pertains to the faith, the general concept of life, rituals, morals and dealings, values and standards, politics and assembly, principles of economics, explanations of the promptings of human activities or interpretation of human history.[56]

Equally, although non-Muslim sources are permissible, if used with caution and circumspection, for abstract learning such as chemistry, biology, physics, and medicine, such sources, together with Muslim sources of doubtful faith and sincerity, are forbidden the true Muslim for matters relating to

> the principles of his faith, the foundations of his concept of life, commentary of the Holy Quran, explanations of the sayings of the Holy Prophet (SAW), philosophy of history, philosophical interpretation of [the] movement, ways and habits of his society, his system of government, the manner of his politics and motivations of his art and craft.[57]

Sayyid Qutb has clearly returned to the classical formulation in its most rigid form.

It has been argued that Sayyid Qutb is a powerful and creative thinker on two grounds. First, *fi zilal al qur'an* is perceived as a masterpiece of sustained and subtle exegesis and as evidence of a powerful intellect. Second, he has extended the concept of *jahiliyya*, has set out his views coherently and has identified much more clearly than, for example, Maududi, both the need for active *jihad* against the enemies of Islam and the identification of those enemies as bad Muslims and corrupt rulers. The argument may be valid in respect of his commentary on the *Qur'an*, but seems excessive in respect of his elaboration of the *jahiliyya* concept and his related political thinking: for in both cases, he has pushed the argument too far and ends up divorced from reality, destructive in effect, perilously close to a form of nihilism, and exhibiting profound pessimism. He has, it seems, rejected not only speculative rationalism, reformist movements, and modernist trends, but also almost the entire historical, doctrinal, and practical experience of the Muslim world. Worse, by characterizing modern Muslim societies and governments as *jahili* and by cleaving to a particularly rigid and authoritarian interpretation of the Golden Age, he has in effect excommunicated the entire Muslim world, including, by implication, himself and his adherents, since he nowhere claims to be that individual with whom the renewal of pure Islam will commence.

When reduced to essentials, his message is clear, simple, and not very attractive. The whole world is on the brink of catastrophe, since all societies and social systems are corrupt and ungodly. However, mere human endeavour will not suffice to correct the situation. Only when God so wills will a new Muslim order be established in which everything is subordinated to God's command as set out in the *Qur'an* and the *Sunna*. This new Muslim order will, automatically, be superior to other systems, since Islam is superior to other ideologies, but there is no guarantee that this will be translated into material improvements for Muslims. Finally, there can be no compromises between Islam and *jahiliyya*, though no one can authoritatively decide who falls into which category. Although, therefore, his writings have been widely read and form the jumping-off point for a number of extremist movements, he has little in practical terms to offer today's Muslim beyond the politics and ideology of despair, a prescription for desperation, and a fundamentally flawed world view.

Conclusions

The analysis in this chapter and the preceding chapter shows a number of recurring themes, of which four are particularly significant: the continuing paramountcy of the *shari'a*, the insistence on the use of *ijtihad*, the development of the concept of *jahiliyya*, and the proper manner of managing the relationship between faith and power. Not even the speculative rationalists are prepared to reject the concept of the *shari'a* as the corpus of God's commands. Yet even the conservatism of Rashid Ridha and Maududi acknowledges that the traditional definition of the *shari'a* as comprising the detailed rules and regulations contained in the authoritative collections of the schools of law sits uneasily with the more complex and constantly changing modern world. The response is a pragmatic attempt to redefine the *shari'a* in such a way as to maintain the relationship with the revelation but to distinguish between generalized principles which are the form in which God's command was revealed and the manner in which man has sought to apply those principles. The point of separation between the immutable essence of the *shari'a* and the interpretations which may be modified differs, of course, from individual to individual, but all have seen the need for a more flexible definition and have sought to provide one which is doctrinally sound. Having done so, it was logical to stress the need for *ijtihad*, though once again there are differences in precise interpretation of the term, in the conditions under which it may legitimately be exercised, in the categories of people who are qualified to exercise it, and in the manner in which it should be exercised. It was, in effect, a move towards the Shi'a distinction between *shari'a* and *fiqh* and towards the Hanbali view that acts were to be deemed permissible in the absence of a specific prohibition. There is, however, an additional factor, in that public interest and social justice figure increasingly as significant modifiers of existing theory. Interestingly, there is little sign, except in Sayyid Qutb and perhaps Maududi, of the extremists' rejection of centuries of gradual change in favour of an idealized though ill-defined return to the Golden Age. However, the other figures discussed were all, in their own way, realists.

Managing the relationship between faith and power was more difficult, since the requirement was to reconcile the reality of colonial domination and the illusory superiority of Islam by finding a rational and doctrinally sound explanation of the functional separation of the spiritual and temporal functions of the *khilafa*. Again the approaches differed, but, in practical terms, all resulted in elaborate and ingenious plans to incorporate democratic political institutions and structures by finding respectable Muslim antecedents, rather than in attempts to develop suitable indigenous institutions and structures from Muslim practice — and, of course, theory. The arguments and justifications become particularly strained in the attempts to reconcile democracy and God's sovereign prerogative. The relationship between the reality of colonial domination and the ideal of Islam's superiority also prompted the development of the concept of *jahiliyya* as a means of explaining the actual inferiority of Muslims. Thus, the traditional ascription of the Muslim world's ills to deviation from *al sirat al mustaqim* espoused by Shah Wali Allah changed imperceptibly through a number of stages to Sayyid Qutb's world of *jahiliyya* in which, though 'no man is an Island, entire of itself', the true Muslim must seek so to be. The development of this doctrine was accompanied by a change from the essentially reconciliatory and gradualist political philosophy of the early thinkers to the essentially confrontational and revolutionary views of Maududi and Sayyid Qutb. Yet, despite their rigidity and aridity, they too, though in their own way, were following their predecessors in seeking to bridge the gap between reality and the ideal, thus unconsciously admitting that the gap exists. However, what Maududi and Sayyid Qutb were not prepared to do, as were others, was to recognize, if not acknowledge, the influence of practice on theory; and it is this, perhaps, which will be the most trenchant criticism levelled against them in future assessments of their writings.

8

The Islamic Revival

Introduction: fundamentalism defined and the historical context

Before considering the phenomenon generally characterized as the 'Islamic revival', 'the resurgence of Islam', 'Islamic militancy', or 'Islamic fundamentalism' there are two points to be addressed: the use of the term 'fundamentalism' and its cognates, and the historical context.

The Oxford English Dictionary defines fundamentalism as 'strict adherence to traditional orthodox tenets held to be fundamental to the Christian faith'. Webster's Ninth New Collegiate Dictionary offers

> a movement in 20th century Protestantism emphasising the literally interpreted Bible as fundamental to Christian life and teaching; the beliefs of this movement; adherence to such beliefs; a movement or attitude stressing strict and literal adherence to a set of basic principles.

Translating any of these definitions into a Muslim context and applying a narrow definition of the basic precepts and principles of Islam leads inescapably to the conclusion that all devout Muslims are 'fundamentalists': all devout Muslims must, by definition, believe in the oneness and uniqueness of God, accept that the *Qur'an* is the Word of God, and believe in the duty to fulfil certain obligations in accordance with God's command. This is, admittedly, an unsatisfactory and unhelpful conclusion, but not more unsatisfactory and unhelpful than the use of a term which has no exact equivalent in Arabic. A Jordanian journalist has commented that the term, as

155

used by the media, 'signifies abhorrent extremism and religious narrow-mindedness. In the mass media the term eroded to become associated with terrorist bloodshed and political assassination.'[1]

We do well to remember, however, that the vast majority of those regularly labelled 'fundamentalist' seek to achieve their ends not by spectacular (and generally counter-productive) acts or conspiracies of violence but by peaceful persuasion and pressure; by co-opting, infiltrating and assimilating the political establishment, not by challenging it directly; by constitutional and evolutionary methods, not by revolution. He further suggests that, in Jordan at least, fundamentalism 'means a return to the fundamental principles of Islam, a return to the pure moral ethics of morality and positive integrity; a return to balanced relationship between man and God, man and society, and man and his inner self'. Moreover,

> Jordan's fundamentalists believe that centuries of foreign occupation, culturally and politically, have corrupted the ethical criteria of political behaviour, have eroded the ethos of religious values, and have degenerated the rules of spiritual conduct to become subservient to a hegemony of a materialistic culture with its ramifications of abhorrent delinquency, decimation of spiritual values and eradication of man's innate instinct to live in a multi-racial, multi-credal, multi-lingual society.[2]

The language may be flamboyant, but the image is very different to that conjured up by, say, the *New York Times*, and is more characteristic.

The term can, of course, be applied validly to the rigidly orthodox 'born-again' bigot who wishes to turn the clock back to a concept of the seventh and eighth century or to a concept of the classical doctrine (the re-affirmers of Chapter 1), and this grouping can be stretched to include the extremists who are prepared to resort to violence to achieve their ends. If shorn of its pejorative overtones, however, the term could also apply to the reformer, who wishes to return to the fundamentals of Islam (or at least to his concept of what those fundamentals are) and to reinterpret those fundamentals so as to reform Islam into something which is both faithful to the fundamental tenets and at the same time 'in tune with the spirit of the age' (the synthesizers of Chapter 1). Finally, the term could equally well be applied to those Muslims who adhere to a relatively orthodox and conservative interpretation of Islam, but who cleave to the implications of the Qur'anic injunction 'Obey God and obey the Apostle and those in authority from among you' (the 'conventional' trend discussed in Chapter 1). The term can thus be applied to a wide range of individuals and organizations. At one end of the range there are extremist revolutionaries such as those responsible for the assassination of President Sadat, those terrorist organizations which operate under the umbrella title 'Islamic Jihad' (though their religious credentials must be questionable), those responsible for the seizure of the Grand Mosque in Mecca in 1979, Khomeini and his followers, Qadhdhafi, and certain elements of the Muslim Brotherhood. At the other extreme are the conventional accepters of the *status quo*, subject to certain modifications to government practices. In between lie those who believe that violence is not sanctioned by the divine revelation, and who, though committed to the recreation of conservative medieval Islam and the practice of the early community, seek to achieve their ends by peaceful means. There are also, of course, the synthesizers who, by definition, are not violent. There is no really satisfactory way of distinguishing between the different groupings, and therefore I prefer to eschew the use of the term fundamentalist and to distinguish between the activists and the extremists, the former comprising the more peaceful groupings and the latter those dedicated to the use of violence. This chapter will deal with the activists and with the broader aspects of the revival and the next chapter with the extremists.

The historical context is important since many observers are surprised by the current revival and see it as a new and worrying phenomenon. However, there has been, in history, a regularly recurring series of similar revivalist, or renewalist, movements, though it must be admitted that the present revival does differ in significant respects from the earlier versions. In other words, there is nothing particularly new or startling about the present revival, which should be seen as part of a regularly recurring cycle consisting of four phases:

(a) synthesis — that is, an attempt to conflate the basics of orthodox Islam and the changing needs of a changing world;
(b) the perceived failure of phase (a);
(c) revival, or a return to a relatively conservative and orthodox interpretation of Islam, inclusive of the purging of Muslim society of un-Islamic practices and accretions, as a natural consequence of phase (b); and

(d) the perceived failure of phase (c), leading naturally back to phase (a).

Though simple, the model is a practical working model, as a brief examination of Muslim history indicates, and it is clear that the Muslim world is, at present, in phase (c). It is a moot point whether the cycle will continue or will be broken. As already suggested, there are significant differences between the current revival and earlier versions. Earlier movements have been very limited geographically — for example, the Wahhabis in the Arabian Peninsula, the Mahdists in the Sudan, Uthman dan Fodio in West Africa, and Shah Wali Allah in India. However, the current revival is very widespread, touching all parts of the Muslim world, though it needs to be stressed that there is nothing co-ordinated about the present ferment beyond the obvious effects of mass communications. Moreover, the circumstances are different, and the current revival is both an inward looking attempt at purification and an outward-looking reaction to modernization and economic development. Other differences will emerge in the course of this chapter.

The Islamic revival: differing views

As suggested in Chapter 1, the current revival has sparked off a voluminous literature which seeks to identify, describe, and explain the trend. Much of the literature is, however, misleading, in that the revival is seen as essentially religious in tone, form, and motivation, notwithstanding the conventional protestations that Islam is more than a question of faith. Furthermore, many observers seek to identify a single cause, frequently secular in nature. One argues, for example, that

> the current Islamic resurgence, with its reassertion of an essentially religious political identity in the sense of a declared adherence to the ethic and values of Islam, is the result of the disorientation caused by the rapid economic development and the disaffection with social change brought about by the transplantation of certain aspects and appurtenances of modernity.

Another refers to 'a growing disillusionment with various aspects of the process of modernisation and development', while a third suggests that the process of adaptation (i.e. synthesis) has gone too far and triggered a reaction, and a fourth has constructed an elegant theory to the effect that 'the development of Muslim revivalist movements is primarily related to the rate of modernisation, and especially urbanisation'. Finally, it has been argued that the oil boom of the 1970s was responsible for a greater political activism in the Muslim world, for an improved standing in world affairs for Muslims, and for changes in perceptions of Islam among Muslims. Thus, the psychological importance of the events of the 1970s cannot be overestimated.[3]

To be sure, most of those cited have indicated elsewhere that the matter is more complex, and implicitly agree that 'it would be erroneous to continue to attribute every change (or for that matter, lack of change) in Muslim societies to Islam' and that it would be 'a serious error to describe the problems and responses of the Muslim peoples [solely] in terms of the religion and ethos of Islam'.[4] Nevertheless, there is a tendency to seek a single cause for the revival, to define the revival as essentially religious, and to gloss over the proposition that although Islam had been 'abandoned as a political ideology' in many Muslim countries, it was never abandoned as a belief system and therefore as the normative system. It follows that there is something in the perceptive comment that 'the renewed role of Islam, since the 1970s merely refers to the process of *political* revival of Islam, to its re-emergence as a political ideology legitimising political action' (original emphasis).[5] However, given that 'Islam, in its precise sense, is a social order, a philosophy of life, a system of economic principles, a rule of government, in addition to its being a religious creed in the narrow Western sense',[6] it is dangerous to compartmentalize too much. It is more helpful to define the revival more generally, as an increased consciousness of and reaffirmation of belief in the values and ethic of Islam in all aspects of life, and a more assertive and active expression of that consciousness and reaffirmation in most parts of the Muslim world. In particular, the re-emergence of Islam as the preferred framework for political and social activism suggests that the process has included a higher profile for the political and social sub-systems defined in Chapter 1. However, this must be qualified in three important ways.

In the first place, although Islam has never, as suggested already, been abandoned as a system of belief, there has undoubtedly been a genuine reaffirmation of faith, an individual religious renewal, particularly among the more sophisticated and better-educated sections of society, many of whose members had earlier neglected or even rejected Islam as a political, social, and religious norm — those frequently described as 'secularists'. As one authority observes:

> Educated people relaxed their observance of the Ramadhan fast, ate pork, rarely if ever prayed, and rarely entered a mosque. They had largely turned their back on Islam as a dominating force in their life, although remaining steadfast in their self-image as Muslims. As one observer put it, they were cultural Muslims but not pious believers.[7]

Second, although it is tempting to seek to identify a unified, transnational leadership and movement,

> the ferment among Muslims and the current resurgence of Islamic fundamentalism, while widespread, do not appear to be the result of a universal Muslim revival movement, nor do they proceed from a single centre. Islamic fundamentalism is not dominated by a few key countries, and it lacks a unified leadership or a philosophy that transcends national boundaries.[8]

The revival is no more monolithic than is Islam itself, and although there are common strands, each country's experience is unique, reflecting the remarkable social, cultural, economic, political, and historical diversity of the Muslim world.

Third, as suggested in Chapter 1, there is no distinctively 'Islamic' set of premises governing human activities, though the manner of articulation, the symbolism, and the manner of interpretation and application will have an 'Islamic' flavour.

> Muslims are people who share with all other humans the same basic needs, and who are motivated by more or less the same aspirations and fears. What happens in Muslim countries today cannot be taken out of, and artificially separated from, the general context of the Third World with all its current agonising problems.[9]

There are, it would appear, three major questions concerning the revival:

160

(a) what form has it taken — that is, what has happened?
(b) why has it happened — that is, what are the causes?
(c) what have been the effects?

A subsidiary, though for many equally important, question is, of course, what are the implications, both long- and short-term? Since, however, the distinction between the first three is at least to some extent artificial, the answers are bound to overlap.

The revival: what has happened

The first question can be disposed of relatively simply. Given that the Muslim world is in the conservative reactive phase of the cycle, it would be appropriate to apply a conventional definition of fundamentalism to the revival: 'the reaffirmation, in a radically changed environment, of traditional modes of understanding and behaviour'.[10] Not surprisingly, therefore, the more obvious manifestations have been generally conservative. At the individual level, there has been a much greater degree of personal piety, including a greater insistence upon and willing performance of the traditional duties: regular performance of the prescribed prayers, including regular attendance at the mosque for Friday midday congregational prayer, fasting during Ramadhan, voluntary alms-giving, and pilgrimage to Mecca. However, the adoption of 'Islamic' dress, abstention from alcohol, increased participation in the activities of religious societies, regular calls for the introduction or re-introduction of *shari'a* law (rarely defined) and for the abrogation of 'un-Islamic' legislation, and the ostentatious avoidance of acts, places, and things which are deemed to be contrary to Islam, often because they are foreign imports (for example, playing football and music), and an increase in the purchase of religious tracts and tomes — all these have been noted.

At the collective level there has been a dramatic increase in the publication of religious writing, both modern and classical, an increase in the number of religious societies and organizations and in their active membership, considerable peer pressure to conform to Muslim norms, greater intolerance of non-Muslims, amounting at times to discrimination and even xenophobia, a rise in the incidence of protests against cultural and economic 'imperialism', much more *da'wa* (missionary) activity (e.g. the activities of the Muslim World League), and a spectacular growth in the number of Islamic banks.

At the governmental level, apart from the establishment or increased influence of Muslim political parties, school curricula have been modified to give greater emphasis to Muslim studies, radio, television, and the press (all normally government-controlled) have now a greater religious content, and there is an increasing and disturbing trend towards the imposition of Muslim law (generally in a particularly conservative form) on non-Muslims, despite the clear provision for separate treatment in certain respects. However, it is in political life that the greatest change has occurred, since the re-emergence of Islam as a political factor — or political framework — has resulted in a change in the language of politics throughout the Muslim world, and Muslim symbolism has become more prominent both among the ruling elites and among the opposition, although for ruling elites concepts of national unity and national identity are still dominant. Existing regimes have adopted or promoted a more identifiably Muslim style of government, partly in order to pre-empt the religious opposition where it exists, partly as a response to the perceived attitudes of the population, and partly as a result of sincere and devout adherence on the part of the ruling elite to a particular concept of Islam as a faith and as a guide. Where this has occurred it has generally prevented the establishment of extremist Muslim groups dedicated to a change of regime by violent means: but regimes in, for example, Pakistan, Saudi Arabia, and the Gulf states have had to walk a very precarious tightrope.

Muslim symbolism is the natural language of opposition movements which could, if injudiciously handled, develop into serious threats to the regime. Muslim movements do exist in such countries but they are normally conservative in view and are dedicated to the peaceful establishment of a truly Muslim society. In some cases, Islam has been incorporated into the predominantly secular political power structure — almost as if it was a domino to be fitted in — either as an act of deliberate policy, as in Algeria, or as a result of the transformation of a particular Muslim movement into a political party — for example, the Muslim Brotherhood and the Ansar in the Sudan. Finally, in some countries (for example, Egypt, Syria, Lebanon, and Iraq) where the regime has been essentially secular in motivation and, to a greater or lesser extent, repressive, highly political and radical 'Islamic' groupings have developed with the stress on Islam acting as the catalyst or as the focal point around which more secular political, social, and economic grievances coalesce. Only in Iran, however, have such groups been able to impose their (often idiosyncratic) concept of a Muslim state.

The revival: why did it happen?

In this connection, a number of organizations are worth noting. In Afghanistan, the emergence of the *mujahidin* groups as the main focus for resistance to the Russian occupation may be essentially political — that is, their primary aim is to free the country of foreign occupation and domination. However, there can be no doubting that the *mujahidin* are also motivated by the desire for a Muslim state for Muslims. Superficially, there are similarities to the Afghan situation in the case of the Moros in the Philippines, but there Islam appears to be more of a focus for regional discontent. In Egypt, the spread of the revival was undoubtedly assisted significantly by President Sadat's espousal of the 'Islamic groups' as a counter to the left-wing political groupings in Egypt, though it would be wrong to question Sadat's personal piety at the time. It might be said that in this case Sadat's head (i.e. his political instinct) and his heart (i.e. his personal belief) ruled jointly. Pakistan is often cited as a state in which activist pressure, including that of Maududi's *Jamaat-i-Islami*, has significantly changed the political framework of the country. Yet a recent, albeit selective and as yet unpublished, survey suggests that the support for the religious political parties was relatively small, but that it was strongest among the middle classes. In more pluralist societies, although there has been a growth in the number of Muslim political parties, it is clear that the more rigid and conservative organizations have caused a backlash among those who fear the imposition of a Maududi type of government: Malaysia, Indonesia, and, though in more muted form, Syria are typical examples of this response.

The variety of possible answers to the question 'why?' has already been demonstrated, but most observers seek to define as 'causes' social, economic, cultural, or political factors which are more properly 'triggers' or 'catalysts'. This does not mean that the matters at issue made no significant contribution, since they patently did: it would be foolish to assert that economic problems, political discontents, social strains, the effects of the urban drift, or concern about the implications of modernization and development were unimportant. However, such matters, though intrinsically important, were important because they served to 'concentrate the mind wonderfully' on what might be the root causes of the problems facing the countries and communities of the Muslim world and on possible solutions, and that this concentration inevitably defined the solution as a return to more or less traditional Muslim attitudes. One observer once summed the matter up elegantly when he commented that in times of crisis, people inevitably resort to their primordial influences, which must be for Muslims, even 'cultural' Muslims, some form of Islam. He has a more structured and elaborate version in his explanation for what he calls 'some increase in the strength of religious consciousness, or at least self-identification in religious terms'. He comments:

> This can be partly explained by the need (felt not only in Muslim countries) to give meaning and direction to the process of rapid and irreversible change in which we are all involved. In such a situation, men and women look for beliefs and symbols which will give them the possibility of behaving rationally, and the assurance that what they are doing, or what is being done to them, is somehow intelligible and in accordance with the nature of the universe. Some may find this assurance in a philosophy of history which holds out the hope that, in spite of appearances, the world can move forward and good can overcome evil; others fall back on inherited beliefs and loyalties which carry with them the conviction that there is some kind of eternal order which controls or judges the chances of natural life.[11]

This is an important point, since it suggests that, however distasteful the language of the extremist ideologues might be, however irrational their argument, however unfairly selective their use of history, and however unpalatable their conclusions, there is a strong psychological attraction about their basic premise that deviation from *al sirat al mustaqim* must be seen as the fundamental error of the Muslim societies. Over the past century or so, Muslims, both individually and collectively, have flirted with other political philosophies and systems, both on their own initiative and under duress. Capitalism and socialism alike have been tried, as have variations of them, mixes containing elements of both, and various forms of synthesis (such as Nasser's Arab Socialism or Ba'athism); but all have in the long run failed to meet the emotional, moral, and spiritual aspirations of both intellectual and peasant. Nor have they dealt with the material problems while political aspirations have been unrealized. On all counts, therefore, they have been found wanting, and have come to be perceived as alien, corrupting ideologies, seeking at least influence, or, more likely, hegemony.

Despite the apparent secularity of this process, however, it has occurred in a milieu which, though drastically altered and still changing, had, and still has, one enduring familiar feature — the all-pervading flavour and influence of Islam, whatever its form. For even the most avowedly secular or agnostic, the cultural, social, and intellectual environment has been moulded to a greater or lesser degree by the local forms of Islam and even more by its norms. A reaffirmation of Hourani's 'primordial influence' can only be a reaffirmation of the norms, values, and beliefs of Islam, for, as the Jesuits have said, 'Give me the child until he is seven and he is mine for life.' Since, however, it is the alien ideology or the synthesis which is perceived to have both failed and corrupted, it is natural to ascribe current and past ills to a failure to comply with God's revealed will, to deviation by the community of the faithful, and to the adulteration of an ideal which is believed to be realizable in practice through the acceptance of innovations, practices, ethics, and modes of thought which are not part of, or consistent with, the original revelation. It is perhaps also natural, though not really justified, to perceive the colonial experience as the imposition by force of such deviating and corrupting factors.

However, we should beware of accepting at face value the entire argument elaborated by people like Maududi and Sayyid Qutb, for although the revival is a natural consequence of the perceived failure of other 'isms', the subsequent argument seems flawed on at least four counts. First, it suggests a remarkably superficial conversion to Islam for all except the first generation who knew the Prophet personally (unless, of course, it was foreordained that this should be so). Second, it suggests that the *umma*, which is composed of fallible men and women, is being punished for its inevitable failure to live up to the ideal by a God who is defined as 'the Compassionate and Merciful' — surely a contradiction in terms. Third, it seeks to mitigate the bleakness of this explanation by identifying a contributory scapegoat. Finally, it fails to come to grips with the vexed question of the relationship between free will and predestination. Admittedly, earlier generations of Muslim intellectuals have done no better on this issue, and it may be that no satisfactory argument is possible. Nevertheless, the failure to attempt to address the issue is a shortcoming. Notwithstanding these strictures, the argument is both attractive and strongly held, and it must therefore be taken seriously.

It has been argued that other observers' 'causes' should be seen as 'triggers' or 'catalysts', but that they are important. As such some consideration is necessary. Again, however, it must be remembered that different countries have had different experiences; that there is no single, universal catalyst; and that in each case a different spectrum of catalysts applies. There are, nevertheless, a number of factors which are general, though all do not necessarily apply in all countries. Some are clearly interrelated, and the importance varies as the experience does. No particular order or priority will be followed.

There has been a greater confidence in the indigenous social, cultural, and political structures of Muslim society. This derives in part from the new, though inevitably temporary, accession to economic power of the predominantly conservative Muslim oil-producing states, coupled with a perception that that economic power carries with it a degree of political clout (though this is a very doubtful correlation). In particular, this power, together with the numerical strength of the Third World and the imputed power of various regional and confessional multinational organizations, is believed to have undermined the historical material and psychological advantages of the industrialized Western world over the less-developed Muslim world. Allied to this has been the deep-seated conviction that Muslim societies were exploited by the imperial powers and a desire to redress the injustice so created. Although the colonial experience is now part of the history of a generation or more ago, the conviction remains strong and has been reinforced by the more recent 'cultural and economic imperialism' which, it is believed, is practised by the West, and in particular by the United States. Thus the external factor as a cause for the decline and continued weakness of the Muslim world remains significant.[12] Despite the confidence referred to above, however, the continuing need to identify an external scapegoat does suggest a collective inferiority complex. It may be argued that some support for this proposition will be found in the manner in which the increased consciousness has both influenced, and been influenced by, perceptions of past Muslim military, political, cultural, and political eminence. There is, admittedly, much in which to take pride, but the manner of articulation does often suggest a need to bolster the self-confidence which serves to hide an unwelcome realization that the power is largely illusory, as recent events have shown clearly, and that the argument about the effects of the colonial experience is wearing thin.

Balancing the foregoing to some extent is a clear need for a focus of identity and pride. The need is, of course, in part a reaction to the flirting with other philosophies and ideologies, but it does go further, in that it reflects the continuing debate about whether modernization and economic development necessarily mean Westernization and secularization. One observer has rightly argued that it is misleading to equate modernization and development with Westernization. However, it is equally misleading to assume that simply because the process of modernization and development in the Western world did result in a degree of secularization, similar processes in other societies will have the same effect. Furthermore, although his definitions of tradition and modernity are not persuasive, he does have a valid and important point in his argument that the process of modernization (and by implication, development) in non-Western societies 'has taken place because of factors within these societies and was neither imposed by the West, nor induced by interaction with the West, nor facilely copied from the West'.[13] However, this assertion, though fundamentally sound, requires some qualification. First, the polarization of international society into a 'balance of superpowers' highlights the need for a superpower relationship, with all that that implies for national feeling, dependence, and separate identity. Both the Western partners of the United States and the Eastern partners of the Soviet Union have found it difficult to come to terms with these implications, and there seems no reason to assume that Muslim nations will be different. Second, the world is now a much more complex place and interdependence is a fact of life. Though some choose to ignore this, they do so at their own peril, as Iran has been discovering. Third, the multilateral aid and development agencies spawned particularly by the United Nations are essentially Western in their philosophies, practices, and attitudes. Fourth, many Muslim nations chose deliberately to embark upon a process of rapid modernization and development despite their lack of the requisite resources — skilled manpower, experience, technical knowledge, and so on. This applied particularly in the Middle East, as a consequence of capital resources accruing from oil revenues.

One effect of this last qualification was the deliberate importation, mainly from Western sources, of the resources not available indigenously, and the use of Western-provided capital. Inevitably, therefore, the process brought not only material improvements and changes, but also certain — though by no means all — Western values, moralities, and modes of thought, which in due course became identified as alien, corrupting, and materialistic. It is unfortunate, though probably inevitable, that the undesirable side effects of rapid modernization and economic development, and of the methods adopted to achieve them, became popularly identified with the process itself, and with the intrusive Western element of the population. Disillusion with the process and resentment against the chosen instruments became the norm, particularly in poorer countries where expectations of improved material conditions were disappointed. The disillusion and resentment were exacerbated by other factors, such as imbalances in the distribution of wealth, conspicuous material consumption, and widespread and evident corruption, all of which were popularly identified with the foreign population and hence with the process they were imported to carry out.

Furthermore, 'urban drift', particularly related to the modernization and development process, became a feature in many countries. It has been pointed out that the stereotype characterization of the 'new urban immigrant' as 'some unwillingly uprooted peasant driven by misery to seek employment in a town, where he falls victim to Durkheimian despair' is often false in that he 'tends to be an enterprising rural worker who often moves to the city in two steps and sometimes two generations via a small town where he is also numbered among those most ready for a change'.[14] This is not universally the case, however, and many have made the change, whether of their own volition or not, in a single, sudden change to 'the relative *anomie* of the urban slums'.[15] Even where the change has occurred via the two stages and two generations, the sheer size of urban centres, the rapid increase in their population, and the inability of governments to satisfy increasing demands for basic necessities (housing, water, sewage disposal, etc.) do lead to an identity crisis. Nor should this be surprising since it occurs in relatively sophisticated societies: the anonymity of the big city and the traumas it engenders are regularly featured in the national press of the Western world.

It is in fact necessary to take into account elements of the more widely held view that

> for rural immigrants seeking security, employment, or wealth in the city, cut off from the ties of kinship or neighbourliness which made life in the village bearable, victims of urban processes they can neither understand nor control, and living in a society of which the external signs are strange to them — for these the religious community may provide the only kind of world to which they can belong. Its spokesmen use a language which is known and appeals to

moral values deeply rooted in their hearts, its rituals and ceremonies are familiar.

In addition, and closely bound to the question of identity, however, is the significant factor that if the immigrants 'do not find what they need in the city, they will bring it with them from the country-side; if rural immigrants have become city dwellers, the cities, or at least the immigrant quarters, have been "ruralised" '.[16] Whatever the manner and pace of the move to the urban centres, the change is traumatic, and the immigrant does seek a focus for identity, which is almost bound to be centred on the belief system: either the symbols and trappings available in the city, or an impor-tation of the familiar village or small town *mores* or, more likely, a mixture of the two. However, the crux is the need for a focus of identity, and the focus most often chosen is Islam.

This complex of issues related more or less directly to the process of modernization and development amounts collectively to two reactions: a disillusionment with and an alienation from imported, normally Western, values, attitudes, and practices; and a perceived failure of earlier attempts at synthesis. The consequent need for a focus for identity — and indeed pride — has resulted in the reaffirmation of the traditional belief system, morality, values, and ethics of Islam, and the identification of Islam as the indigenous focus for individual and collective identity and for individual and collective pride at a time when both have faced considerable problems.

Other general triggers have been identified. The establishment of the State of Israel and the failure to resolve the Arab–Israel Dispute are regarded as both the creation of Western imperialism (and therefore as proof positive of continued imperialist efforts) and as clear evidence of the weakness and debility of the Arab — and by extension, the Muslim — world, which derives from disunity and disregard for the values, norms, and ethics of Islam. Govern-ments and ruling elites have also voiced concern about the long-term effects of rapid and possibly uncontrolled modernization on traditional social, cultural, and political structures. This concern is not, of course, restricted to the ruling elites, but has been voiced more widely, but the concern has served to highlight the importance and general acceptability of those structures and hence of their Muslim identity and the importance of maintaining them, albeit in a modified form. Indeed, some governments have responded actively, if somewhat undirectedly, to calls for greater 'Islamization' of administrative, executive, and judicial processes and institutions. Finally, the effect of 'peer pressure' should be noted, exerted by both individuals and governments. It is sometimes genuine, sometimes a cynical attempt to demonstrate 'Islamic' credentials, and occasionally a frivolous matter of fashion. (The incidence of 'Islamic' dress among university students has been likened to the manner in which blue jeans swept the universities of the United States and Europe in the 1960s.)

In addition to these general considerations there are factors affecting individual countries alone. In Iran, for example, the 'clericalization' of the polity was in part a reaction to the threat to the traditional ability of the mullahs to influence general government policies posed by the Shah's modernizing secular policies. The mullahs also opposed the increased emphasis on the non-Muslim Iranian tradition and there was the emergence of Khomeini as a charismatic leader with a coherent political philosophy. Special factors affecting Egypt include serious economic difficulties, a reaction against the more provocative intrusions of Western culture, particularly since 1973, the need to develop a replacement for Nasser's socialist ideals, and the late President Sadat's support for Muslim movements as a counterbalance to left-wing activists. In Syria, Islam, particularly in the shape of the Muslim Brotherhood, has been the only possible focus around which more generalized political and other dissent could coalesce. The emergence of conservative views in Indonesia is in part attributable to the belief strongly held among the Muslim majority of the population that they did not enjoy a political status commensurate with their numbers and importance and there has been concern about the activities of Christian missionaries as well as opposition to the secular nature of the regime. Similar instances can be found throughout the Muslim world, but this partial listing suggests that the underlying problem is, as is the case with the more general factors, largely a matter of identity, of disillusion and of opposition, with the process of modernization and its effects playing the double role of cause and target.

The foregoing may lead to the conclusion that the major trigger or catalyst has indeed been the process of modernization and economic development, as many have argued, though this seems to be too narrow. There is, for example, the thesis that the contemporary revival may be explained as a natural consequence of the process of modernization and that it differs from earlier revivals in that the latter were elitist intellectual movements which had little or no impact on the masses and had little or no participation by them, while the current revival stems from 'the involvement of the masses through modernisation [which] is an unprecedented event in the Islamic world. It does not occur before the 1920s', and that 'it was modernisation, most conspicuously in the form of urbanisation, which involved the masses and led to the formation of a reaction different from those of the nineteenth — and early twentieth — century elites'.[17]

Admittedly, the process has brought with it significant strains in the social fabric of Muslim countries. It has also failed to deliver the promised improvements and has become identified with Westernization and secularization. Admittedly, too, there is a difference between the recent revival and earlier versions; but to argue that 'modernisation is a necessary condition of the appearance of the phenomenon [Muslim revivalist movements]'[18] is to ignore the absence of modernization or urban drift as a background to earlier movements such as those led by Shah Wali Allah, Muhammad ibn Abdul Wahhab, Uthman dan Fodio, and Muhammad Ahmad (the '*Mahdi*'). Nor does the view that it is the involvement of the masses in politics which is the significant difference between the present revival and earlier movements, which were essentially movements of the elite, ring true. One proponent of this line of argument comments:

> Whereas in the past attempts at the regeneration of Islam and its claims for a leading role in the affairs of state were led by elites of intellectuals and religious teachers, concerned with theological-philosophical disputations and religious reform, today these are carried out by militant leaders who can mobilise and directly involve the armed masses of the population.[19]

Were these views to be valid, however, it could be expected that significant changes would have occurred in the political direction of Muslim states and that these changes would have the active and vociferous support of the majority of the population; or that regimes would have prevented such changes by repression and brute strength and that the failure to engineer changes would be a universal focus for complaint. Yet only in Iran — and, for a brief interlude, in the Sudan — has there been any real change, and it is clear that the change does not enjoy universal approbation, and that complaints are voiced by a remarkably small, if vocal, segment of the population in other states. Furthermore, the current revival continues to be a movement of the elites — particularly among the better-educated; and it is from them, rather than the mass of the population, that the calls for change originate. However, the striking improvement in mass communications systems and the ready availability of transistor radios, television sets, cassettes, and newspapers and journals has greatly enlarged the potential audience which can be easily reached by the activist intellectual elite. In addition, illiteracy, though still a problem, has decreased and is no longer the limiting factor it was, given other means of communication. Also, the activities of *da'wa* (missionary) organizations throughout the Muslim world have further extended, in a trans-national framework, the potential audience of the activist.

Although the activist movement is essentially an elite movement, however, there has been popular participation in the revival, in that the majority of the Muslim populations at all levels has manifested some degree of reaffirmation and in that the message disseminated on radio, television, cassette, and in the press has been couched in familiar, if emotionally charged, language, using traditional symbolism. The message has been easy to understand, emotionally satisfying, and eloquently presented — an important factor for those who are easily swayed by rhetoric. It is thus a relatively simple matter to mobilize the masses and to direct their energies. However, such participation is far from being active commitment to a readily identifiable set of goals, while the appeal across national frontiers is not, and should not be construed as, evidence of concerted action. There is no pan-Islamic co-ordinating body and no real pan-Islamic co-ordination, except to a limited degree between governments operating through the activities of the Organisation of the Islamic Conference (OIC); and the OIC is a *political* organization seeking solidarity, not unity.

To sum up, there has been a genuine reaffirmation of belief in the ideals, values, precepts, practices, and ethics of Islam which, though uncoordinated, has been manifest in most, if not all, Muslim states and Muslim communities, and in all levels of society. The activist leaders are still, however, drawn from the intellectual and educated elites: it is there that are found the detailed articulation of demands, desires, and aspirations, and it is from their ranks that such leaders as have emerged have been drawn — people like Muhammad Natsir in Indonesia, Hassan al Turabi in the Sudan, Nabih Berri in the Lebanon, Khurshid Ahmad in Pakistan, and Salim Azzam of the Islamic Council of Europe. The most significant feature of that articulation has been the reassertion of the social and political sub-systems of Islam, but this has generally occurred within existing political structures: most activist leaders are evolutionary and not revolutionary. The general reaffirmation has been triggered (not caused) by a number of factors, varying from country to country and community to community.

These factors are all different facets of an identity crisis combined with a reaction against the continued decline and weakness of the Muslim world, and the perceived failure of, and therefore disillusion with, a modernization and development process which is in form, though not in inspiration, Western. Inevitably, therefore, much of the rhetoric is couched in anti-Western or anti-imperialist terms (for the two are seen as synonymous). Furthermore, some ruling elites are seen as tools of that imperialism, and the language of politics, whether that of the establishment or of the opposition, has become more overtly Islamic in flavour. However, we need to bear in mind the percipient observation that:

> Language is never a neutral medium through which to express the world, and wherever the political language of Islam is used it brings with it certain attitudes and tendencies: a heightened sense of the difference between Muslims and non-Muslims; a certain alienation from Western power, and suspicion of imported ideas; an increased respect for the great ritual obser-vances of the faith, the annual Pilgrimage, and the annual fast; a tendency to hold on to what is left of the *shari'a*, not as a rigorous system of laws but at least as a repository of moral values regarded as typically Muslim; and an emphasis on certain symbolic acts.[20]

Although the present revival does differ in important respects from earlier movements, it is essentially part of a regular cycle. The most important differences are:

(a) the current phenomenon has touched all parts of the Muslim world, while earlier movements have been geographically limited;
(b) technical advances in mass communications have greatly enlarged the potential audience;
(c) changes have occurred in the style and structures of govern-ment, though they are so far relatively minor, Iran and Pakistan notwithstanding.

In any consideration of the many Muslim groupings and organizations with a particular interest in politics, it is as well to avoid the simplistic conclusion that the motivation is more often than not a cynical pursuit of political power for its own sake. In the first place, many leaders recognize that politics is the 'art of the possible' and that political power is an indispensable necessity for translating a vision or a dream into reality. In the second place, many Muslim organizations are government-controlled, government-inspired, or have a legitimate place in the political structure of the state. In such cases, they undoubtedly influence government policies, but do not necessarily represent a threat to the stability of regimes. Thus, for example, the Muslim Brotherhood in Jordan and in the Sudan have a recognized role in the system, as do the Ansar and the Sufi brotherhoods in the Sudan, and are permitted a fair degree of latitude. The limits to their freedom of action are clearly understood and it is rare for them to overstep the mark. Since, however, they are committed to the Islamization of the political structure, they may find it necessary to change their policies if and when they are disillusioned by the rate of change.

The revival: goals and implications

What then do the activist leaders seek? What are their goals? Are the goals attainable in practice? Why do they seek them? And what are the implications? The answers to these questions will necessarily differ depending upon whether the leader in question is a reaffirmer or a synthesizer, and although most appear to be reaffirmers, there are occasional clear hints of synthesis in particular areas of life and in particular countries.

There is a clearly expressed passionate desire to establish or re-establish a genuinely Muslim polity in which Muslims can freely and without restriction fulfil their individual and collective obligations to God; a polity in which government and governmental institutions are inspired and regulated by the principles, precepts and injunctions revealed by God; a polity in which society is likewise inspired and self-regulated; a polity in which Muslims rule. For only thus can the political, social, economic and cultural weakness of the Muslim world be halted and reversed and the first steps towards the recreation of the universal *umma* be achieved.

The historic consciousness as well as the perception of that history of the vast majority of the population is Islamic, comprising a glorious past which was lost with the loss of power. It has been impossible to restore that power by the adoption of Western, or European, means. It may be possible to do so by a strict adherence to the ethic and values of Islam.[21]

For some, this process implies a recreation of the ideal and idealized polity of the Golden Age of the *Rashidun*, or, more accurately, of their perception of what that ideal polity was; even for those who are less dogmatic, that ideal remains a paradigm.

In practical terms, this idealistic formulation means, for the affirmers, a state in which the entire political elite should be devout and practising Muslims. Non-Muslims do, of course, have certain rights and liberties which must be respected, but these are granted on the basis of acceptance of certain obligations and of a status of second-class citizens from whom certain rights and privileges are necessarily withheld: but so are certain obligations and it is instructive to compare this arrangement with, for example, the position of the non-Jewish Arab population in Israel. The synthesizer, though sympathetic, has some difficulty with this line of reasoning, since he is normally committed to the concept of equality of citizenship. Nevertheless, the synthesizer too seeks to establish a state in which the ethic and values of Islam underlie and regulate the complex of reciprocal rights and obligations. As a result he tends to debar non-Muslims from certain sensitive or symbolic positions — head of state and head of government, for example — while allowing free access and equality of opportunity in other areas, subject always to the qualification that no action or decision by a non-Muslim can be valid if it is repugnant to or inconsistent with the ethic, values, and injunctions of Islam. Both necessarily seek justification in the historical experience, which both for many purposes seek to disregard.

A similar dichotomy occurs in consideration of the preferred system of law, since there is general acceptance of the idea that the state exists to facilitate and ensure compliance with the revealed law. The *shari'a* is, therefore, necessarily the primary law of the land. For the reaffirmer, the *shari'a* normally comprehends the orthodox concept of the code of laws enshrined in the codices of one or other of the schools of law which may not be modified, re-interpreted, or otherwise tampered with, since it represents the law of God. Problems arise, however, as they always have done, where the theoretical comprehensiveness of the *shari'a* is not borne out in practice. In such instances, the state authorities may issue regulations which are at one and the same time binding legal provisions but not part of the *shari'a*: but the powers of the state are severely limited and there is no inherent autonomous legislative power. It follows that the *ulama* retain an important but independent role as the final arbiters of the content of the *shari'a* and of the permissibility or otherwise of the regulatory practice of the state. Some affirmers go further, and seek to disregard the corpus of law as elaborated over the centuries and to stand upon the *Qur'an* and the *Sunna* alone, unconsciously echoing the underlying principles of the Hanbali *madhhab*, though taking them much further than the Hanbalis do in practice. The synthesizer naturally prefers to define the *shari'a* in such a way as to afford the maximum flexibility and adaptability, in order to cope with constantly changing circumstances, and does so by emphasizing the distinction between the principles (and the few clear instructions) contained in the *Qur'an* and the *Sunna* and man's fallible interpretation of them as developed in the works of the jurisprudents. Underlying this line of reasoning is acceptance of the general concept of man's vice-regency on earth, and the corollary that the people in whom limited sovereignty on behalf of God inheres are empowered to delegate their collective authority to their representatives, including the power to derive positive law from the principles, taking into account past interpretations, changing circumstances, and that most elastic of concepts, the public interest.

For the synthesizer, the ulama clearly have a role to play in the legislative process: they must be involved since they are best placed to rule authoritatively on what the fundamental principles are and on the validity or otherwise of a particular interpretation. However, it is inherent that they too are, in effect, the delegated representatives of the *umma*, from whom they derive their power and to whom they are accountable. It is also inherent that, if they are to carry out their functions effectively, they must be 'devout doctors of Islamic law and jurisprudence who shall be at the same time conversant with the exigencies of their age'.[22] It is, however, important to note that both approaches are based on the centrality of the *shari'a*, however that is defined, and that the ultimate purpose is not to 'make law' as the term is generally understood, but to identify, clarify, and interpret the detailed content of God's law.

Forms of government and governmental institutions are less clear-cut for reaffirmer and synthesizer alike. Clearly, the original concept of the universal *umma* ruled by the universal and rightly guided *khalifa* is even more unattainable now than it has been for much of the historical experience of the Muslim world. Even the rationalization of the medieval jurists that '*any* government, however it came to power, was legitimate so long as it ruled in full accord with the *shari'a* and framed policy through close consultation with the *shari'a*'s recognized interpreters, the '*ulama*'[23] (original emphasis) needs some modification to conform with changed circumstances: this was achieved by adding the argument that the process of consultation is best accomplished in today's Muslim state through some form of elected representative assembly which will also be the regulatory authority and the expression of delegated collective authority to the ruler or rulers.

The revival and the relationship between faith and power

The brief outline set out above serves to highlight once again the vexed question of the relationship between faith and power, and in particular the nature and legitimacy of the institutions of authority first raised in Chapter 1, and touched on periodically since. It is at first sight surprising that the institutional structures of government and of political power in Islam should be so ill-defined and that Muslims — and observers — should be so confused about the issues, when it is clear from an examination of administrative arrangements throughout the Muslim world at its heyday and subsequently that not only was the need perceived early on but that appropriate administrative arrangements were developed as necessary.

What, then, is the argument about? Professor Vatikiotis has argued cogently that, protestations to the contrary notwithstanding, the separation between faith and power, between religious and political authority, occurred very early on in Muslim history.[24] Professor Lambton has suggested a reason for the confusion and dichotomy when she commented that the basis of the Islamic state was 'ideological, not political, territorial or ethical and the primary purpose of governments was to defend and protect the faith, not the state'. She also suggests that by the eleventh century, the jurists had reached the point at which they denied the existence of the state as a separate institution and, somewhat confusingly, both recognized reality and also regarded all states as temporal and therefore as an intrusion.[25] As Professor Gibb has suggested,

Consequently, not only is all discussion on the institution of government in Muslim political thought concentrated on the caliph, who alone is considered to represent that authority, but also the State as such is regarded as a merely transient phenomenon, and although possessed of temporal power, lacking any intrinsic authority of its own.[26]

Malise Ruthven follows a different line of reasoning in arguing that the distinctive characteristic of Islam as compared to Christianity lies in the fact that 'the division between the religious and the secular occurs at a different point, between the legal and political realms', and that 'the failure of the caliphal state to realise the Islamic vision of a politically unified Umma extending throughout the known world had the effect of placing politics *outside* the purview of religion' (original emphasis).[27] The clear implication of those arguments, if taken to their logical conclusion, is of a separation between the source of political legitimation — religion — and the actuality to be legitimized — government institutions and political theory.

In *Usul al Shari'a* (The sources of the law) Muhammad Said al Ashmawi, a leading Egyptian lawyer, argues that the *Qur'an* offers no guidance about the Islamic state and the nature of its government, since religion, including Islam, 'is concerned with man and society, not with states and empires'. Indeed, until the death of the Prophet, the state, as the term is normally understood, did not exist in Islam: there was the community, the *umma*, whose locus of loyalty was belief, not a national or territorial entity. 'The Qur'an and the *Shari'a* always addressed themselves to the faithful, not the citizens.' Neither the *Qur'an* nor the *Sunna* dealt specifically with the form of government in Islam, although legislative verses were revealed to the Prophet as and when necessary to provide for the regulation of the community's domestic life and its relations with others. God remained the sole sovereign ruler, however, and chose the Prophet to lead the community and to execute His will. Clearly, for these purposes the Prophet enjoyed certain rights and privileges deriving from his selection by God, but these inhered in him alone and were not transferable, despite the fact that he was neither infallible nor sinless. This was, in fact, 'God's government', which differed from government of the people, which is 'any earthly government based on social conditions and economic circumstances, and imposed by the realities of power'. The *khalifas* after Abu Bakr represented their rule as a continuation of 'God's government', but they had, in fact, arrogated to themselves the rights and privileges of the Prophet, and their rule was essentially a 'government of the people'. For Ashmawi, therefore, there was only one brief period of 'God's government' under the Prophet during which the *shari'a* was the guide for the dynamic working out of rules to meet specific problems and circumstances rather then a rigid and immutable code. The dynamism disappeared, however, and

> it was the obfuscation of the essence of the meaning of the *shari'a* and its transformation from a guide and ethic, a way to a better life and a means to salvation to a body of permanent rigid and immutable rules which created the central difficulty in the relation between Islam and power.[28]

There is something in all these lines of reasoning, but there seems to be a missing step. Professor Vatikiotis, for example, is content to assert that Islam 'has failed to provide a formula for a flexible political order which could cope with change. It never quite managed to establish an acceptable relation between religion and state, power and belief';[29] but he does not explore the implications. Malise Ruthven too is content with the straight assertion and fails to make the point that the discontinuity is both spatial and temporal: spatially, the point of apparent separation is between the law and the political sub-system, and temporally, in the clear discontinuity between the early rudimentary political order and the later reality, partly for the reasons adduced by Professors Lambton and Gibb, but also because the concept of the nation-state rarely figured in Muslim political thought. Political theory and political institutions are in practice closely linked to the concept of the nation-state in one form or another; there was therefore no real impetus to incorporate them into the Muslim world view. In this connection, it may be significant that the development of an empire elsewhere has normally followed the establishment of an identifiable polity, be it a nation-state or a city state, and the development of both institutions of political power and a political order — for example, the Greek, Roman, Spanish, British, and French Empires. In the case of the Muslim world, however, the emergence of the empire was contemporaneous with the early stages of defining political authority, and was in many ways the root cause of that process of definition. Both Professors Gibb and Lambton set out the problem but do not address the relationship, while Ashmawi is both uncompromising and relatively traditional in his views. By his distinction between religion and religious thought, between political institutions and the revelation, he in fact perpetuates the impractical views of the medieval jurists.

An alternative view

Fortunately, there is a more satisfactory and practical formula which starts with the not very startling proposition that the locus of the legitimizing force — or otherwise — of any act, fact, theory, or institutional framework in the Muslim world lies in the faith subsystem, and that the acid test is whether or not it is in accord with the revealed command as set out in the *Qur'an* and the *Sunna* and as codified in the *Shari'a* (no subjective judgement is made here on the precise meaning to be attached to that elastic concept). However, as all authorities have recognized, these sources do not offer any real practical advice about political theory, about political and government institutions and order, and about the relationship between faith and power. Nevertheless, state authority and institutions are a necessary component of any social order and their function is to maintain and protect that social order by enforcing compliance with its social, ethical, legal, and other norms. In the case of the Muslim state, state authority and institutions are necessary to maintain, defend, and protect the faith by enforcing compliance with the norms of Islam as set out in the *Qur'an*, the *Sunna*, and the *shari'a*. This applies even though many of the norms of Islam relate to individual and personal duties and obligations. However,. this necessarily implies some degree of separation of 'Church' and 'State', though that separation is both limited and specific: it is not, and indeed cannot be, a total separation since it is essentially a separation of function rather than of theoretical inspiration. There is thus a requirement to manage the relationship — and, if necessary, to rationalize the form. For the arrangement to work reasonably effectively and be able to develop, however, the progress of managing and rationalizing must be one which does not question the legitimacy of the theory, of political structure and institutions, or of the political functions of the government. The motivation for particular acts may, however, be called into question.

Now, Muslim jurists and intellectuals have consistently refused to accept the necessary functional separation and have inevitably denied the corollary set out above. However, the actuality was very different to their views, for political institutions, structures, and practices — indeed, political theories and principles — necessarily developed in the Muslim world — a fact frequently cited by modern Muslim apologists and polemicists as evidence of the all-embracing nature of Islam. However, it never proved possible to define in any satisfactory manner the relationship between doctrine and practice: indeed, it could not be possible, given the jurists' denial of the separation of function. As a result, the rational and dynamic development of the institutions of the state could never be accorded legitimacy — and, more importantly, neither could the institutions themselves or the theories underlying their establishment and development. They did, however, exist, and needed to be explained: lacking legitimacy, the only explanation possible was that they were temporal, transient, irrelevant, and certainly not doctrinally acceptable.

Hence, the only legitimate paradigm is that in which the separation of function had not yet occurred — the idealized *post eventum* vision of the Golden Age. It is not, therefore, a failure to 'institutionalize' — to develop a dynamic political order and political theory that is the real problem. Rather, the real problem lies in the refusal to recognize the distinction between 'separation' and 'functional separation', the failure to provide a workable institutional and theoretical linkage between the source of legitimizing power and the instruments necessary for the implementation of God's plan. That this should be so is surprising since the concept of *din wa dawla* (the domain of religion and the domain of politics and government) necessarily implies a functional separation, with Islam, which includes both, forming the essential link. Yet only in the Islamic Republic of Iran and in the relationship between the Ansar and the Umma Party in the Sudan has this been recognized in practice. It seems that Muslims have become conceptual prisoners of the *din wa dawla* model: that is, because political institutions were *a priori* illegitimate according to the theory, they in fact became illegitimate in practice and their further development, though not precluded, was made more difficult; and such institutional structures as did evolve and such further development as did occur remained outside the theoretical framework and therefore always vulnerable to attack on doctrinal grounds. This problem still besets the Muslim world generally, even in more traditional and conservative countries, like Saudi Arabia, and can be seen starkly delineated in Pakistan and Iran. Until the problem has been resolved, it cannot be said that the Islamic revival has succeeded.

Conclusions

It follows logically that the goals of the activists are not attainable unless and until the issues discussed above are satisfactorily addressed and resolved, and a number of intellectuals have begun to attempt to deal with them. Considerable attention has been devoted to them, and in particular to the precise definition of the *shari'a*, to the relationship between temporal and spiritual authority, and to the patent impracticality of attempting to govern a state in the modern world in accordance with a set of idealized general principles. It is however significant that no one has questioned the centrality of the *shari'a* (except, possibly, Qadhdhafi), though the term is variously defined. Non-separation of 'Church' and 'State' is frequently a major premise and is often couched in familiar Christian terms: the injunction to 'render unto Caesar the things that are Caesar's, and unto God the things that are God's' is impossible in Islam because separation is impossible. However, that assumes only one interpretation of the injunction — that is, the one normally used in the Christian world (consider the argument normally adduced concerning the First Amendment to the American Constitution). However, practice in the Christian world has generally been based upon the interpretation set out in the first verses of the thirteenth chapter of St Paul's Epistle to the Romans, which clearly recognize a linkage and a relationship which is both familiar and unexceptionable to Muslims:

1. Let every soul be subject unto the higher powers. For there is no power but of God: the powers that be are ordained of God.
2. Whosoever therefore resisteth the power, resisteth the ordinance of God: and they that resist shall receive to themselves damnation.
3. For rulers are not a terror to good works, but to the evil. Wilt thou then not be afraid of the power? Do that which is good and thou shalt have the praise of the same.
4. For he is the minister of God to thee for good. But if thou do that which is evil, be afraid; for he beareth not the sword in vain: for he is the minister of God, a revenger to execute wrath upon him that doeth evil.
5. Wherefore ye must needs be subject, not only for wrath, but also for conscience sake.

Since, however, received views are difficult to challenge anywhere, the paradigm of the early community and the impossibility of even functional separation is found even in the writings of synthesizers. Furthermore, though there are notable exceptions to this generalization, the dichotomy between 'Islamic' and 'non-Islamic' remains strong. Among the exceptions are Sadiq al Mahdi, who has commented:

> The traditionalist Islamic thesis is a historically conditioned understanding by Muslims of the teachings of the Quran and the Sunna. To transcend that thesis (in its various forms) in favor of Islam in a modern context is both Islamic and national.[30]

Even a man as traditional in his views as Hassan al Turabi has been able to assert:

> Any form or procedures for the organisation of public life that can be ultimately related to God and put to his service in furtherance of the aims of Islamic government can be adopted unless expressly excluded by the *shariah*. Once so received, it is an integral part of Islam whatever its source may be. Through this process of Islamisation, the Muslims were always very open to expansion and change. Thus, Muslims can incorporate any experience whatsoever if not contrary to their ideals. Muslims took most of their bureaucratic forms from Roman and Persian models. Now, much can be borrowed from contemporary sources, critically appreciated in the light of the *shariah* values and norms, and integrated into the Islamic framework of government.[31]

Such views are unhappily the exception and certainly do not inform the minds of the general public, for whom the identification of 'Western' and 'modernizing' with 'un-Islamic' is virtually unshakeable. Until such time as this state of affairs changes — and it will be an internally generated change if it does occur — the prognostication must be that the current revival, which is reaffirmatory rather than synthesizing in inspiration, will in due course fail to overcome the problems facing the Muslim world and will be perceived as having failed to fulfil the wishes and aspirations of individual Muslims and of groups of Muslims, and the cycle will be resumed. To break the cycle clearly requires a profound change in traditional interpretations, modes of thought, and attitudes, which will come, if it comes at all, slowly, painfully, and piecemeal. In particular, the tension between Islam and modernization, which is based upon the perception that modernization is alien and secular in motivation will have to be transformed by the assimilation and incorporation of the process into a credible Muslim framework. Furthermore, the end-result will not be monolithic: despite the common factors, it will be as diverse as are current perceptions and will be influenced not only by the common strands but also by the very different historical, social, economic, cultural, and political experiences.

Whatever the direction of future developments, there are a number of obvious truisms. There will continue to be a profound conflict of values, ideologies, and practices which will occasionally erupt into the sort of disorder and unrest which has been characteristic of the past few years. Governments of all complexions will need to deal sympathetically with not only the catalysts and reactions to them, but with the domestic implications of the increased use of Muslim symbolism. They will, for one reason or another, be more or less influenced by the strength of Muslim feeling, but are likely to continue to give priority to economic development and modernization: the balancing act will not be easy. However, the recreation of the idealized Golden Age community is not a practical proposition: some accommodation will be necessary, and is likely to be achieved.

9

The Extremists

Introduction

At the beginning of Chapter 8, a rough and ready distinction was made between the 'activist', who normally works within the existing social and political order to attain his objectives, and the 'extremist', who is prepared to resort to violence to achieve those aims. This generalization needs further refinement in a number of areas, however, since there is a regrettable tendency to lump all extremists together as either mindlessly violent or committed to revolution in a cynical and self-seeking pursuit of power. It is necessary to distinguish between, on the one hand, those who resort to violence deliberately, with premeditation, and for ideological reasons — for example, the group responsible for the assassination of President Sadat, other followers of Sayyid Qutb, the Moros of the Philippines, and the religiously oriented *mujahidin* in Afghanistan; and, on the other hand, those who may have drifted into violence inadvertently — for example, the communal rioting in India. In addition, distinctions must be drawn between different groups whose espousal or use of violence is deliberate on the basis of motivation.

Motivations for violence and types of organization

Thus, the religiously oriented Afghan *mujahidin* have taken to violent action in order to fight against the Soviet attempt to impose an alien culture by force:

Current violence reflects Afghan resentment at foreign control — whether in the form of native rulers espousing foreign

185

(Communist) doctrine, or in the more blatant Soviet tanks and troops patrolling highways leading to Kabul. Rather an already deeply entrenched ideology is being marshalled by Afghan tribesmen in an attempt to expel foreign influence.[1]

The moderate wing of Amal, under the leadership of Nabih Berri, engages in violent activity for quite different reasons — partly a question of collective self-preservation, particularly among the Shi'a of southern Lebanon, partly to achieve a political, social, and economic position within Lebanon commensurate with the size of the Shi'a population, and partly on the basis of 'if you can't beat 'em, join 'em'. The feudal and sectarian nature of Lebanese politics has forced violence upon them, but 'it is clear that they do not seek an Iranian-style takeover of the Lebanese system. In November, 1983, for example, Nabih Berri told an American journalist: "I want a new Lebanon where every Lebanese has the same rights and the same obligations — no difference between Christian and Muslim".'[2] Different again are the motivations of the Muslim Brotherhood in Syria and, subsequently, the Higher Command of the Islamic Revolution in Syria. In part, their violence represents Sunni hostility towards 'the sharpened Alawi bias of the regime and the deepening erosion of the status and power of the Sunni community',[3] but it also represents a deep-seated antipathy towards what is seen as the repressive and sectarian nature of that regime. The Declaration and Program of the Islamic Revolution in Syria summed this up as follows:

> The experiment of the Ba'ath party in power was, and still is, a total disaster. On the internal level, the party squashed freedom, abolished political parties, rationalized the press, threw people into prisons, and hanged those who dared to voice their disapproval of its injustice and aggression against the interests of people. The party which turned against the simplest values of political work, exiled the honest ones and favoured the agents and corrupt ones who found, by living on the fringe of the regime and rotating in its orbit, an easy way to unlawful earning and illegal richness. The result of this was that the party was converted into a peculiar collection of people with nothing to bind them except mutual interests and suspicious loyalty. Furthermore, after the series of coups which had helped to empty the army of its scientific and fighting capabilities, the party pushed it into politics and

made it forget its main duty as a defender of the borders and an instrument for regaining lost rights. It became instead a guard for the regime. The image of democracy was also distorted by the party; the constitution became a lie, referendums changed to comedy acts and the so-called people's organisations were something to be ashamed of.

The Command went on to say that

> the Syrian regime fell into the swamps of secretarianism . . . Hafiz Asad and his brother Rifaat and those who bowed their heads to them have, with the help of certain sectarian elements, taken absolute control of power. With their autocratic rule they transgressed beyond bounds in the lands and heaped therein mischief on mischief. They enslaved the Muslims and stripped them of their wealth, deadened the hearts and spread corruption. Whenever they used up a group of mercenaries and graspers they spat them out, forgot about them, and replaced them with another group which would face the same fate as its predecessors, and so on indefinitely.[4]

The Moros in the Philippines appear to be essentially a secessionist movement in which Islam is the cement but they do not appear to be intent upon imposing an 'Islamic' government upon others. The motivations of the more violent groups in Egypt — for example, *Munadhdhamat al Tahrir al Islami* (The Islamic Liberation Organization, also known as the Technical Military Academy Group and as *Shabab Muhammad*), *Jama'at al Muslimin* (The Society of Muslims, also sometimes known as *al Jihad al Jadid*)[5] — represent in part a stretching to the limit of the views of Sayyid Qutb and in part a break with those views. Hizballah and Islamic Jihad in Lebanon, though their inspiration may be qualitatively different, one from the other, share a perception that violence was introduced into the area by the establishment of the state of Israel, that the United States is responsible both for the continued existence of that state and also for continued aggression against the inhabitants of the area, and that violence against the United States government and its agents is both legitimate and reactive. The Islamization of Pakistan under Zia ul-Haq seems to be a combination of personal belief on his part, a means of legitimizing his rule, and a response to perceived (though not necessarily actual) desires of the Pakistani population. Strictly speaking, Pakistan does not resort to violence, but Zia ul-Haq is certainly prepared to use force to impose his policies on a population which is not solidly behind him. Finally, where does Ayatollah Khomeini fit? On the one hand, he has repeatedly gone on record as opposing the violent export of the revolution, while on the other, he either tacitly supports, or condones, attempts by his subordinates to do just that; on the one hand, he came to power essentially as a leader opposing the ungodly and repressive nature of the Shah's regime, but on the other hand, has accepted the necessity for the use of even more brutal repression of all who oppose his long-term aims.

Once again the remarkable diversity of interpretations of Islam and the remarkable diversity of triggers are evident, but there are certain common factors, if Afghanistan and Lebanon are set on one side. The broad aims of the activists described in the preceding chapter are equally those of most extremists, though precise interpretations of those aims do vary: and most spokesmen tend to present actions as essentially in *defence* of Islam. This diversity does pose problems of categorization; but these are more apparent than real. Perhaps the most rational division is one recognizing four broad categories:

(a) Instances where organizations have achieved power, as in Iran; or where pressure for Islamization has come from the existing government, as in Pakistan;

(b) Instances where organizations are broadly based and genuinely represent significant numbers: for example, the *mujahidin* in Afghanistan; Amal in Lebanon; possibly the Moros in the Philippines; and the opposition in Syria (though Syria sits uneasily); and instances where the confrontation or opposition is related to a non-Muslim government;

(c) Instances where organizations are small, generally clandestine, radical, and inclined to view all who do not share their views and commitment as unbelievers rather than as fellow Muslims, as in the case of *Takfir wa Hijra* and *al jihad* in Egypt; but unlike group (b), the focus is on opposition to an avowedly Muslim government;

(d) Small, shadowy, clandestine groups, such as Islamic Jihad in Lebanon, who are distinguished from group (c) by the manner in which they have internationalized the issue by their willingness to 'eliminate anyone — Israeli, American, Christian, Arab or pro-Western Muslim — who appears to stand in the way'.[6]

Islamization imposed by government fiat

Group (a) may well share the broad ideological framework of the others, but its members have had to learn that accession to power is a remarkably powerful modifying force: 'creeping pragmatism' is more evident in Iran today than it was in the heady days of 1979, for example. They have also had to grapple with the problems of internal opposition, particularly when expectations have been disappointed. Thus, the process of Islamization in Pakistan, claimed to be in response to the wishes and aspirations of the Pakistani people, has caused more conflict, questioning, and opposition than it has unity and harmony. 'The use of Islam to legitimate military rule, cancel elections, outlaw political parties, impose Islamic taxes and punishments, and ban certain forms of entertainment has caused many to ask "Whose Islam?", and "What Islam?", and "To what ends?" ' Similarly, the establishment of the Islamic Republic of Iran has brought with it restrictions, repression, hardship, intolerance, and capricious penal sentences (not to mention the continued conflict with Iraq) which seem at odds with the true spirit of Islam. 'Although the experiences of Pakistan and Iran are in many ways dissimilar, the respective efforts at Islamisation raise similar questions: "Whose Islam is this?" and "Why emphasize a negative Islam?" '[7]

Nevertheless, it is possible to argue that this group, to the extent that its chief actors do genuinely represent the majority of the population of a given state, are legitimate: the methods employed to achieve certain ideological objectives may be validly criticized or questioned, but ideology, motivation, and inspiration may not, although this does not preclude disputation concerning interpretation. Thus, one can validly and justifiably lodge strong objections to the manner in which the leadership of the Iranian revolution has implemented its ideological objectives, on grounds of abuse of human rights, capricious application of the law, and the wholesale use of the accusation 'corruption on earth' to justify executions and less condign punishments imposed on persons whose sins appear to consist mainly of dissent or consorting with others deemed to be enemies of the regime, and so on.[8] However much one might disagree with Khomeini's interpretation of doctrine and with his concept of *velayat-i-faqih*, however, that interpretation and that concept are both justifiable and valid in terms of Shi'a jurisprudence: criticism or objections must be qualitatively very different to those levelled against his methods. Nor can his sincerity be questioned in relation to his ideological or religious motivation and inspiration — though his continued refusal to compromise over the continuation of the conflict with Iraq is a very different matter.

It may be argued that Qadhdhafi in Libya strictly forms part of this group in that he has certainly employed violence and has equally certainly used Islam to legitimize his regime. In addition, his personal devotion is unquestionable. However, this is an incorrect inference. In the first place, Qadhdhafi's concept of Islam is idiosyncratic in that he takes the argument of the reaffirmers to its logical conclusion and rejects the proposition that the *shari'a* is at least divinely inspired. The only source is the *Qur'an*: the entire corpus of law elaborated over the centuries can be rejected if it is no longer appropriate, for it is neither Muslim nor licit:

> le Coran n'autorise pas l'existence de telles lois en dehors de ses propres prescriptions! Le Coran existe, et tout autre livre qui se proposerait de légiférer au nom de l'islam serait par la force des chose en contradiction avec le Coran . . . [les lois musulmanes] doivent donc être considérées comme l'oeuvre de l'esprit humain et non comme quelque chose de divin.[9]

Second, although Qadhdhafi continues to invoke his concept of Islam as the inspiration and basis for his actions, this is because Islam is both his own cultural environment and that of the Libyan population — a tool rather than an inspiration. Furthermore, by stressing the need to 'purge Islam of historically inaccurate accretions, of specialized classes of jurists, of tradition and the tradition-bound, he was undermining the political power of the competing religious establishments in Libya'[10] and thus further strengthening his grasp on the levers of power. Finally, his views have been regularly denounced as heretical by many Muslims. He has clearly crossed the limits of what is generally held to be acceptable, and 'his personal interpretation increasingly set him apart from the mainstream of Islamic thought and at odds with both the religious establishment and the fundamentalist reformers in the wider Muslim world'.[11] There is a strong case, therefore, for the argument that Qadhdhafi 'only needs Islam in order to remind himself that what he believes and does must be right because he is devout'.[12] As such he — and Libya — are not true members of this group.

However, even accepting the contrary view[13] and associating Libya with Iran and Pakistan in this group, a number of pertinent questions arise — but remain unanswered. In particular, how much genuine and lasting popular support is there for the imposition of a particular concept of Muslim society by a government or a leader? The incidence of failed *coups d'état* in Libya, evidence of opposition in Iran to the policies and ideology of the revolutionary authorities, and signs of lack of support in Pakistan evinced in, for example, the extremely low polling for Zia ul-Haq's recent referendum, and in the poor performance of the *Jamaat-i-Islami* and candidates closely identified with Zia ul-Haq's regime in the subsequent elections for national and provincial assemblies — all suggest that popular support is waning, and is not particularly enduring. Coercion is not popular in the long term, however emotionally satisfying the message may be in the short term.

Broadly based and popularly supported organizations

Group (b) is essentially oppositional in character, but, it may be argued, does have some element of legitimacy, coherence, and respectability, in that there is broad-based support and the organizations are seeking — at least ostensibly — to oppose alien cultural and ideological patterns of thought, or to obtain social, economic, political, and cultural justice. In other words, one may deplore the use of violence by members of this group, but even more deplorable is the fact that they have been driven to the use of force and violence to achieve legitimate — even laudable — objectives. There are, however, differences between possible members of this group.

The Afghan *mujahidin*, as already noted, are seeking to prevent the coercive imposition of an alien political and cultural ideology on a country whose inhabitants are overwhelmingly — an estimated 99 per cent — practising Muslims.[14] However, the Afghan resistance also represents a long tradition of opposition to attempts by any central government to establish control over the disparate ethnic and tribal groupings, which remain important foci for particularism. It is, of course, partly for this reason that the Afghan resistance has lacked cohesiveness, despite the easy identification of a common enemy.

Amal, originally *Afwaj al Muqawama al Lubnaniya* (Battalions of the Lebanese Resistance) but better known by the acronym which, conveniently, is the Arabic for 'hope', was, in the first instance, the military wing of a mass organization called 'The Movement of the Deprived', founded by Musa Sadr, the then undisputed head of the Lebanese Shi'a community, in 1974. Its original intended function was to defend South Lebanon from Israeli attacks, but it quickly developed its own political and social infrastructure and became, in effect, the political manifestation of the Lebanese Shi'a, complete with the mandatory (in Lebanese politics) militia. That this was possible was the result of a number of factors. First, as a result of the economic development policies of successive Lebanese governments, the hitherto scattered and disunited Shi'a community began to develop a coherence and a collective identity. As a result, political, economic, and social aspirations became more overt among the Shi'a, and concentrated heavily on the perceived discrimination against the Shi'a in the political structure of Lebanon and on antipathy towards the traditional leaders of the Shi'a community, who were seen as collaborating with the Maronites for personal gain. Furthermore, the first Israeli invasion of South Lebanon in March 1978 caused the Shi'a in that area to define — and pursue — their own collective interests in distinction to those of the Palestinians in South Lebanon, whose presence and activities had prompted the Israeli action. In addition, the success of the Iranian revolution caused many Lebanese Shi'a to contemplate a confessionally based political movement while the economic and social development of previous years meant that there was a corpus of well-educated, articulate Shi'a who concluded that the structure of Lebanese politics no longer reflected the demographic reality of the country.

Thus, although Amal had originally been established as a non-sectarian organization, it quickly became a Shi'a organization. No doubt the close connection with the Shi'a religious hierarchy resulting from Musa Sadr's leadership of the movement encouraged and assisted that trend. However, despite the religious orientation, Amal remains relatively moderate and committed to a continuation of secular rule in Lebanon, though with some modifications to reflect demographic changes. This is not to suggest that there were no calls for more radical solutions: there were, and there is still, a debate over whether the goal should be an Iranian-style Islamic Republic; but so far its advocates have been relatively few in number and have carried little influence, although they continue to put pressure on the Amal leadership. However,

> Berri's base of support has remained a core of Shia professionals, *ulama* and long time Amal activists who have tried, as Sadr usually tried, to find a viable middle course between pragmatism and the all-out radicalism that parts of their constituency were demanding.[15]

Violence, inter-sectarian fighting, Israeli raids, and Palestinian attacks and counter-attacks have been endemic features of Lebanese political history for many years now, and it is inevitable that Amal, in seeking to change the political structure and to protect the Shi'a community, should join in. However, it may be argued, though without condoning violence and excesses, that Amal were forced by circumstances, as were the Afghans, to 'take arms against a sea of troubles and by opposing end them', or at least seek to end them. However, Amal has generally eschewed the type of terrorist activity regularly claimed by the extremist movements using the appellation 'Islamic Jihad'. These will be covered later.

Another widely known member of group (b) is the Moro National Liberation Front (MNLF) in the Philippines, though its aims differ from those of the Afghans and the Lebanese Shi'a. There has for a long time been a sizeable Muslim population concentrated in the southern islands of the Philippine archipelago which has resisted central government attempts to establish control since at least the sixteenth century. This historic opposition was given a sharper focus as a result of a movement by non-Muslims into the predominantly Muslim areas and consequent conflict over land, local political control, and identity. By 1970, Moro demands for autonomy had become commonplace and led in due course to open rebellion and violent clashes between the Moros and government forces and to the signature of the Tripoli Agreement of 1976 under which internal autonomy was to be granted. Clashes have continued, however, because President Marcos made little effort to implement the terms of the agreement. But although the MNLF has an element of Muslim identity and has (successfully) appealed to the wider Muslim world for assistance, it is essentially a separatist movement with more secular motivations than other organizations in this group. The Pattani separatist movement in Thailand appears to be similar, though it also has an ethnic strand in that the Thai Muslim community is made up of Malays.

Muslim extremists in Syria represent a number of factors, as already noted. The core of the extremist opposition is the remnant of the Syrian Muslim Brotherhood which operated legally for a number of years, particularly before the Ba'ath coup in 1963, but the Syrian Brotherhood during that period was not particularly dynamic or effective. Their 1954 manifesto, for example, was restricted to generalities. 'It committed them to such objectives as "the combating of ignorance, disease, want, fear and indignity" and "the establishment of a virtuous polity which would carry out the rules and teachings of Islam''.' Their central slogan, borrowed from the Egyptian Brotherhood, was no more definite: 'God is our End; His Messenger our Example; the Quran our constitution; the Jihad our Path; and Death for God's Cause our Highest Desire.'[16] However, after the Ba'athist accession to power in 1963, the Brotherhood became active in opposition to the regime and was in due course outlawed. Thereafter a split occurred in the organization, initially between the followers of Isam al Attar, who had been elected Superintendent-General of the Brotherhood in 1961, and the followers of Marwan Hadid, who had imbibed the ideas of Sayyid Qutb during a period of further education in Egypt in the early 1960s.

Attar and his group operated outside Syria and gradually moved from a purely Syrian to a more global and pan-Islamic focus. Marwan Hadid, however, returned to Syria and began actively to attempt to overthrow the Ba'ath regime. Strikes, demonstrations, and disturbances became a regular feature of life in Syria, particularly after the Alawi take-over of the Ba'ath regime. However, the significant change in the Brotherhood's approach came with the provision of military training to Hadid and some of his adherents by *al Fatah* in 1968. The trend towards armed struggle subsequently accelerated and by 1979, a campaign of sporadic guerrilla warfare commenced, culminating in major disturbances in Aleppo and Hama in 1980, and the brutal suppression of the uprising by the Syrian army. It is not clear to what extent these events can be ascribed to the Brotherhood or to other dissident elements of Syrian society who chose to ally themselves with the Brotherhood — the only organized (if underground) opposition force in Syria. However, it has been demonstrated clearly that 'a number of Syrian "*ulama*" and their relatives played a leading role in the armed struggle against the regime',[17] and the establishment of the Higher Command of the Islamic Revolution in Syria appears to owe as much to non-Brotherhood Muslims as to the Brotherhood itself.[18] Further clashes between the Front and the Syrian government followed, the most explosive incident being the rebellion in Hama in February 1982, during which vast areas of Hama were reported to have been destroyed and thousands of people killed.[19]

The Front's claims to enjoy the support of the majority of the Syrian population seem exaggerated, though such judgements must be made with considerable caution. Nevertheless, as one observer comments, 'the Hama revolt, for all its fierceness and brutality, demonstrated that the Islamic revolutionaries did not enjoy the support of the entire Sunni community in Syria.' He rightly rejects the fear of retaliation and poorly co-ordinated planning as inadequate explanations for the failure of the Sunni community in Syria to support the Islamic Front. Although the Iranian example may have deterred some — the more liberal-minded — from active support for the Front, the failure to attract the support of the technocratic elite (which contains many Sunnis as well as Alawis) and of the public at large is better explained by the stark fact that 'it appears that the great majority of the Syrian people, in spite of considerable dissatisfaction with the Asad regime, were disinclined to participate in an Islamic revolution'.[20]

This suggests that there is something in the argument that 'it is not the beliefs of the Sunnis that have been in danger or under attack since the Ba'athist take-over in 1963, but the social interests of the upper and middle elements of their landed, mercantile, and manufacturing classes'.[21] However, proponents of this view go too far in implying that the conflict is not about religion: for it does reflect antipathy towards a particular faith, towards that faith's alliance with a secular ideology, and towards the nature of the resultant regime. In all this the perennial problem of the relationship between faith and power can be clearly seen, but it is a more complex relationship in the case of Syria, given the plurality of society there. Perhaps the real conclusion to be drawn is that Syria's experience shows more clearly than any country so far considered that the tolerance characteristic of most 'main-stream' Muslims often manifests itself in a marked distaste for extremism of any kind and an equally marked preference for the middle of the road.

Before moving on to group (c), it is worth considering the demographic characteristics of group (b). There is a consistent pattern: the leadership tends to be young — 25 to 35 years old — well-educated, middle-class, and their disciplines tend towards the sciences rather than traditional Muslim theology and jurisprudence. In Lebanon, for example, Helena Cobban refers to 'hundreds of fully-trained professionals, now well established in their chosen fields', to the 'new Shia business and professional classes', and to doctors, bankers, and lawyers.[22] As for Syria, Batatu points out that the activists were young men — in their twenties and early thirties — and predominantly students, teachers, engineers, and so on. Of a total 1,384 taken into custody by the Syrian authorities between 1976 and May 1981, 27.7 per cent were students, 7.9 per cent teachers, and 13.3 per cent members of the professional classes, 'including 79 engineers, 57 physicians, 25 lawyers and 10 pharmacists'. He notes that the leadership of the military sections of the Brotherhood have a similar profile.[23]

Small clandestine but discrete groups

Group (c), the generally small, extremist clandestine groups, are perhaps the best documented, despite the obvious problems of establishing the true facts about them. Unlike the groups discussed above, however, this group is found mainly in the Middle East: elsewhere, activity has been noted in Indonesia, Malaysia, Nigeria, and Thailand. Furthermore, such activity has been by one or two groups only in these countries, while a recent study has identified some 28 groups in Egypt alone.[24] However, statistical evidence should be treated with some caution since, as a number of observers have pointed out, membership is fluid and individuals move from one to another — and the suppression of one group often results in the reappearance of its leadership under a new name.

> It appears that new groups are being formed continually, as frustrations intensify especially among the youth and the unemployed. A pattern of appearance and disappearance characterizes these societies as they are unearthed by the government, the suppressed or contained, only to return to Egypt's omnipresent underground.[25]

Although motivations, actions, and ideology do differ from country to country and even from organization to organization, there are certain common characteristics. In the first place, most add to the general aims and beliefs of the activists of Chapter 8 a number of additional assumptions and beliefs. For most extremists, these are all closely related to two issues:

(a) the duty laid upon all Muslims to strive actively for the establishment of a true Muslim state and, for some, the re-establishment of the *khilafa*;[26]

(b) the need for all true Muslims to engage in *jihad* (in the sense of active warfare) in order to achieve (a).

Jihad is seen as a positive duty, the rejection or neglect of which is seen as the primary cause of the ills besetting the Muslim world and of the successive humiliations suffered by it and of the disunity and weakness so prevalent in it. These are, of course, all seen as factors which have been exploited by the Western Judaeo-Christian conspiracy to the detriment of the Muslim world. All governments which do not follow the dictates of the *shari'a* (as usual not defined in any detail) are both illegitimate and un-Islamic and as such are appropriate targets for *jihad*. Indeed, they are a first target on the grounds that it is more important to fight the enemy who is near than it is to fight the enemy who is distant. All governments in the Muslim world (with the possible exception of the Iranian government) are seen as governments led by unbelievers, and are therefore all to be attacked, as are all their supporters and employees. Jews and Christians are also fair game, partly because they are unbelievers and partly because they are supportive of the *jahili* governments of Muslim countries and are therefore directly responsible for the parlous state of the Muslim world. Fanatical belief in the rightness of the cause is normal and all those who do not subscribe to the particular articles of faith of the organization are unbelievers and apostates: they are an evil which must be ruthlessly extirpated.[27]

Second, the leadership is almost always charismatic, whether it is collective or individual, except in the case of groups of rather longer standing, in which case the leadership tends to be bureaucratic. In addition to charisma, however, the leadership, particularly of the younger groups, exhibits 'a strong sense of alienation from society and a powerful compulsion to compensate for personal sufferings or deprivation by seeking the destruction or the radical transformation of the ruling order'.[28] Other typical character traits are authoritarianism, aggressiveness, intolerance, austerity, and an almost paranoid distrust of others. Third, most extremist groups in the Middle East are offshoots or lineal descendants of the Muslim Brotherhood, although their ideologies and philosophies are often far removed from the original views of Hassan al Banna. The transition is normally via the views of Sayyid Qutb but group attitudes and aims have taken his essentially sterile and bleak world view to its logical conclusion. Fourth, most groups are relatively small: a recent survey indicates that only 20 per cent of the organizations considered had a membership in excess of 5,000, and many of those seek to achieve their objectives peacefully — they are activist, not extremist, in orientation. Finally, the socio-economic background of most leaders shows a common pattern — as does that of many of the members; and many members exhibit common characteristics. Typically, they are young, well educated (many have university backgrounds), scientific, or technical specialists rather than humanists and often immigrants from rural or small-town environments to the major cities. Political, social, and economic discontents figure largely — they are the disoriented, disaffected, discontented, and dissatisfied of Chapter 1 — but they have concluded that their own particular solution is the only one, and that that solution can be achieved only by violent, revolutionary means — that is, by 'actual violent group behaviour committed collectively against the state or other actors in the name of Islam'.[29] Commitment to and acceptance of martyrdom are endemic.

The terrorist groups

The distinction between organizations in group (c) and those in groups (d) is a fine one since violence is characteristic of both. Those in group (d) might be described as a combination of terrorist group and suicide squad. Like group (c), their objective is to establish a Muslim state, though this is often left implicit and to be deduced from the name: Islamic Jihad, Hussein Suicide Commandos, Defender of the Islamic Revolution, the Revolutionary Organization of Socialist Muslims, and so on. However, these groups have taken the *jahiliya* argument a stage further (though not, let it be said, in print) in that they ascribe all ills to the malign influence of the West, and in particular the United States, whether it be directly, through policies, or indirectly, through indigenous non-Muslim communities. However, the obsessive nature of this point of view leads to a conspiracy theory to end all conspiracy theories and to an ascription of motives for apparently innocent actions which can be bizarre in the extreme. Thus, Mehmed Ali Agca, who unsuccessfully attempted to assassinate the Pope in 1981, saw the Pope's visit to Turkey in 1979 in the following terms:

> Out of fear of seeing Turkey and its Arab brothers create a new political, economic and military force across the Middle East, the West has sent John Paul II to Turkey as commander of the crusades. If this untimely and meaningless visit is not cancelled, I will certainly kill the Pope . . . Someone has to pay for the attack on the Great Mosque of Mecca in 1979, provoked by the United States and Israel.[30]

In practice, organizations in this group — if indeed they are organizations (a moot point) — concentrate their venom on the United States, the United Kingdom, France, and Israel. Lesser targets are Muslim countries which are seen as collaborating with those four or which have incarcerated members of the organization for criminal offences — for example, Egypt, Jordan, Saudi Arabia, and Kuwait. In the case of the major targets, there is no discrimination between citizens and governments: all are deemed to be equally guilty. Tactics include kidnapping, bomb attacks, assassination attempts, hijacking, straightforward murder, and both psychological and physical torture of kidnap victims. Furthermore, they appear to have locked into the international terrorist network and to be available for hire. An instructive listing, albeit biased towards the American audience, is contained in the 1985 Hearings of the Subcommittee on Europe and the Middle East of the Committee on Foreign Affairs of the House of Representatives concerning 'Islamic Fundamentalism and Islamic Radicalism'. Some fifty-five incidents are listed, covering the period from July 1982 to September 1985, and including the kidnapping of individuals, suicide bomb attacks, bombs in restaurants frequented by Americans, bomb attacks on airline offices, the assassination of the British Deputy High Commissioner in Bombay, and the attempted assassination of the Amir of Kuwait. The pattern is clear. Any and every manifestation of the imperialist is an enemy and may be attacked anywhere. In practice, attacks seem to occur in countries which are either in turmoil, as in Lebanon, or where security precautions are inadequate or difficult to implement effectively, as in Greece, Spain, Saudi Arabia, and Kuwait.

The Egyptian experience

Not surprisingly, the Egyptian experience has been the best documented: extremist activity in Egypt is of longer standing than elsewhere; coverage of trials of extremists in the media has been extensive; spectacular action, whether successful, as in the case of the assassination of Sadat, or not, as in the case of the attack on the Technical Military Academy in 1974, have caught the public attention; and extensive fieldwork by sociologists, political scientists, and others has resulted in a sizeable corpus of literature on the subject. However, the literature throws up a number of sometimes surprising points. In the first place, 'there are few observers, regardless of their ideological inclinations, who will not agree with the notion that religious extremism is alien to Egyptian values and norms':[31] a somewhat surprising conclusion, given the history of violence connected with the later years of the Muslim Brotherhood. Second, there seems to be common ground that extremism is an epiphenomenon, despite the variety of 'causes' adduced.[32] Yet available evidence indicates clearly that extremism is deeply entrenched as far as its adherents are concerned, though the degree of committed popular support is questionable. Third, the extent to which extremists can be and have been 'desensitized' or 'cured' is hotly debated. Available evidence does not provide a clear answer, although it does seem to deny a high rate of 'cures'. Finally, there is no generally agreed view on 'how wide-spread and deeply embedded is the militant phenomenon in Egyptian society'.[33] Yet religious extremism, which implies militancy, is apparently 'alien to Egyptian values and norms'. However, a note of caution would be wise: not only is the corpus of evidence in all four issues insufficient to permit a proper conclusion, but in addition, and perhaps more importantly, it is impossible to forecast the effects of the passage of time on the views of a relatively small proportion of the total population. However, it may be significant that the Muslim Brotherhood is generally regarded as an old man's organization and as insufficiently radical and active, and that it is for this reason that many of the clandestine extremist movements have broken away from them.

There appear to be two main streams of thought among Egyptian extremist movements, typified by the views of the *Jamaat al Muslimin* (the Society of Muslims, popularly known as *Takfir wa Hijra*) and the *Munadhdhamat al Tahrir al Islami* (the Islamic Liberation Organization). The former, though ostensibly founded by Shukri Mustafa, drew its ideological inspiration from the thinking of Ali Abduh Ismail, a graduate of al Azhar. However, the latter subsequently repudiated his doctrines, and it was left to Shukri Mustafa to elaborate them and attempt to put them into practice. Essentially he followed Sayyid Qutb's view of *jahiliya* but argued that the proper interpretation to be placed upon Sayyid Qutb's term *mufasila* or *'uzla* (separation or withdrawal) was an actual, physical separation from society. Furthermore, there was no salvation for any Muslim who failed to recognize this fact and join what was in effect an embryo Muslim society totally divorced and separated from the existing sinful society, which could then be excommunicated. Shukri Mustafa and his followers in fact consciously modelled their behaviour on that of the early Muslim community.

Until such time as they had gained sufficient strength to impose their beliefs on others, violent action, in the cause of *jihad*, would be eschewed. In short, they advocated the establishment of a new and envigorated Society of Muslims in a gradualist manner, in emulation of the early community. Indeed, he actually did withdraw into the Egyptian desert following the arrest of a number of adherents in 1973, though at this stage they were not perceived as dangerous by the state authorities.

The concentration on withdrawal or separation from the surrounding *jahili* society meant that Shukri Mustafa had to take on responsibility for housing, food, and other necessities of life, for material matters as well as spiritual matters. The Society, therefore,

> provided a total environment for its members, who were kept occupied in prayer, study, athletics, propaganda and work in the Takfir's enterprises. Thus the membership was insulated from society and made dependent on the group for all its needs. Errant members would be excommunicated and suffer physical punishment. If a member left the society he would be considered a *kafir* (infidel) since there could be no salvation outside the group.[34]

The Islamic Liberation Organization, *per contra*, though sharing Shukri Mustafa's views on the evil nature of iniquitous and infidel rulers, did not hold that all society was *jahili*: the blame for the weakness and debility lay squarely on the ruler and the government. The solution was the seizure of power and the imposition of the Muslim order from above. Accordingly they mounted a failed *coup d'état* in 1974, involving an attempted take-over of the Technical Military Academy in Helicopolis which was to be followed by the assassination of President Sadat.

In 1976, Shukri Mustafa attracted the serious attention of the security forces by mounting a series of punitive expeditions to chastise certain members of the *jama'at al muslimin* who had been won over to a rival leadership and who, by leaving the Society, stood accused of apostasy. The police intervened, arrested fourteen members, and issued a warrant for Shukri's arrest, thus precipitating a chain of events which led to the kidnapping and murder of a former Minister of *Awqaf*, Shaikh Husain al Dhahabi, in 1977. Some extremists have apparently claimed that the murder was the work of the police, who were attempting to implicate the Society to give an excuse for strong action against them. This seems implausible, since the group claimed responsibility for the kidnapping and threatened to execute the ex-Minister if their demands were not met. At all events, the police rounded up some 400 adherents, and the five leading members, including Shukri Mustafa, were executed in March 1978. The membership of the Society has been variously estimated at between 3,000 and 5,000 at its height. However, although the Society was in theory broken after the events of 1977–8, there are claims that it is still in existence, though underground. Its leadership is also, according to some, in exile. It seems likely that the 1977 round-up did not pick up all active members, that they still adhere to the basic beliefs of Shukri Mustafa, but that they have joined or founded other clandestine extremist groups.

A more shadowy group, known variously as *al jihad* and *al jihad al jadid* ('holy war' and 'new holy war') emerged towards the end of the 1970s. Dekmedjian suggests that it was first brought to public notice in 1978 following involvement in anti-Coptic activities, while Ansari claims that it represented a reorganization of the remnants of the Islamic Liberation Organization and 'was liquidated in 1978 after a bloody confrontation with the security forces in Alexandria', and Kepel implies that it had no real organization but was the result of splits between other groups, and began to coalesce in 1980.[35] However, Ansari also points out that the confession statements submitted to the public prosecutor in the wake of the assassination of President Sadat are inconsistent and concludes that 'some organised activity began to take place in 1980'. Dekmedjian offers a fairly detailed organizational chart.[36] It seems more plausible that *al jihad* or *al jihad al jadid* were both loose coalitions of small groups and individuals with similar political views, and that broadly the same individuals and views (subject always to the activities of the Egyptian security services) were to be found in both.

It is, of course, a moot point whether there is any clear distinction between them. Whatever the truth, it was this grouping, under the inspiration of Muhammad Abdul Salam Faraj, to whom reference has already been made, which mounted the successful attack on President Sadat. The central focus of his views was on the absolute necessity of *jihad* inclusive of armed revolt if the situation warranted it, combined with the rejection of any world view which was not in complete accord with his own. Since he believed that Egypt was an 'atheist' state and that 'Muslims who joined the government or are serving the state in the police and the military services must be fought for the role they play in strengthening the arm of an atheist state', it follows that he believed that 'the primary responsibility of the Jihad group is the overthrow of the government of unbelievers and the substitution of Islamic laws for positive laws'.[37] In due course, the logic of this argument led to the assassination of President Sadat in 1981, followed by the inevitable massive crack-down by the security forces.

As with organizations already considered briefly, the three main Egyptian extremist groupings exhibit what has now become the characteristic demographic and socio-economic features: predominantly students and graduates, and mainly from lower-middle and middle-class backgrounds; a rural or small-town background, but recent migrants to the larger conurbations; scientific and technical training; and the majority under thirty years of age. However, many of the rank and file, as opposed to the leadership, appear to be remarkably ignorant about the fundamentals of not merely the organization's ideologies but also of the faith they profess. In addition, there seems to be little in the shape of a practical policy or series of policies to be implemented once power is achieved: sweeping generalities are the norm. Nor has much thought been given to the structure of government and administration. These appear to be matters which will resolve themselves as a matter of course once the message has been accepted by sufficient people and the new, genuine, universal *umma* has been established. The rationale appears to be that once a genuine Muslim order or Muslim state has been created in which all citizens follow *al sirat al mustaqim* forms and structures will evolve as necessary.

In addition to the major organizations covered briefly above, there have been many others — for example, *junud Allah, shabab Muhammad, junud al rahman, qif wa tabayyin* (God's warriors, Muhammads' youth, warriors of the Merciful One, Halt and Expound) — but they appear to be relatively small and to disappear after suppression by the security forces — only to rise again, phoenix-like, under a new name and possibly a new leadership, but with the same beliefs and aims. Although as dedicated to violence as the three more important groupings, these small organizations seem unlikely, on grounds of size alone, to be capable of much more than limited local insurrections and possibly assassinations.

Iraq, Bahrain, and South and South-East Asia

Although violence has been seen in most Muslim countries and has often been supported by clandestine Muslim organizations, the incidence of 'actual violent group behaviour committed collectively against the state or other actors in the name of Islam' in the sense intended by Saad Eddin Ibrahim and committed by organizations falling into group (c) is remarkably small. The activities of *hizb al da'wa* (the Call or Missionary Party) in Iraq, for example, have been generally ineffective and have been related more to the position of the Shi'a in Iraq and to more secular concerns than to a desire to impose a particular form of order on the country. Nevertheless, it is as well to remember that Ayatollah Sayyid Mahdi al Hakim, the son of the founder of *hizb al da'wa*, stated publicly that

> the main objective of this party is to establish an Islamic state . . . The leaders of the Da'wah party had also consulted the leaders of al-Ikhwan al-Muslimun who broadly agreed that the objective of establishing an Islamic state constituted the best programme of cooperation between the Shi'i and Sunni Muslims.[38]

Furthermore, there were open calls for social reforms and the establishment of an Islamic state during the Muharram demonstrations in 1979, and there were massive demonstrations following the arrest of Ayatullah Sayyid Muhammad Baqr al Sadr, the recognized leader of the Shi'a community and of *al da'wa*, later the same year.

Notwithstanding the Iranian connection — most clandestine Iraqi groups have their headquarters in Iran and are connected with the Higher Council of the Islamic Revolution — the failure of such organizations to garner much popular support in Iraq itself is suggestive that the Iraqi Shi'a are collectively more akin in their objectives to Amal under Nabih Berri in Lebanon, but are relatively docile. Similarly, the violent activities of the Movement of the Forces of Allah in Malaysia appear to be related to a question of identity with more than a touch of racism and xenophobia: in Malaysia, the Malay community and the Muslim community are virtually identical. A similar pattern can be discerned in Thailand, where it is significant that the major opposition movements among the Malay (and therefore Muslim) community in Thailand do not, in their names at least, appeal to Islam — the Pattani National Liberation Front, the National Liberation Front, and the Pattani United Liberation Organization. There are, however, two organizations which do merit further consideration: the Islamic Front for the Liberation of Bahrain and the Hizballah in Lebanon.

The Islamic Front for the Liberation of Bahrain is essentially a Bahraini Shi'a movement with strong links with Iran, which mounted an abortive *coup d'état* in December 1981, the conspiracy having been picked up by the security forces. In terms of Bahraini politics, however, the Front really represents real or imagined grievances by a section of the Shi'a population concerning political, social, and economic discrimination. They are, it might be argued, today's equivalent of the National Liberation Front of the 1950s and 1960s which drew its inspiration from Nasser's philosophy and which was essentially a vehicle for violent protest by the Bahraini Shi'a. In other words, the Islamic Front for the Liberation of Bahrain should be seen as an organization which was originally geared to relatively secular and political objectives, but which has been taken over by individuals, such as Hadi Modarrasi, who are committed to the ideals of the Iranian revolution. In this there is an interesting parallel with the manner in which the Dhofar Liberation Front in Oman, originally established to seek greater Dhofari involvement in the administration of Dhofar, was taken over by left-wing ideologues and transformed into the Popular Form for the Liberation of Oman and the Arabian Gulf. Notwithstanding this, the Islamic Front for the Liberation of Bahrain is now ideologically committed to the establishment of an Islamic Republic on the Iranian pattern and is clearly ready to use violence to achieve that end. It equally clearly depends on the Iranian connections, and the strength of real support among the Bahraini Shi'a seems less than full and whole-hearted. In this connection, the Bahraini 'establishment' contains a sizeable number of well-to-do Shi'a.

The Lebanese experience: Hizballah

The Hizballah in Lebanon is a shadowy organization competing with Amal for the leadership of the Lebanese Shi'a. Hizballah is dedicated to the establishment of an Islamic Republic in Lebanon, on the pattern of Iran. Its main demands were listed in a manifesto or declaration issued in February 1985 as:

(a) Complete evacuation of the Israeli Army from the Lebanon 'as a prelude for the removal of Israel from existence and liberating Jerusalem from the claws of occupation';
(b) 'America, France and their allies must leave Lebanon once and for all, and any imperialist influence in the country must be terminated';

(c) 'The Phalangists must be subjected to trial for all the crimes they have committed against Muslims and Christians with encouragement from America and Israel';

(d) 'All our Lebanese people must be given the chance of determining their future and choosing the system of government they want, bearing in mind that we will not give up our commitment of the rule of Islam.'

The manifesto went on to state that Hizballah feared no one but God and would not tolerate injustice, aggression, and humiliation and commented that

> the United States and its NATO partners and the Zionist state which has usurped the holy Islamic land of Palestine have exercised, and are still exercising, aggression on us with a view to humiliating us. We, therefore, are always on the alert and constantly girding ourselves to repel the aggression and defend our religion, existence, and dignity.[39]

The underlying philosophy has been set out in greater detail in a recent interview with Ayatollah Muhammad Husain Fadhlallah, who is held to be the organization's spiritual leader, though he has regularly denied that he is the Hizballah leader.[40] He believes that the violence endemic in the Middle East is the result of the establishment of the state of Israel, and that Muslim extremism is violence forced upon Muslims when all other means of resolving problems have failed. He clearly does wish to see an Islamic Republic in Lebanon, but appears to be realistic in recognizing that it can be no more than a dream for the foreseeable future. He has also condemned kidnapping, hijacking, and other terrorist acts, although he indicated that he understands and sympathizes with the reasons why such acts are committed. He is, nonetheless, thought by many to be connected with Islamic Jihad, an even more shadowy group which has claimed responsibility for numerous acts of violence in Lebanon. There is no clear proof either way, but he is known to be 'close to Hussein al-Musawi whose involvement in the bombing of the US Embassy in April 1983 and of the US and French military headquarters in October 1983 is also suspected'.[41]

Hizballah does engage in violence, and does so not purely for practical reasons, as does Amal, but for ideological reasons. In assessing the extent to which this is true, however, we do well to remember that Hizballah appears to be an umbrella organization representing views of great diversity and that it is not a well-defined organization with lists of members and membership cards: rather, it is a sphere of influence; and within that sphere of influence lies Islamic Amal, led by Hussain al Musawi, and the more militant and extremist followers of Subhi al Tufaili, Abbas al Musawi, and Hassan Nasrullah. James Piscatori has defined the relationship between Hizballah, Islamic Amal, and Islamic Jihad neatly. 'In short', he comments, 'Islamic Amal seems to be the military wing of Hizballah, and the Jihad groups the commando wing of the Islamic Amal. Despite these roots in Lebanon, the Jihad groups are essentially transnational in character'.[42]

Conclusions

A number of general conclusions can be drawn from this necessarily brief survey of extremists, but none will apply to all four groups. As far as the imposition by force of an Islamic order is concerned, I have already argued that this has a certain valid legitimacy, however much the methods may be objectionable. However, failure to understand the real concerns of non-Muslims, of Muslims of a different sect, or of nominal Muslims is bound to lead to opposition. Most countries today are pluralist societies and pluralist societies tend to be less doctrinaire and more tolerant. Both attitudes are under attack when an Islamic order is imposed from above against the wishes and aspirations of the greater part of the population, and also when there is a fear that this might happen, however unjustified that fear might be. Donald K. Emmerson commented on this with great percipience in his discussion of Islam in Indonesia, suggesting that

> So long as practising Muslims remain a qualitative minority in a statistical majority, in a diverse society, in a fragmented environment the temptation to enforce piety from the 'top down' will remain. And because of those very conditions, non- and nominal Muslims will continue to fear that 'political solution'.[43]

With suitable adjustments, that comment can apply throughout the Muslim world, with the qualification that control of or support from the armed forces (or the lack) is a crucial factor. Finally, the difficulties implied in the foregoing are not exclusive to the Muslim world nor to faith-based political systems: India, Israel, the Philippines, Namibia, South Africa, and Zimbabwe, to note but a few, seem sufficient proof.

Group (b) is perhaps best seen in terms of the classic freedom fighters — that is, of groups who seek to oppose the imposition of unwelcome political systems, or who seek to redress an imbalance in a political system, having failed to achieve this through more peaceful means. The crucial factor here, it seems to the present author, is the degree of external support combined with the degree of internal cohesion. In neither case, therefore, is there any real difference between Muslims and non-Muslims.

The important factor to bear in mind about the third group is that though the number of organizations is large and is, apparently, still proliferating, their actual membership is small, and they are representative neither of the majority of Muslims, nor of the majority of the activist trend. 'Though effective in political agitation, disruption, and assassination, they have generally not been successful in mass mobilization.'[44] That judgement might have to be amended, however, in the event of an alliance between activists and a broadly popular movement and an extremist group, though it seems likely that the former would prevail. In any case, the experience of the Muslim Brotherhood in Egypt suggests that violence is a two-edged weapon. Another possible modifier of this judgement resides in the fact that proscribed organizations frequently became more sophisticated in their structure and learn to plug into the international black market in armaments. On both counts, it will be less easy to identify and to deal with them, and they may become more attractive if social, economic, and political problems remain unsolved.

The fourth group will, by all accounts, be with us for many years. A successful resolution of the Arab–Israeli dispute is unlikely to affect the issue, since fanatics are by definition impervious to reason and their aims are more comprehensive than the mere destruction of Israel. The same applies to their other aims, and since their acts of violence seem to be random, precautionary measures such as those already being implemented in many countries can do little more than attempt to contain the level of violence. Fadhlallah's denunciation of some of the acts of this group may in due course have an effect, but this seems unlikely, given the context in which it was made.

Finally, we do well to remember that the extremists, as the term has been used, are an extreme and violent manifestation of the more law-abiding activist trend. As long as the latter continue to seek their version of paradise on earth, as long, that is, as the present phase in the cycle identified in Chapter 8 continues, there is bound to be an extremist wing. Nevertheless, the judgement that the extremists constitute a minority and are likely to remain so, despite the cautious note sounded above, remains broadly correct for a number of reasons, not least because they are extreme in their views: for man is generally inclined towards moderate attitudes, and the violence of the extremists militates against the orderly regulation of society which is necessary. Moreover, their views, when stripped of all the eloquent phraseology, are remarkably barren and sterile, offering nothing tangible to the average person. It is, perhaps, no surprising matter that the only two broadly based movements to have achieved a degree of success were the Muslim Brotherhood before the onset of violence and the Iranian revolution, since their leaders understood only too well the need to satisfy the material as well as the spiritual desires of their followers. In addition, it is significant that the more peaceful activist groupings in many parts of the Muslim world have recognized this fact and have embarked upon a policy of economic self-help as a valuable means of gaining support. Furthermore, extremism and violence are distasteful and alienating, particularly when they appear to be used not *fi sabil Allah* — in the path of God — but in an almost naked pursuit of power by groups whose devoutness must be suspect because their knowledge is scanty.

10

Envoi

The Introduction suggested that both newer and older scholarship about Islam was in some ways unsatisfactory and reasons for this view were set out briefly. The reasons for the dissatisfaction were discussed in Chapter 1, as were a number of points which should infuse any *practical* generalized view of Islam. The subsequent analysis drew out a number of regularly recurring themes which collectively suggest that Muslims have a more practical concept of what Islam comprehends than would appear to be the case from much of the literature, particularly the more recent Muslim literature. Can any conclusions be validly drawn, and in particular, does a different way of looking at Islam emerge, a way which may have more practical value? — and if so, what is it?

The first issue that needs to be addressed is the implications of the argument that it does not matter greatly what non-Muslims may think, since in the last analysis, Islam is what Muslims believe it to be. This argument might have some validity if Islam could be considered *in vacuo*; but the interrelationship between the Muslim and the non-Muslim world requires that Islam should be considered (for practical purposes at least) *coram populo*. Thus, the manner in which non-Muslims manage their relationships with Muslims, at individual, communal, and national levels, is conditioned by how they think of Islam and Muslims; and the manner in which Muslims manage their relationships with non-Muslims is conditioned by their own views of what Islam is, their perceptions of how the non-Muslim world sees Islam, and the manner in which non-Muslims deal with them. This is, admittedly, a gross over-simplification, but it does serve to emphasize two important points: the better the understanding non-Muslims have of what Muslims believe Islam to be, the better they are likely to be at managing the relationship at all levels; and the better Muslims are at identifying both their own and others' actual understanding of Islam, the better they will be, in their turn, at managing the relationship.

However, a brief examination of the relationship between Muslims and non-Muslims at all levels suggests that the relationship, despite its importance to both sides, has been generally mishandled (though, as always, there are exceptions). Thus, the Western world and the USSR are still perceived in the Muslim world as seeking to impose cultural, economic, and intellectual imperialism, and in so doing demonstrating at best a belief in the inherent inferiority of Islam and at worst a contempt for it and for its followers. The West and the USSR are perceived as hostile, lacking real understanding, failing to comprehend what Islam means to Muslims, and as feeling more comfortable with either the crude stereotypes noted in Chapter 1, with conventional views, and with academic discussion of doctrine and theory which is demonstrably divorced from the real world. Western perceptions of the Muslim world are similarly flawed: crude stereotypes abound and the more enlightened tend to accept simple black-and-white images. Thus, Muslims are arrogant, militant, greedy, insincere, lacking in proper understanding of the West's position, often naive, and prone to blaming their misfortunes on others: but in reality, neither perception is true. Although the Muslim view is a defensive and not always justified perception, there is some justification for it and to this extent there is some validity in Edward Said's criticism of the 'orientalists'. It must, however, be said that he offers just as stereotyped a picture as do those he criticizes and that the Muslim world cannot be absolved from blame. The conclusion is simple but very important: those who have to deal with Islam and the Muslim world should cease to try to define what Islam is and what Muslims are; they should, rather, seek to understand what Muslims believe Islam to be and how it conditions their thoughts, actions, and attitudes. Correspondingly, Muslims might be well advised to show greater understanding of the non-Muslim world and to avoid the generalized statements and condemnations which all too often hit the headlines: for in an interdependent world, understanding and tolerance are essential attributes.

This leads naturally into the second issue: what do *Muslims* believe Islam to be, and how can the non-Muslim identify it? It is clearly insufficient either to concentrate on doctrine and theory or to concentrate on what Muslims say, since both approaches have been shown to be demonstrably wanting in the preceding analysis.

This is not to suggest, however, that either is unimportant, since clearly the doctrine and the theory represent the unattainable ideal to which all Muslims aspire; and what Muslims say may represent at the least what they may wish others to hear, and may even represent their own true beliefs. Whichever it be, it is important to recognize that what Muslims say should not necessarily be taken uncritically at face value; it is also necessary to consider the practice, for what Muslims show by their actions and attitudes as forming part of their understanding of Islam is a significant pointer to what Muslims believe Islam to be. Thus, we seem to have three guides to what Muslims believe Islam to be: doctrine and theory; what Muslims say; and what Muslims do. However, the relationship between these three is not static and varies according to circumstances, geography, history, and so on; and no single monolithic perception can be adduced. The implied, and very real, diversity of doctrine and theory is not merely a reflection of the differences between Sunni, Shi'a, Zaidi, Ismaili, and Ibadhi; it also reflects the diversity of national, communal, and individual experience, all of which, as the analysis clearly shows, are significant modifiers of the doctrine and the theory, both universally and also in a more limited territorial manner. Thus, for example, Ismaili doctrine was at one stage such that Ismailis were regarded as heterodox even by Shi'a standards, if not downright heretical, yet Ismaili doctrine as exemplified today by the Aga Khan has pragmatically adjusted to circumstances and is hardly distinguishable in practice from mainstream Muslim doctrine. Doctrine and theory are thus rarely straightforward; are certainly not as straightforward and monolithic as some Muslim intellectuals suggest they are; and have exhibited continuous multi-stranded development and reaction to reality.

Similarly, what Muslims say (or write) exhibits, and has exhibited over the centuries, a great diversity for similar reasons. There is, however, a difference, in that what Muslims say and write very often reflects what they think Islam ought to be and derives largely from the particular interpretation of the doctrine and theory to which they adhere, and from their view of the relationship between the ideal doctrine and the real world. Like the doctrine, therefore, what Muslims say is often a description of the unattainable ideal, though dressed up as realizable in practice. However, it may also be an attempt to reconcile doctrine and reality; or even (e.g. Sayyid Qutb) a total rejection of reality and of developments over the centuries. Although different schools, or individuals, generally claim that their particular interpretation represents the only true Islam, they normally stop short of identifying the others as deviant, erroneous, or heretical, preferring to accuse the entire community of deviation and error, and leaving the reader or listener to draw the right conclusion. Indeed, in much of the modern literature, it is often governments who stand accused: by implication, the *umma* is compelled to follow false interpretations and deviance as a result of the coercive power of government. However, just as no single authoritative statement of doctrine and theory can be offered, so no single authoritative expression of what Muslims believe Islam to be can be identified on the basis of what Muslims say. Indeed, all views expressed, save only those which can be authoritatively rejected as contrary to the revelation, have validity and legitimacy for some part of the *umma* at least, at some time in history.

At a more practical level, practice — that is, what Muslims do — is important in that it shows clearly what different Muslim communities recognize as part of their understanding of Islam. Moreover, if it is accepted, as it should be, that the ideal is unattainable, practice surely represents attempts to live up to that ideal in a constantly changing and diverse world. Inevitably, therefore, there are considerable differences, but to define all differences in practice and all changes as un-Islamic merely because they fall short of the ideal, or because they are not consistent with a particular vision, seems quite unjustified. This applies not only to the individual, but also to communities and governments in the Muslim world, since both are often influenced by collective perceptions of what Islam really comprehends; their practice is often a creditable attempt to reconcile the ideal and reality in a manner consistent with general principles; and may represent a genuine, if occasionally cynical, attempt to govern in accordance with an imprecise revelation. More importantly, practice is a significant modifier of the theory. However, modern modifications should not be regarded as merely cynical attempts to bring theory into line with actual practice. Rather, they should be seen as part of a pragmatic and dynamic process reflecting the changed circumstances of the *umma*: for example, the manner in which state plurality has been incorporated into the doctrine; the gradual acceptance of *zakat* as a state-imposed tax whose proceeds form merely one part of government revenue; the change in the theoretical basis of international relations; and the participation of Muslim states in multinational organizations without significant criticism.

It may, however, be argued that this suggests that Muslims, collectively or individually, are entitled to their own interpretation of what Islam is and that this runs counter to the fundamental tenet that Islam comprehends God's will in all areas of human activity. There are, however, few who have in the past insisted, or who now insist, that the *Qur'an* is a detailed exposition of God's command: the more generally accepted view is that it contains general principles and the argument is directed more to the validity of the application of those principles and the extent to which divine ordination or inspiration have been vouchsafed to those undertaking the task of interpretation and application. Indeed, it may be argued that the very imprecision and opacity of the revelation constitute clear evidence of its genuineness, on the grounds that Allah, who is omniscient, would not be so misguided as to lay down detailed instructions for all time when He would have known that circumstances would inevitably change. Furthermore, if the developments in doctrine and practice, which represent fourteen centuries of gradual change, and the emergence of differing concepts and practices among the Muslims which are clearly influenced by differing historical, geographical, social, and cultural experiences were not part of the grand plan, this fact and Allah's displeasure would surely have been made manifest early on. It is easy and comfortable to talk of deviation and error, but it does not in any way offer an explanation.

The next issue follows on naturally. The notion of consensus has been part of Muslim doctrine for centuries, but the term has been variously defined and does not necessarily mean complete unanimity. It is reasonable to accept that what the majority of the Muslim population of a particular state or community accepts as consistent with their understanding of Islam represents the consensus within that state or community. Thus, if, as has been suggested, 'the great majority of the Syrian people, in spite of considerable dissatisfaction with the Asad regime, were disinclined to participate in an Islamic revolution',[1] it is reasonable to conclude that the particular manifestation of Islam represented by the Syrian Muslim Brotherhood and the Higher Command of the Islamic Revolution in Syria was not acceptable to the general consensus among Syrians. Similarly, the lack of general support for extremist movements in Egypt, the failure of the ultra-conservative political parties in Malaysia in the recent elections, and the general lack of support in Saudi Arabia for the group led by Juhaiman al 'Utaibi, who were responsible for the seizure of the Grand Mosque in 1979, suggest that the particular forms of Islam represented by the Egyptian extremists, the ultra-conservatives in Malaysia, and the followers of Juhaiman al 'Utaibi in Saudi Arabia are not generally acceptable to the communities in question. However, there is a further significant point here. To the extent that consensus has a legitimizing force, it may be argued that lack of active popular opposition to governments in the Muslim world on doctrinal grounds means tacit acceptance that such governments are at least not contravening the local consensus in any large measure; and that such acceptance may have the force of providing practical and functional legitimacy which, in the absence of doctrinally valid legitimacy, is better than nothing — and is, in any case, yet another example of practice influencing doctrine.

The notion of consensus may also explain the relative lack of success of the activists, who in general seek in practical terms to jettison some fourteen centuries of development which are part of the cultural, social, and historical heritage of a variety of Muslim societies. This denial offends the susceptibilities of the majority; it is not recognized as valid by the consensus; and therefore has little lasting appeal. It also plays a role in the attitude of the Shi'a in Pakistan who oppose the particular form of Zia ul-Haq's drive towards the Islamization of the Pakistani polity. They prefer to live in a more secular polity, one which is less rigidly oriented towards a particular form of Islam, on the grounds that only in this way will they be able to live in accordance with their own particular form of Shi'ism. Khomeini's *Velayat-i-Faqih* is not for them, but neither is Zia ul-Haq's uncompromising Sunnism. Similarly, the Shi'a and the Ismaili communities in Saudi Arabia seem prepared, within limits, to co-operate with the Al Saud government, provided there is not too much interference with their rituals and practices, or too much active discrimination against them. Furthermore, in Iraq, notwithstanding the objectives of the Da'wa Party, the Shi'a are generally accommodationist in political terms, except when the Ba'ath government seeks to impose overly discriminatory and oppressive measures. The conclusion, of course, is unexceptionable: consensus, like doctrine and theory, is rarely straightforward.

The framework set out above suggests that Muslims in general do in fact believe Islam — or their own particular understanding of it — to be dynamic and susceptible to change, while insisting against the evidence that it is static and unchanging; a seeming inconsistency. The explanation appears to lie in a relationship similar to that between the complete separation of Church and state and the functional separation discussed in Chapter 8. For Muslim insistence on the unchanging and static nature of the revelation as universally applicable in any age serves to obscure the changes which have actually taken place until such time as they have been given respectable antecedents and have been effectively incorporated into the authorized version. It is important to emphasize that in this Muslims do not generally act out of cynical self-interest and deliberate falsification. Rather, the process is largely unconscious and the result of Muslims being conceptual prisoners of the doctrine of immutability: they find it difficult, therefore, to distinguish between a holistic immutability and a functional immutability, other than in the distinction between *ibadat* and *mu'amalat*. Moreover, if Muslims are confused, is it any wonder that outside observers are too?

What, it may be asked, about the Islamic revival and the more extreme and violent manifestations of Islam? Once again, no precise and universally applicable conclusions can be offered. The revival is neither monolithic nor co-ordinated, despite a measure of trans-national appeal by certain popular ideologues. The particular triggers differ from country to country, and may even differ within a particular country. Hence, the form taken by the revival is varied, and is affected not least by demographic characteristics: it appeals most to the young and is therefore more overt in countries with a predominantly young population. However, whether that appeal will carry forward into middle age is an open question. All that can be said with any certainty about the present revival is that it is part of a regularly recurring cycle and that it is qualitatively different from its predecessors. Whether it will remain part of the cycle and will be succeeded by another attempt at synthesis, or represents the beginning of a break in the cycle, cannot be forecast at this juncture. However, a tentative conclusion may be drawn on the basis of recent events in Malaysia and Pakistan: in some countries at least the revival appears to have peaked, and although activists continue to press for Islamization, the public response is critical. On the other hand, the recent Saudi decision to replace *sahib al jalala* (His/Your Majesty) with *khadim al haramain al sharifain* (Servant, or Protector, of the two Holy Places) indicates continuing sensitivity and a concern to placate the activists. Not surprisingly, there is no sign of the emergence of a unified ideology: for despite the apparent unifying force of conservative orthodoxy, abetted by the mass media and the spread of literacy, the unity of the Muslim world remains a pious fiction and individual states must be considered separately.

There is no universal truth, save the profession of faith.

Whether or not the cycle continues or is broken, activist and extremist views will continue to be voiced, since doctrine is open to differing interpretations and they will always be able to rest their case on their own interpretation and to find doctrinal justification for it. Given the role of consensus discussed earlier, however, the degree of popular support they will receive will always be less than they claim, and will be influenced by other more mundane considerations. Only the emergence of a more practically oriented approach to theory, such as that advocated by Rashid al Ghanoushi, the leader of the Islamic Tendency in Tunisia, and a realistic appraisal of the causes of the disarray of the Muslim World, such as that of Dr Rashid al Mubarak,[2] are likely to reduce the prospects of continued emergence of theory-bound activism — and the chances of that happening across the Muslim world seem slight. Until then, difficulties such as those encountered in doing business with Iran today will continue to surface from time to time. It is therefore important to understand that the root cause of those difficulties is Khomeini's insistence on playing the game according to his own rules and his rejection of the rules generally accepted by the rest of the world. He has thus rejected any accommodation with internationally accepted norms and reverted to classical doctrine — albeit his own version of it. An underlying point of some significance is that such action can normally be justified in doctrinal terms, thus pre-empting potential opposition.

Given the diversity and imprecision regularly noted in this study, can any general conclusions be drawn on the apparently simple, but infinitely complex question: how do Muslims perceive Islam and how should the non-Muslim approach the issue? It is surely right to accept the regularly repeated claim that Islam is more than just a matter of faith and ritual, but provides guidance in all areas of human activity. However, the assertion does need elaboration for it is clear from what Muslims do, individually and collectively, that Islam is for them an overall framework within which normal human activity takes place, and that the general principles influence the manner in which such activities are conducted. In this, they are not greatly different to adherents of other ideologies, either faith-based or otherwise, except that the relationship is generally more overt and recognizable. However, the degree of influence is, inevitably, affected by more pragmatic and familiar considerations — the imperatives of power, wealth and poverty, status, self-interest, and public interest, and the need for generally acceptable rules for regulating man' relations with his fellow man at both the domestic and the international levels.

The vision of Islam presented briefly above is not, it must be admitted, an easy one for the non-Muslim observer to comprehend, since there are few clearly defined premises. It is exactly this lack of precision and sharp definition, however, which is the most significant feature, comprehending, as it does, the diversity of doctrine, the diversity of interpretation, and the diversity of practice, which overlays the fundamental unity of Islam. Indeed, Islam is protean, taking different forms in different places, according to the historical, social, cultural, geographical, and intellectual experience; and until this is fully recognized and incorporated into Western (and Russian, for that matter) perceptions, misunderstandings are all too likely in dealing with the Muslim world. Palmerston commented in a despatch to the British Minister in Lisbon in 1836:

> Political Connections between Governments are neither useful nor lasting unless they are rooted in the Sentiments and Sympathies of Nations; and it is only by extensive Commercial Intercourse that a Community of Interests can be permanently established between the People of different Countries.[3]

This might legitimately be modified to read:

> Political connections between the governments of the Muslim and non-Muslim world are neither useful nor lasting unless they are rooted in a deep understanding of what Islam means to its followers; and it is only by extensive and sympathetic understanding of Islam that a community of interests between them can be permanently established.

That deep understanding must include recognition that Islam is much more complex than it is represented to be; that the views of both Orientalist and Muslim intellectuals which have become conventional wisdom are defective; that Islam is diverse in form and imprecise in articulation; that the revelation provides general principles which are immutable but that it is legitimate to apply those principles in a manner appropriate to time and place; that Islam forms both the framework within which normal social, economic, political, and intellectual activity takes place and, simultaneously, a source of guidance for that activity; that it does not preclude other pragmatic considerations and may indeed encourage them; that practice does modify theory; that Muslims accept change largely by a process of obscuring its existence; that the Muslim world today cannot be divorced from the fourteen centuries of change, development, and experience which have made it what it is; that Islam is not intrinsically antipathetic to the process of economic development and modernization; that how non-Muslims think of Islam conditions the manner in which they deal with Muslims, which in turn conditions how Muslims think of and deal with non-Muslims; that some Muslims are as confused about their real beliefs about Islam as are non-Muslims; that individual and collective interpretations of Islam range from dogmatic assertion of the classic doctrine through attempts at synthesis to speculative rationality; that the imprecision and opacity of the revelation permits interpretations which are rigidly doctrinaire, unrealistic, and doctrinally not opposable; and that no single authoritative and universally accepted definition is possible. As James Piscatori put it succinctly:

> The only definite thing one can say about the term 'Islam' is that it is Protean and imprecise. Every Muslim can agree that the profession of faith, 'there is no God but God and Muhammad is his Prophet', is an article of faith and not susceptible to differing interpretations, but there is little agreement that many other principles and ideas mean the same to everyone and are beyond question and change.[4]

This quotation, which encapsulates the approach followed in this volume, is a fitting conclusion.

Notes

Introduction

1. Compare, for example, Karen House's article 'The West will remain hostage', *The Wall Street Journal*, 20 June 1985; John Laffin, *The Dagger of Islam*, London: Sphere, 1979; Leon Uris, *The Haj*, New York: Doubleday, 1984; Wael B. Hallaq, 'Was the Gate of Ijtihad closed?', *International Journal of Middle Eastern Studies* 16 (1984); Yvonne Y. Haddad, 'The Quranic justification for an Islamic Revolution: the view of Sayyid Qutb', *Middle East Journal* 37 (3) (Winter 1983); Mohamed S. El-Awa, *Punishment in Islamic Law: A Comparative Study*, Indianapolis: American Trust Publications, 1982; James P. Piscatori, *Islam in a World of Nation-States*, Cambridge: Cambridge University Press, 1986; Malise Ruthven, *Islam in the World*, Harmondsworth: Penguin Books, 1984.

2. Nabeel Abraham, 'The lived reality of Islam', *Middle East International*, 28 September 1984, p. 19.

3. See, for example, Salem Azzam (ed.) *Islam and Contemporary Society*, London and New York: Longman in association with the Islamic Council of Europe, 1982; Khurshid Ahmad (ed.) *Studies in Islamic Economics*, Leicester: The Islamic Foundation, 1980; Muhammad Asad, *The Principles of State and Government in Islam*, Gibraltar: Dar al-Andalus, 1980; Abul A'la Maududi, *Islamic Law and Constitution*, trans. Khurshid Ahmad, Lahore: Islamic Publications, 8th edition, 1983; Sayyid Qutb, *Milestones*, trans. S. Badrul Hasan, Karachi: International Islamic Publishers, 1981.

4. For example, H.A.R. Gibb, *Mohammedanism*, London: Oxford University Press, 1949; Ignaz Goldziher, *Introduction to Islamic Theology and Law*, trans. Andras and Ruth Hamori, Princeton and Guildford: Princeton University Press, 1981; A.S. Tritton, *Islam*, London: Hutchinson, 1951; W. Montgomery Watt, *What is Islam?*, London: Longman, 2nd edition, 1979; Sir W. Muir, *The Caliphate: Its Rise, Decline and Fall*, ed. T.H. Weir, Edinburgh: John Grant, new and revised edition, 1915.

5. The names cited have been selected at random and are merely illustrative. Many other eminent scholars figure in the notes. John Voll, Professor of History at the University of New Hampshire, has produced a masterpiece of compressed writing and an extremely useful quarry in his *Islam: Continuity and Change in the Modern World*, Boulder and Harlow: Westview Press and Longman, 1982. The late Hamid Enayat was Professor of Political Science at Tehran University and later taught at Oxford University. His *Modern Islamic Political Thought*, London: Macmillan, 1982 is a useful and clearly written introduction to a complex subject. John Esposito is a Professor at the College of the Holy Cross in Worcester, Massachusetts, and has written extensively on Islam. His *Voices of Resurgent Islam*, New York and Oxford: Oxford University Press, 1983 and (with J.J. Donohue) *Islam in Transition*, New York and Oxford: Oxford University Press, 1982 are useful compilations, the first of current scholarship and the second of Muslim views. Mohamed S. El-Awa has produced a

meticulous study of Muslim criminal law in his *Punishment in Islamic Law: A Comparative Study*, Indianapolis: American Trust Publications, 1982. Albert Hourani taught for many years at Oxford University where he was a major influence on oriental studies in the UK generally. He has written extensively on Middle Eastern and Islamic topics. For this study, his *Arabic Thought in the Liberal Age, 1798–1939*, London: Oxford University Press, 1962 has been invaluable. The late Noel Coulson (1928–86) was Professor of Oriental Laws at the School of Oriental and African Studies, University of London, from 1967 until his death. He has written the standard introductory text on Muslim law in his *A History of Islamic Law*, Edinburgh: University Press, 1964. Majid Khadduri (1908–) was Professor of Middle Eastern Studies at the School of Advanced International Studies of the Johns Hopkins University from 1949 to 1970 and has written widely on Muslim law, and the Muslim law of nations. His *The Islamic Law of Nations: Shaybani's Siyar* (1966), *War and Peace in the Law of Islam* (1955), and *The Islamic Conception of Justice* (1986), all published by the Johns Hopkins Press, are magisterial contributions to the literature. James Piscatori, currently Associate Professor at the School of Advanced International Studies, is one of the leading members of the new generation of scholars of Islam. He has published widely, and his most recent volume, *Islam in a World of Nation-States*, Cambridge: Cambridge University Press, 1986 is mandatory reading for students of Islam and international relations.

6. Ignaz Goldziher (1850–1921) is generally regarded as the founder of the modern school of Islamic studies. His views are somewhat dated in places, but his *Vorlesung über den Islam*, translated by Andras and Ruth Hamori under the title *Introduction to Islamic Theology and Law*, Princeton: Princeton University Press, 1981 is still well worth reading. Sir Hamilton Gibb (1895–1971) was Professor of Arabic at the School of Oriental and African Studies, University of London, Oxford University and Harvard University successively from 1930 to 1964. During this period he was a major influence on the study of Arabic and Islam. His publications include *Mohammedanism*, London: Oxford University Press, 1949 (later retitled *Islam*); *Modern Trends in Islam*, Chicago: University of Chicago Press, 1950; and *Studies on the Civilisation of Islam*, Boston: Beacon Press, 1962. All are standard, if somewhat dated, introductory texts. Joseph Schacht (1902–69) was Professor of Arabic at the University of Leiden, 1954–9, and Professor of Arabic and Islamics at Columbia University, 1959–69. The leading authority on Muslim law in his day, he built on the earlier work of Goldziher in formulating a thesis on the origins of Muslim law which remains irrefutable in its broad outline. His major works include *The Origins of Muhammadan Jurisprudence*, Oxford: Oxford University Press, 1950, and *An Introduction to Islamic Law*, Oxford: Oxford University Press, 1964. Muhammad Abduh (1849–1905) is generally regarded as the father of Egyptian modernism and as a major influence outside Egypt. His contribution is discussed in Chapter 7. Rashid Ridha (1865–1935) was a follower of Abduh but later became a conservative reformer emphasising the importance of the faith and practice of the first generation of Muslims. His contribution is also discussed in Chapter 7.

Chapter 1: Ways of Looking at Islam

1. Abd al Monein Said Ali and M.W. Wenner, 'Modern Islamic reform movements: the Muslim Brotherhood in contemporary Egypt', *The Middle East Journal* 36 (3) (Summer 1982): 336.

2. For example, Abdur Rahman I. Doi, *Shari'ah: The Islamic Law*, London: Ta Ha Publishers, 1984; Farouq Hassan, *The Concept of State and Law in Islam*, Lanham: University Press of America, 1981; Abul A'la Maududi, *Islamic Law and Constitution*, trans. Khurshid Ahmad, Lahore: Islamic Publications, 8th edition, 1983.

3. Nabeel Abraham, 'The lived reality of Islam', *Middle East International*, 28 September 1984, p. 19.

4. John L. Esposito (ed.), *Voices of Resurgent Islam*, New York and Oxford: Oxford University Press, 1983, p. viii; James P. Piscatori, *Islam in a World of Nation-States*, Cambridge: Cambridge University Press, 1986, p. 3.

5. Hamid Enayat, *Modern Islamic Political Thought*, London: Macmillan, 1982, p. 1.

6. See, for example, H.A.R. Gibb, 'Constitutional organisation' and Asaf A.A. Fyzee, 'Shi'i legal theories', both in M. Khadduri and H.J. Liebesney (eds) *Law in the Middle East, Vol. I, Origin and Development of Islamic Law*, Washington, DC: Middle East Institute, 1955, pp. 3–27 and 113–131 respectively; and Moojan Momen, *An Introduction to Shi'i Islam*, New Haven and London: Yale University Press, 1985, p. 147ff. *Taqiyya* is discussed in Enayat, *Modern Islamic Political Thought*, p. 175ff.

7. John O. Voll, *Islam: Continuity and Change in the Modern World*, Boulder and Harlow: Westview Press and Longman, 1982, p. 281, quoting J. Berque, *Cultural Expression in Arab Society Today*, trans. R.W. Stookey, Austin: University of Texas Press, 1978, p. 62.

8. Khurshid Ahmad, 'Islam: basic principles and characteristics' in Khurshid Ahmad (ed.) *Islam, Its Meaning and Message*, London: Longman for Islamic Council of Europe, 1976, p. 37; and Muhammad Qutb, 'Islam as a supreme doctrine' in Salem Azzam (ed.) *Islam and Contemporary Society*, London and New York: Longman, 1982, p. 1.

9. P.J. Vatkikiotis, *Arab and Regional Politics in the Middle East*, London: Croom Helm, 1984, p. 61.

10. Respectively, Abul A'la Maududi, 'What Islam stands for' in Altaf Gauhar (ed.) *The Challenge of Islam*, London: Islamic Council of Europe, 1978, p. 3; M. Hamidullah, *Introduction to Islam*, London: MWH London Publishers, 1979, p. 8; E.I.J. Rosenthal, *Islam in the Modern National State*, Cambridge: Cambridge University Press, 1965, p. 7.

11. The grammatical form is significant. The word Islam is the verbal noun of the fourth, causative derived form of the verb stem.

12. Muhammad al Faisal, Inaugural address to the International Conference on 'Islam and the challenge of our age' in Gauhar, *The Challenge of Islam*, pp. xxx-i.

13. W. Montgomery Watt, *What Is Islam?*, London: Longman, 2nd edition, 1979, p. 4.

14. For variations in grouping and nomenclature, see, for example, Fazlur Rahman, who distinguishes between pre-modernist revivalism,

Notes

classical modernism, neo-revivalism, and neo-modernism: 'Islam: challenges and opportunities' in Alford T. Welch and Pierre Cacchia (eds) *Islam: Past Influence and Present Challenge*, Edinburgh: Edinburgh University Press, 1979, pp. 315–30. Yvonne Haddad refers to normativists, acculturationists, neo-normativists, and secularists: *Contemporary Islam and the Challenge of History*, Albany: State University of New York Press, 1982, pp. 7–23. Malise Ruthven speaks of the archaic, modernist, reformist, and neo-traditionalist responses: *Islam in the World*, Harmondsworth: Penguin Books, 1984, pp. 294–5. Ali Merad refers to fundamentalists, reformists, orthodox modernists, and radical modernists: 'The ideologisation of Islam' in Alexander S. Cudsi and Ali E. Hillal Dessouki (eds) *Islam and Power*, London: Croom Helm, 1981, p. 38. John O. Voll uses adaptationist, conservative, fundamentalist, and individualist: *Islam: Continuity and Change*, pp. 29–31.

15. J. Schacht, 'The schools of law and later developments of jurisprudence' in Khadduri and Liebesney, *Law in the Middle East*, p. 74.

16. ibid., p. 78.

17. George C. Anawati and Maurice Borrmans, *Tendances et courants de l'Islam arabe contemporain, Vol. I Egypt et Afrique du Nord*, Munich and Mainz: Kaiser Verlag and Matthias-Grunewald Verlag, 1982, p. 179.

18. Piscatori, *Islam in a World of Nation-States*, p. 101ff.

19. Anon, 'Kaddafi et l'Islam', *Jeune Afrique* 1236, 12 September 1984, pp. 55–61.

20. See, for example, James A. Bill, 'Resurgent Islam in the Persian Gulf', *Foreign Affairs* 63 (1) (Fall 1984): 108–27.

21. P.J. Vatikiotis. The definition was given in private discussion.

22. See, for example, Emmanuel Sivan, *Radical Islam: Medieval Theology and Modern Politics*, New Haven and London: Yale University Press, 1985; and *Islamic Fundamentalism and Islamic Radicalism*, Hearings before the Subcommittee on Europe and the Middle East of the Committee on Foreign Affairs, House of Representatives, 24 June, 15 July, and 30 September 1985, Washington, DC, 1985.

23. See also Eqbal Ahmad, 'Islam and politics' in Yvonne Haddad, Byron Haines, and Ellison Findly (eds) *The Islamic Impact*, Syracuse: Syracuse University Press, 1984, pp. 20–1.

24. For a description, see Gerd Baumann, 'Conversion and continuity: Islamization among the Nuba of Miri (Sudan)', *British Society for Middle Eastern Studies Bulletin* 12 (2) (1985): 157–71.

25. Seriatim: Richard P. Mitchell, *The Society of the Muslim Brothers*, London: Oxford University Press, 1969, p. 233; Qutb, 'Islam as a supreme doctrine', p. 1; Maududi, *Islamic Law and Constitution*, p. 52; John J. Donohue and John L. Esposito (eds) *Islam in Transition: Muslim Perspectives*, New York and Oxford: Oxford University Press, 1982, pp. 84–5.

26. See Robert Stewart (comp.) *A Dictionary of Political Quotations*, London: Europa Publications, 1984, p. 18.

27. Enayat, *Modern Islamic Political Thought*, p. 1.

28. Vatikiotis, *Arab and Regional Politics in the Middle East*, pp. 61 and 73 respectively.

29. For an extreme version of this line of argument, see The Islamic Student Association of Cairo, 'Lessons from Iran' (mimeographed, 1979) in Donohue and Esposito, *Islam in Transition*, pp. 246–50.

30. Doi, *Shari'ah*, p. 39.

31. Fazlur Rahman, *Islam and Modernity: Transformation of an Intellectual Tradition*, Chicago and London: University of Chicago Press, 1982, p. 20.

32. M.E. Yapp, 'Contemporary Islamic revivalism', *Asian Affairs* XI (O.S. vol. 67) (II) (June 1980): 178.

33. al Faisal, Inaugural address in Gauhar, *The Challenge of Islam*, pp. xxx–i.

Chapter 2: The Law

1. For the third definition, see Murtada Mutahhari, *Jurisprudence and its Principles*, trans. M.S. Tawheedi, Albany: Muslim Students Association (Persian Speaking Group), no date, pp. 7–8.

2. Noel J. Coulson, *Conflicts and Tensions in Islamic Jurisprudence*, Chicago: University of Chicago Press, 1969, p. 3.

3. Asaf A.A. Fyzee, *Outlines of Muhammadan Law*, Calcutta: Oxford University Press, 1949, p. 16. See also S.G. Vesey-Fitzgerald, 'Nature and sources of the Shari'a' in Khadduri and Liebesney, *Law in the Middle East*, pp. 85–6.

4. Abdur Rahman I. Doi, *Shari'ah: The Islamic Law*, London: Ta Ha Publishers, 1984, p. 5.

5. Vesey-Fitzgerald, 'Nature and sources of the Shari'a', p. 87.

6. ibid., p. 88.

7. Doi, *Shari'ah*, p. 47.

8. Vesey-Fitzgerald, 'Nature and sources of the Shari'a', p. 92.

9. Abul A'la Maududi, 'What Islam stands for' in Altaf Gauhar (ed.) *The Challenge of Islam*, London: Islamic Council of Europe, 1978, p. 9.

10. See, for example, Sadiq al Mahdi, 'Islam: society and change' in John Esposito (ed.) *Voices of Resurgent Islam*, New York and Oxford: Oxford University Press, 1983, pp. 230–40; Khalid M. Ishaque, 'Islamic law — its ideals and principles' in Gauhar, *The Challenge of Islam*, pp. 155–75.

11. See Maududi, 'What Islam stands for', p. 10; and Subhi Mahmasani in J.J. Donohue and John Esposito (eds) *Islam in Transition*, New York and Oxford: Oxford University Press, 1982, p. 186 for variant translations.

12. See Sadiq al Mahdi, 'Islam: society and change', p. 233.

13. Vesey-Fitzgerald, 'Nature and sources of the Shari'a', p. 94, quoting G.H. Bousquet, *Précis de droit musulman*, Algiers: 2nd edition, 1947, p. 31.

14. ibid., p. 95.

15. Doi, *Shari'ah*, p. 94.

16. Ignaz Goldziher, *Introduction to Islamic Theology and Law*, trans. Andras and Ruth Hamori, Princeton: Princeton University Press, 1981, p. 52.

17. ibid., pp. 50–1.

18. Muhammad Asad, *The Principles of State and Government in Islam*, Gibraltar: Dar al-Andalus, 1980, p. 38.

19. Mutahhari, *Jurisprudence and its Principles*, p. 48.
20. See, for example, Noel Coulson, *A History of Islamic Law*, Edinburgh: Edinburgh University Press, 1964, p. 80ff; Vesey-Fitzgerald, 'Nature and sources of the Shari'a', p. 105; John L. Esposito, 'Law in Islam' in Yvonne Haddad, Byron Haines, and Ellison Findly (eds) *The Islamic Impact*, Syracuse: Syracuse University Press, 1984, p. 74; M. Jamil Hanafi, *Islam and the Transformation of Culture*, New York: Asia Publishing House, 1974, p. 108.
21. John O. Voll, 'Renewal and reform in Islamic history — *Tajdid* and *Islah*' in Esposito (ed.) *Voices of Resurgent Islam*, p. 38, quoting Arnold H. Green, *The Tunisian Ulama, 1873–1915*, Leiden: Brill, 1978, pp. 188–9.
22. Wael B. Hallaq, 'Was the Gate of Ijtihad closed?', *International Journal of Middle East Studies* 16 (1984): 3–41.
23. ibid., p. 18.
24. J. Schacht, 'Pre-Islamic background and early development of jurisprudence' in Khadduri and Liebesney (eds) *Law in the Middle East*, pp. 30–1.
25. Fazlur Rahman, *Islam and Modernity: Transformation of an Intellectual Tradition*, Chicago and London: University of Chicago Press, 1982, p. 20.
26. Coulson, *A History of Islamic Law*, p. 11.
27. Schacht, 'Pre-Islamic background and early development of jurisprudence', in Khadduri and Liebesney (eds) *Law in the Middle East*, p. 35.
28. ibid., p. 39.
29. Coulson, *A History of Islamic Law*, p. 40.
30. ibid., p. 56.
31. Majid Khadduri, *Islamic Jurisprudence: al Shafi'i's Risala*, Baltimore: The Johns Hopkins Press, 1961, pp. 119 and 112 respectively.
32. Coulson, *A History of Islamic Law*, p. 134.
33. ibid., pp. 147–8. See also Hallaq, 'Was the Gate of Ijtihad closed?', *passim*.
34. See, for example, Doi, *Shari'ah*, pp. 453–4; and Esposito, 'Law in Islam', p. 83.
35. Coulson, *A History of Islamic Law*, p. 105.
36. Mutahhari, *Jurisprudence and its Principles*, p. 11.
37. Kashif al-Ghita, *The Shiah Origin and Faith*, trans. M. Fazal Haq, Accra/Bombay/Freetown/Karachi/London/New York: Islamic Seminary Publications, 2nd edition, 1985, p. 139.
38. Momen, *An Introduction to Shi'i Islam*, pp. 185–6.
39. ibid., p. 186.
40. A.K.S. Lambton, *State and Government in Medieval Islam*, Oxford: Oxford University Press, 1981, p. 228.
41. Momen, *An Introduction to Shi'i Islam*, p. 187.
42. See James P. Piscatori, 'The roles of Islam in Saudi Arabia's political development' in John L. Esposito (ed.) *Islam and Development*, Syracuse: Syracuse University Press, 1980, p. 132.
43. Fazlur Rahman, 'Islam in Pakistan', *Journal of South Asian and Middle Eastern Studies* VIII (4) (Summer 1985): 41.
44. ibid., p. 40.
45. Joseph Schacht, *An Introduction to Islamic Law*, Oxford: Oxford

University Press, 1964, p. 90.

46. See Hallaq, 'Was the Gate of Ijtihad closed?', *passim*. The question has been touched on by others. See, for example, Coulson, *A History of Islamic Law*, p. 142; Esposito, 'Law in Islam', p. 74; Abul A'la Maududi, *Islamic Law and Constitution*, trans. Khurshid Almad, Lahore: Islamic Publications, 8th edition, 1983, pp. 58–60 and 63–4.

47. Mohamed S. El-Awa, *Punishment in Islamic Law: A Comparative Study*, Indianapolis: American Trust Publications, 1982, p. 85.

48. See, for example, Yusuf al-Qaradawi, *The Lawful and the Prohibited in Islam*, trans. Kamal El-Helbawy, M. Moinuddin Siddiqui, and Syed Shukry, London: Shorouk International (UK) Ltd, 1985 (previously published in Indianapolis by American Trust Publications), p. 14ff.

49. Doi, *Shari'ah*, p. 468.

50. Asad, *The Principles of State and Government in Islam*, pp. 11–17. Quotations are seriatim at pp. 11–12, 13, and 14.

51. Richard P. Mitchell, *The Society of the Muslim Brothers*, London: Oxford University Press, 1969, pp. 236–41.

52. Maududi, *Islamic Law and Constitution*, p. 52.

53. ibid., p. 59.

54. ibid., p.74.

55. See Donohue and Esposito (eds) *Islam in Transition*, p. 186.

56. ibid.

57. Rahman, *Islam and Modernity*, p. 101.

58. ibid., pp. 101–16. Quotation is at p. 115.

59. ibid., p. 39.

60. ibid., p. 69.

61. Mutahhari, *Jurisprudence and its Principles*, p. 7.

62. Coulson, *Conflicts and Tensions*, pp. 106–7.

63. Mohamed S.El-Awa, *On the Political System of the Islamic State*, trans. Ahmad Naji al Imam, Indianapolis: American Trust Publications, 1980, p. 80.

Chapter 3: Concepts of State Government and Authority

1. A.K. Brohi, 'Islam: its political and legal principles' in Salem Azzam (ed.) *Islam and Contemporary Society*, London and New York: Longman, 1982, p. 87.

2. E.I.J. Rosenthal, *Islam in the Modern National State*, Cambridge: Cambridge University Press, 1965, p. 48.

3. A.K.S. Lambton, 'Khalifa: (ii) In Political Theory' in *Encyclopedia of Islam*, 2nd edition,Vol. IV, Leiden: E.J. Brill, 1978, p. 948.

4. H.A.R. Gibb, 'Constitutional organisation' in M. Khadduri and H.J. Liebesney (eds) *Law in the Middle East, Vol. I, Origin and Development of Islamic Law*, Washington, DC: Middle East Institute, 1955, p. 5.

5. E.I.J. Rosenthal, *Political Thought in Medieval Islam*, Cambridge: Cambridge University Press, 1962, p. 26.

6. Moojan Momen, *An Introduction to Shi'i Islam*, New Haven and

London: Yale University Press, 1985, p. 192.

7. ibid., p. 33.

8. Rosenthal, *Islam in the Modern National State*, pp. 14–15.

9. H.A.R. Gibb and H. Bowen, *Islamic Society in the West, Vol. 1, Part 1, Islamic Society in the Eighteenth Century*, London, New York, and Toronto: Oxford University Press, 1950, p. 28.

10. H.A.R. Gibb, 'Heritage of Islam in the modern world', *International Journal of Middle Eastern Studies* I (1970): 12–13.

11. Gibb and Bowen, *Islamic Society in the Eighteenth Century*, p. 27.

12. Gibb, 'Constitutional organisation', p. 3.

13. Hassan al Turabi, 'The Islamic state' in John Esposito (ed.) *Voices of Resurgent Islam*, New York and Oxford: Oxford University Press, 1983, p. 242.

14. Gibb, 'Constitutional Organisation', p. 4.

15. *These two hadith* are regularly quoted. See, for example, Muhammad Asad, *Principles of State and Government in Islam*, Gibraltar: Dar al-Andalus, pp. 38 and 48.

16. Mohamed S. El-Awa, *On the Political System of the Islamic State*, trans. Ahmad Naji al Imam, Indianapolis: American Trust Publications, 1980, p. 76.

17. H.A.R. Gibb, *Studies on the Civilisation of Islam*, Boston: Beacon Press, 1962, p. 162.

18. Sadiq al Mahdi, 'Islam: society and change' in Esposito (ed.) *Voices of Resurgent Islam*, p. 233.

19. See R. Levy, *The Social Structure of Islam*, Cambridge: Cambridge University Press, 1957, pp. 284–94; Rosenthal, *Political Thought in Mediaeval Islam*, pp. 27–37; Gibb, *Studies on the Civilisation of Islam*, pp. 151–65; A.K.S. Lambton, *State and Government in Medieval Islam*, London: Oxford University Press, 1981, pp. 83–102.

20. See, for example, G.D. Newby, 'Ibn Khaldun and Frederick Jackson Turner: Islam and the frontier experience', *Journal of Asian and African Studies* 18 (3–4) (1983): 275–85.

21. A. Hourani, *Arabic Thought in the Liberal Age, 1798–1939*, London, New York, and Toronto: Oxford University Press, 1962, p. 18.

22. Omar A. Farrukh, *Ibn Taimiya on Public and Private Law* (a translation of *Kitab al siyasa al shar'iya*), Beirut: Khayyats, 1966, p. 187; see also Qamaruddin Khan, *The Political Thought of Ibn Taymiyah*, Islamabad: Islamic Research Institute, n.d., p. 29.

23. Farrukh, *Ibn Taimiya*, pp. 187–8.

24. Khan, *Political Thought*, p. 184.

25. Farrukh, *Ibn Taimiya*, p. 183.

26. ibid., p. 182.

27. ibid., pp. 183–4.

28. Khan, *Political Thought*, p. 183.

29. See, for example, Rosenthal, *Political Thought in Medieval Islam*, pp. 84–113; M. Mahdi, *Ibn Khaldun's Philosophy of History*, Chicago: University of Chicago Press, 1964 (first published in London by George Allen & Unwin, 1957).

30. Gibb, 'Constitutional organisation', pp. 13–14, quoting Ibn Khaldun, *Muqaddima*, Book 3, Chapter 25; see also Ibn Khaldun, *The Muqaddimah*, trans. F. Rosenthal and abridged N.J. Dawood, London and

Henley: Routledge and Kegan Paul, 1967 and 1978, pp. 154–5.

31. Hourani, *Arabic Thought*, p. 24.

32. Rosenthal, *Political Thought*, p. 216; Gibb and Bowen, *Islamic Society*, p. 33ff; Lambton, *State and Government*, p. 181.

33. Lambton, *State and Government*, p. 186.

34. Muhammad Riza al-Muzaffar, *The Faith of Shi'a Islam*, trans. various, London: The Muhammadi Trust, 1982, p. 32.

35. ibid., p. 34.

36. Lambton, *State and Government*, p. 219.

37. ibid., p. 190.

38. Momen, *An Introduction to Shi'i Islam*, pp. 192–3.

39. ibid., p. 190.

40. Malise Ruthven, *Islam in the World*, Harmondsworth: Penguin Books, 1984, p. 180.

41. Abbas Kelidar. The point was made in discussion.

42. Eqbal Ahmad, 'Islam and politics', in Yvonne Haddad, Byron Heines, and Ellison Findly (eds) *The Islamic Impact*, Syracuse: Syracuse University Press, 1984, p. 12.

43. Jean Bodin (1530–96) was a French political philosopher. See *Encyclopaedia Britannica*, Chicago, London, and Toronto: Encyclopaedia Britannica Ltd, 1953, Vol. 3, pp. 770–1 for a brief account of Bodin and his works.

44. Johannes Althusius (1557–1638) was a Swiss professor who wrote extensively on legal and political issues. See Joseph Dunner (ed.) *Dictionary of Political Science*, London: Vision Press, 1964, p. 17 for a brief biography.

45. The United Kingdom has not yet resolved the problems of regional separatism; the United States still has difficulties over the relationship between federal and state authorities — and loyalties; the USSR has a system of 'autonomous' republics; and ethnic and confessional sensitivities are a political hot potato in most parts of the world.

46. P.J. Vatikiotis, 'Religion and state' in Gabriel R. Warburg and Uri M. Kupferschmidt (eds) *Islam, Nationalism and Radicalism in Egypt and the Sudan*, New York: Praeger, 1983, pp. 58–9.

47. In the United Kingdom, Scottish and English law are very different.

Chapter 4: International Relations and International Law

1. Percy E. Corbett, *Law in Diplomacy*, Princeton: Princeton University Press, 1959, p. 3.

2. Majid Khadduri, *The Islamic Law of Nations: Shaybani's Siyar*, Baltimore: The Johns Hopkins Press, 1966, p. 6.

3. ibid., p. 15.

4. Majid Khadduri, *War and Peace in the Law of Islam*, Baltimore: The Johns Hopkins Press, 1955, p. 57.

5. Khadduri, *The Islamic Law of Nations*, p. 16.

6. Maulana Muhammad Ali, *A Manual of Hadith*, Lahore: The

Ahmadiyya Anjuman Ishaat Islam, n.d., p. 261. See also Omar A. Far-rukh, *Ibn Taimiya on Public and Private Law*, Beirut: Khayyats, 1966, p. 27.

7. Mohamed S. El-Awa, *Punishment in Islamic Law: A Comparative Study*, Indianapolis: American Trust Publications, 1982, p. 56.

8. Khadduri, *The Islamic Law of Nations*, pp. 8–9.

9. ibid., p. 40.

10. ibid., pp. xvi–xvii.

11. A.K.S. Lambton, *State and Government in Medieval Islam*, Oxford: Oxford University Press, 1981, p.95.

12. The enduring nature of the close identification between people and territory is particularly striking in North Yemen and in Oman: in the former tribal leaders have been described *Awlad Saba* (sons of Sheba), and in the latter it was not unusual to hear the term *Bani Himyar* (Sons of Himyar) applied to all Omanis. The terms, though used casually, suggest an historical identity of some 2,500 to 3,000 years.

13. V. Minorsky, trans., *Hudud al 'Alam, 'The Regions of the World'*, Karachi: Indus Publications, 1980; originally published by Oxford University Press, 1937, p. 82.

14. James P. Piscatori, *Islam in a World of Nation-States*, Cambridge: Cambridge University Press, 1986, p. 74ff.

15. Shah Mohammed (ed.), *Writings and Speeches of Sir Syed Ahmad Khan*, Bombay: Nachiketa Publications, 1972, p. 256.

16. Khadduri, *The Islamic Law of Nations*, p. 57.

Chapter 5: The Islamic Economic System

1. M.N. Siddiqi, 'Muslim economic thinking: a survey of contemporary literature' in Khurshid Ahmad (ed.) *Studies in Islamic Economics*, Leicester: The Islamic Foundation, 1980, p. 191.

2. ibid., pp. 271–315.

3. See, for example, Muhtar Holland, trans., *Public Duties in Islam: The Institution of the Hisba*, Leicester: The Islamic Foundation, 1982, being a translation of Ibn Taimiyya's *al hisba fi 'l islam*; Ibn Khaldun, *Muqaddima*; Abu'l Fadhl Ja'far Ali al Dimishqi, *kitab al ishara*.

4. M. Rodinson, *Islam and Capitalism*, trans. Brian Pearce, Harmondsworth: Penguin Books, 1977, p. 14.

5. Philip Reiser, unpublished seminar paper, 1985.

6. Timur Kuran, 'The economic system in contemporary Islamic thought: interpretation and assessment', *International Journal of Middle East Studies* 18 (1986): 135.

7. Amir Muhammad al-Faisal al-Saud, 'Banking and the Islamic standpoint' in Salem Azzam (ed.) *Islam and Contemporary Society*, London and New York: Longman, 1982, p. 120.

8. Rodinson, *Islam and Capitalism*, pp. 16–17, quoting M. Hamidullah, 'Le monde musulman devant l'économie moderne', *Cahiers de l'Institute de Science Économique Appliquée*, Supplement no. 120 (Series V, no. 3) (December 1961): 27.

9. S.M. Ghazanfar, 'Development ethics and economics: socio-economic justice in Islam', *Journal of South Asian and Middle Eastern Studies* V (2) (Winter 1981): 28.

10. Amir Muhammad al-Faisal al-Saud, 'Banking and the Islamic standpoint', p. 121.

11. Kuran, 'The economic system in contemporary Islamic thought', p. 139.

12. Samir Shamma, comp. and trans., *The Law of Income Tax and Zakat in the Kingdom of Saudi Arabia*, Beirut: Dar al-Ahad, 1951, p. 44.

13. Government of the Kingdom of Saudi Arabia, *Memorial of the Kingdom of Saudi Arabia* (1955), vol. 2, pp. 297 and 292. In the Arabic version the references are at pp. 278 and 272.

14. Amir Muhammad al-Faisal al-Saud, 'Banking and the Islamic standpoint', pp. 131-2.

15. ibid., pp. 133-4.

16. Charles Issawi, 'The adaptation of Islam to contemporary economic realities' in Yvonne Haddad, Byron Haines, and Ellison Findly (eds) *The Islamic Impact*, Syracuse: Syracuse University Press, 1984, p. 43.

17. ibid., p. 43.

18. M. Uzair, 'Some conceptual and practical aspects of interest-free banking' in Khurshid Ahmad (ed.) *Studies in Islamic Economics*, p. 45. He quotes Sarakhsi, *al Mabsut* Cairo, Matba'a Sa'ada, Vol. XII, p. 17; and Ibn Rushd, *Bidayat al mujtahid wa nihayat al muqtasid*, Cairo: 1329 AH, p. 265.

19. Kuran, 'The economic system in contemporary Islamic thought', p. 157.

20. Ghazanfar, 'Development ethics and economics', pp. 29-30.

21. M. Novak (ed.), *Capitalism and Socialism: A Theological Enquiry*, Washington, DC: American Enterprise Institute for Public Policy, 1979, preface.

22. Some 50 per cent of Majles members is drawn from the ranks of the clerical hierarchy.

23. Ibn Khaldun, *Muqaddimah*, trans. F. Rosenthal, New York: Pantheon Books, 1958, Vol. II, pp. 336-7.

24. Rodinson, *Islam and Capitalism*, pp. 28-75.

25. M. Naimuddin, 'Contemporary thinking on "Islamic economics"' in Anwar Moazzam (ed.) *Islam and the Contemporary Muslim World*, New Delhi: Light and Life Publishers, 1981, p. 116.

26. Ijaz Shafi Gilani, 'The political context of Islamic economics: high and low road strategies' in Khurshid Ahmad (ed.) *Islamic Economics*, p. 141.

Chapter 6: Intellectual Influences, Part I — The Indian Subcontinent

1. Terminology has varied. Revival, resurgence, and reaffirmation figure regularly in the literature. I prefer the formulation used here as a more accurate description. However, for convenience, the term 'revival' will be used.

2. M.E. Yapp, 'Contemporary Islamic revivalism', *Asian Affairs* XI (O.S. vol. 67) (II) (June 1980): 183-4.

3. Abul A'la Maududi, *A Short History of the Revivalist Movement in Islam*, trans. Al Ash'ari, Lahore: Islamic Publications Ltd, 2nd revised edition, 1972, p. 95. The quotation is from the Preface to Shah Wali Allah's *al Musaffa*.

4. Mi'raj Muhammad, 'Shah Wali-Allah's concept of the *Shari'ah*' in Khurshid Ahmad and Zafar Ishaq Ansari (eds) *Islamic Perspectives: Studies in Honour of Mawlana Sayyid Abul A'la Mawdudi*, Leicester and Jedda: The Islamic Foundation and Saudi Publishing House, 1979, p. 349.

5. ibid., pp. 350-2. See also E.I.J. Rosenthal, *Islam in the Modern National State*, Cambridge: Cambridge University Press, 1965, p. 186. The quotation is at Mi'raj Muhammad, p. 350.

6. Aziz Ahmad, 'Political and religious ideas of Shah Wali-Ullah of Delhi', *Muslim World* 52 (1962): 25

7. Rosenthal, *Islam in the Modern National State*, p. 187.

8. Malcolm H. Kerr, *Islamic Reform: The Political and Legal Theories of Muhammad Abduh and Rashid Ridha*, Berkeley: University of California Press, 1966, p. 216.

9. Aziz Ahmad, *An Intellectual History of Islam in India*, Edinburgh: Edinburgh University Press, 1969, p. 8.

10. Rosenthal, *Islam in the Modern National State*, p. 186.

11. S. Moinul Haq, *Islamic Thought and Movements*, Karachi: Pakistan Historical Society, 1979, p. 406.

12. I.H. Qureshi, *The Muslim Community of the Indian Subcontinent, 610-1947*, Karachi: Ma'aref Printers, 2nd edition 1977, p. 215. He is quoting *History of the Freedom Movement*, vol. 1, Karachi: 1957, p. 511.

13. See, for example, Aziz Ahmad, *Islamic Modernism in India and Pakistan (1857-1964)*, Oxford: Oxford University Press, 1967, pp. 40-1; John Voll, *Islam: Continuity and Change in the Modern World*, Boulder and Harlow: Westview Press and Longman, 1982, p. 65.

14. Ahmad, *Islamic Modernism*, p. 41.

15. Rosenthal, *Islam in the Modern National State*, p. 191.

16. W. Cantwell-Smith, *Modern Islam in India*, London: Gollancz, revised edition, 1946, p. 20.

17. Ahmad, *Islamic Modernism*, p. 50.

18. Fazlur Rahman, *Islam*, Chicago and London: University of Chicago Press, 1966, pp. 216-17.

19. ibid., p. 217. For a slightly different version, see Christian W. Troll, *Sayyid Ahmad: A Reinterpretation of Muslim Theology*, New Delhi: Vikas Publishing House, 1978, pp. 313-14.

20. Qureshi, *The Muslim Community*, p. 280.

21. ibid., p. 281.

22. Cantwell-Smith, *Modern Islam in India*, pp. 26-8.

23. Voll, *Continuity and Change*, p. 113.

24. ibid.

25. ibid., p. 224.

26. Muhammad Iqbal, *The Reconstruction of Religious Thought in Islam*, Lahore: Sh Muhammad Ashraf, 1962, p. 148.

27. ibid., p. 168.

28. ibid., p. 167.

29. Muhammad Iqbal, *Speeches and Statements of Iqbal*, comp. A.R. Tariq, Lahore: Shaikh Ghulam Ali & Sons, 1973, p. 5.

30. Seriatim: Iqbal, *The Reconstruction*, p. 159; Muhammad Iqbal, *Stray Reflections*, ed. Javid Iqbal, Lahore: Shaikh Ghulam Ali & Sons, 1961, pp. 26-7; Iqbal, *Speeches and Statements*, pp. 141-2.

31. Iqbal, *Speeches and Statements*, pp. 7-12. Quotations are at pp. 7-8, p. 8, p. 8 and pp. 11-12.

32. Cantwell-Smith, *Modern Islam in India*, p. 100.

33. Iqbal, *Stray Reflections*, p. 94.

34. ibid., p. 109.

35. W. Cantwell-Smith, *Islam in Modern History*, Princeton: Princeton University Press, 1957, p. 234; C.J. Adams, 'Maududi and the Islamic state' in John Esposito (ed.) *Voices of Resurgent Islam*, New York and Oxford: Oxford University Press, 1983, p. 99; Ahmad and Ansari (eds) *Islamic Perspectives*, p. ix.

36. Abul A'la Maududi, *Towards Understanding Islam*, trans. and ed. Khurshid Ahmad, Lahore: Idara Tarjuman-ul-Quran, 14th edition, 1974, p. 3.

37. Khurshid Ahmad and Zafar Ishaq Ansari, 'Mawlana Sayyid Abul A'la Mawdudi: An Introduction to his Vision of Islam and Islamic Revival' in Ahmad and Ansari (eds) *Islamic Perspectives*, p. 365.

38. Abul A'la Maududi, *Islamic Law and Constitution*, trans. Khurshid Ahmad, Lahore: Islamic Publications, 8th edition, 1983, p. 52.

39. ibid., p. 75.

40. Maududi, *A Short History*, p. 24.

41. ibid., p. 24.

42. ibid., pp. 26-7.

43. ibid., pp. 30-3.

44. Maududi, *Islamic Law and Constitution*, p. 56.

45. ibid., p. 49.

46. Majid Khadduri, *War and Peace in the Law of Islam*, Baltimore: The Johns Hopkins Press, 1955, pp. 9-13 discusses this concept.

47. See Maududi, *Islamic Law and Constitution*, pp. 189-200, and Hamid Enayat, *Modern Islamic Political Thought*, London: Macmillan, 1982, pp. 105-7.

48. George C. Anawati and Maurice Bormans, *Tendances et courants de l'Islam arabe contemporain*, Vol. I Egypt et Afrique du Nord, Munich and Mainz: Kaiser Verlag and Matthias-Grunewald Verlag, 1982, p. 179.

Chapter 7: Intellectual Influences, Part II — Egypt

1. Muhammad Iqbal, *Speeches and Statements of Iqbal*, comp. A.R. Tariq, Lahore: Shaikh Ghulam Ali & Sons, 1973, pp. 141-2.

2. Albert Hourani, *Arabic Thought in the Liberal Age, 1798-1939*, London, New York and Toronto: Oxford University Press, 1962, p. 156.

3. ibid., p. 136.

4. ibid., p. 139.

Notes

5. Malcolm H. Kerr, *Islamic Reform: The Political and Legal Theories of Muhammad Abduh and Rashid Ridha*, Berkeley: University of California Press, 1966, pp. 108-9, and Hourani, *Arabic Thought*, pp. 140-1.
6. Hourani, *Arabic Thought*, p. 145.
7. Kerr, *Islamic Reform*, p. 110.
8. C.C. Adams, *Islam and Modernism in Egypt*, New York: Russell and Russell, 1968 (first published 1933), p. 129.
9. Hourani, *Arabic Thought*, pp. 146-7.
10. Kerr, *Islamic Reform*, p. 144.
11. Hourani, *Arabic Thought*, p. 148.
12. ibid., p. 149.
13. Umberto Eco, *The Name of the Rose*, trans. William Weaver, London: Secker & Warburg, 1983, p. 199.
14. M.A. Zaki Badawi, *The Reformers of Egypt*, London: Croom Helm, 1978, p. 81.
15. Hourani, *Arabic Thought*, p. 156.
16. *Seriatim*, Kerr, *Islamic Reform*, p. 149; Badawi, *The Reformers*, p. 48.
17. Kerr, *Islamic Reform*, p. 152.
18. ibid., p. 155.
19. ibid., p. 156.
20. Hourani, *Arabic Thought*, p. 228.
21. Adams, *Islam and Modernism*, p. 191.
22. Hourani, *Arabic Thought*, p. 148.
23. Kerr, *Islamic Reform*, p. 189.
24. ibid., p. 190.
25. Hourani, *Arabic Thought*, p. 237.
26. Badawi, *The Reformers*, p. 120.
27. Kerr, *Islamic Reform*, p. 177.
28. E.I.J. Rosenthal, *Islam in the Modern National State*, Cambridge: Cambridge University Press, 1965, p. 122.
29. Adams, *Islam and Modernism*, p. 204.
30. Richard P. Mitchell, *The Society of the Muslim Brothers*, London: Oxford University Press, 1969, p. 216.
31. ibid., p. 223.
32. ibid., p. 4.
33. ibid., p. 222.
34. ibid., p. 233.
35. Hamid Enayat, *Modern Islamic Political Thought*, London: Macmillan, p. 85; Mitchell, *The Society of the Muslim Brothers*, p. 14.
36. Enayat, *Modern Islamic Political Thought*, p. 85.
37. ibid., p. 85.
38. Mitchell, *The Society of the Muslim Brothers*, p. 235.
39. Enayat, *Modern Islamic Political Thought*, p. 88.
40. Mitchell, *The Society of the Muslim Brothers*, p. 238.
41. ibid., pp. 327-8.
42. ibid., p. 331.
43. *Seriatim*, Sayyid Qutb, *Milestones*, trans. S. Badrul Hasan, Karachi: International Islamic Publishers, 1981, pp. 4-5; Yvonne Y. Haddad, 'Sayyid Qutb: ideologue of the Islamic revival' in John Esposito (ed.) *Voices*

234

of Resurgent Islam, New York and Oxford: Oxford University Press, 1983, p. 69.

44. Gilles Kepel, *The Prophet and the Pharaoh: Muslim Extremism in Egypt*, trans. Jon Rothschild, London: Al Saqi Books, 1985, pp. 39-41. The quotation is at p. 40.

45. Haddad, 'Sayyid Qutb', p. 93.

46. Kepel, *The Prophet and the Pharaoh*, p. 38.

47. Sayyid Qutb, *Milestones*, p. 93.

48. Emmanuel Sivan, *Radical Islam: Medieval Theology and Modern Politics*, New Haven and London: Yale University Press, 1985, pp. 23-4.

49. Sayyid Qutb, *Milestones*, p. 61.

50. ibid., p. 61.

51. Haddad, 'Sayyid Qutb', p. 89.

52. Sayyid Qutb, *Milestones*, pp. 115-16.

53. ibid., p. 190.

54. ibid., p. 191.

55. ibid., p. 194.

56. ibid., p. 196.

57. ibid., p. 202.

Chapter 8: The Islamic Revival

1. Musa Keilani, 'Needed: a new definition of fundamentalism', *Jordan Times*, 5 September 1984.

2. ibid.

3. *Seriatim*, P.J. Vatikiotis, 'Islamic resurgence: a critical view' in Alexander S. Cudsi and Ali E. Hillal Dessouki (eds) *Islam and Power*, London: Croom Helm, 1981, p. 193; P.H. Stoddard, 'Themes and variations' in Phillip H. Stoddard, David C. Cuthell, and Margaret W. Sullivan (eds) *Change and the Muslim World*, Syracuse: Syracuse University Press, 1981, p. 16; John O. Voll, 'The Islamic past and the present resurgence', *Current History* 78 (456) (April 1980): 180-1; M.E. Yapp, 'Contemporary Islamic revivalism', *Asian Affairs* XI (O.S. vol. 67) (II) (June 1980): 194; Daniel Pipes, 'This world is political!', *Orbis* 24(1) (1980): 9-41.

4. Nazih N.M. Ayubi, 'The political revival of Islam: the case of Egypt', *International Journal of Middle East Studies* 12 (1980): 484.

5. Bassam Tibi, 'The renewed role of Islam in the political and social development of the Middle East', *Middle East Journal* 37 (1) (Winter 1983): 5.

6. J.J. Donohue and John Esposito (eds) *Islam in Transition*, New York and London: Oxford University Press, 1982, pp. 84-5.

7. Richard B. Parker, *North Africa: Regional Tension and Strategic Concerns*, New York: Praeger, 1984, p. 90.

8. Stoddard, 'Themes and variations', p. 18.

9. Ayubi, 'The political revival of Islam', p. 484.

10. R. Stephen Humphreys, 'Islam and political values in Saudi Arabia, Egypt and Syria', *Middle East Journal* 33(1) (Winter 1979): 3.

11. Albert Hourani, 'Conclusion' in James P. Piscatori (ed.) *Islam in the Political Process*, Cambridge: Cambridge University Press, 1983, pp. 226-7.

12. For a characteristic exposition of this line of reasoning, see Khurshid Ahmad, 'The nature of the Islamic resurgence' in John Esposito (ed.) *Voices of Resurgent Islam*, New York and Oxford: Oxford University Press, 1983, pp. 218–29.

13. Yapp, 'Contemporary Islamic revivalism', p. 180.

14. ibid., p. 185.

15. Nikki Keddie, 'Iran: change in Islam; Islam and change', *International Journal of Middle East Studies* 3(4) (1980): 530.

16. Hourani, 'Conclusion', p. 227.

17. See Yapp, 'Contemporary Islamic revivalism', *passim*. The quotation is at p. 181.

18. ibid., p. 194.

19. Vatikiotis, 'Islamic resurgence', p. 171.

20. Hourani, 'Conclusion', p. 228.

21. Vatikiotis, 'Islamic resurgence', p. 171.

22. 1907 Amendment to 1906 Iranian Constitution.

23. Humphreys, 'Islam and political values', p. 7.

24. P.J. Vatikiotis, *Arab and Regional Politics in the Middle East*, London: Croom Helm, 1984, p. 61.

25. A.K.S. Lambton, *State and Government in Medieval Islam*, London: Oxford University Press, 1981, p. 228.

26. H.A.R. Gibb, 'Heritage of Islam in the modern world', *International Journal of Middle Eastern Studies* I (1970): 12–13.

27. Madise Ruthven, *Islam in the World*, Harmondsworth: Penguin Books, 1984, pp. 157–8.

28. Vatikiotis, 'Islamic resurgence', pp. 187–8.

29. Vatikiotis, *Arab and Regional Politics*, p. 73.

30. Sadiq al Mahdi, 'Islam: society and change' in John Esposito (ed.) *Voices of Resurgent Islam*, New York and Oxford: Oxford University Press, 1983, p. 240.

31. Hassan al Turabi, 'The Islamic state' pp. 249–50.

Chapter 9: The Extremists

1. Shahin F. Dil, 'The myth of the Islamic resurgence in South Asia', *Current History* 78(456) (April 1980): 167.

2. Helena Cobban, *The Shia Community and the Future of Lebanon. The Muslim World Today*, Occasional Paper no. 2, Washington, DC: American Institute for Islamic Affairs, 1985, p. 10.

3. Hanna Batatu, 'Syria's Muslim brethren', *MERIP Reports no. 110, vol. 2, no. 9* (November/December 1982): 20.

4. The Higher Command of the Islamic Revolution in Syria, *Declaration and Program of the Islamic Revolution in Syria*, Damascus: 1980, pp. 8–10.

5. The nomenclature is taken from R. Hrair Dekmedjian, *Islam in Revolution*, Syracuse: Syracuse University Press, 1985, p. 90.

6. James P. Piscatori, 'The Islamic Jihad groups', in *Islamic Fundamentalism and Islamic Radicalism*, Hearings before the Subcommittee on Europe and the Middle East of the Committee on Foreign Affairs, House

of Representatives, 24 June, 15 July, and 30 September 1985, Washington, DC, 1985, p. 293.

7. John L. Esposito, *Islamic Revivalism. The Muslim World Today*, Occasional Paper no. 3, Washington, DC: American Institute for Islamic Affairs, 1985, pp. 10–11.

8. Hamid Algar has defined 'corruption on earth' as 'a broad term including not only moral corruption, but also subversion of the public good, embezzlement and usurpation of public wealth, conspiring with the enemies of the community against its security, and working in general for the overthrow of the Islamic order'. See Hamid Algar, *Islam and Revolution*, London: KPI, 1985, p. 154.

9. Anon., 'Kaddafi et l'Islam', *Jeune Afrique* 1236, 12 September 1984, p. 58.

10. Lisa Anderson, 'Qaddafi's Islam' in John Esposito (ed.) *Voices of Resurgent Islam*, New York and Oxford: Oxford University Press, 1983, p. 135.

11. ibid.

12. A.C. Goodison, 'The Islamic factor in the thought and internal policies of Mu'ammar al Qadhdhafi' (unpublished research paper), p. 36.

13. See Daniel Pipes, *In the Path of God*, New York: Basic Books, 1983, pp. 220–3.

14. See Esposito, *Islamic Revivalism*, pp. 8–9 for population estimates.

15. Cobban, *The Shia Community*, p. 7.

16. Batatu, 'Syria's Muslim brethren', p. 12.

17. Thomas Mayer, 'The Islamic opposition in Syria', *Orient* 24 (1983): 597.

18. ibid., p. 599.

19. Estimates vary from 8,000 to 30,000 casualties and up to 30 per cent of the town destroyed. See Mayer, 'The Islamic opposition', p. 605, footnote 43.

20. ibid., pp. 605–6.

21. Batatu, 'Syria's Muslim brethren', p. 13.

22. Cobban, *The Shia Community, passim*. See in particular p. 4.

23. Batatu, 'Syria's Muslim brethren', p. 20.

24. See Dekmedjian, *Islam in Revolution*, pp. 102 and 179–80.

25. ibid., p. 102.

26. Interestingly, Abdul Salam Farraj identifies 1924 as the date of the definitive demise of the Caliphate: presumably he accepted the Ottoman Caliphate as legitimate and Islamic, despite the large-scale borrowing of legal codes. See Johannes J.G. Jansen, *The Neglected Duty*, New York: Macmillan, 1986, p. 167.

27. See Esposito, *Islamic Revivalism*, p. 3, and Dekmedjian, *Islam in Revolution*, pp. 100–1 for alternative listings.

28. Dekmedjian, *Islam in Revolution*, p. 63.

29. Saad Eddin Ibrahim, 'Anatomy of Egypt's militant Islamic groups: methodological note and preliminary findings', *International Journal of Middle East Studies* 12 (1980): 427.

30. See Pipes, *In the Path of God*, pp. 242–3.

31. Hamied N. Ansari, 'The Islamic militants in Egyptian politics', *International Journal of Middle East Studies* 16 (1984): 123.

32. These include alienation and loss of identity; government support for and encouragement of 'Islamic groups' as a counter to left-wing extremism; government failure to deal with political, social, and economic grievances; external influence; and a reaction to state-imposed repression. 'Violence invites violent reactions' was regularly offered as a reason by Omar al Tilmisani, the late leader of the Egyptian Muslim Brotherhood, though his view might also be cited in support of government action against violent protests.

33. Ansari, 'The Islamic militants', p. 125.

34. Dekmedjian, *Islam in Revolution*, p. 96.

35. Ansari, 'The Islamic militants', p. 126; Dekmedjian, *Islam in Revolution*, p. 97; Kepel, *The Prophet and the Pharaoh*, p. 204ff.

36. Ansari, 'The Islamic militants', p. 126; and Dekmedjian, *Islam in Revolution*, pp. 97–9.

37. Ansari, 'The Islamic militants', p. 137.

38. R.K. Ramazani, 'Shi'ism in the Gulf' in Juan R. Cole and Nikki R. Keddie (eds) *Shi'ism and Social Protest*, New Haven and London: Yale University Press, 1986, p. 41, quoting an interview in English in *Impact International*, April 25–May 8 1980.

39. See, for example, *The Middle East Reporter*, 23 February 1985, p. 17.

40. See *Middle East Insight* 4, nos 2 and 4 (1984 and 1985).

41. Piscatori, 'The Islamic Jihad groups', p. 294.

42. ibid.

43. Donald K. Emmerson, 'Islam in modern Indonesia: political impasse, cultural opportunity' in Phillip H. Stoddard, David C. Cuthell, and Margaret W. Sullivan, *Change and the Muslim World*, Syracuse: Syracuse University Press, 1981, p. 167.

44. John L. Esposito, prepared statement in *Islamic Fundamentalism and Islamic Radicalism*, p. 14.

Chapter 10: Envoi

1. Thomas Mayer, 'The Islamic opposition in Syria', Orient 24 (1983): 606.

2. See the two-part interview by Rashid al Ghanoushi in *Arabia* (October and November 1986), pp. 13–15 and 14–17 respectively for an indication of his views, and Dr Rashid al-Mubarak's article in *Arabia* (October 1986): 22–3.

3. See Jasper Ridley, *Lord Palmerston*, London: Book Club Associates with Constable & Co., 1970, pp. 185–6. Ridley is quoting Palmerston to Howard de Walden, 25 April 1836 (B.M. Add. 48441).

4. Piscatori, *Islam in a World of Nation-States*, Cambridge: Cambridge University Press, 1986, p. 3.

Glossary of Technical Terms

abangan and santri

Abangan is the term used for nominal Muslims in Indonesia, particularly in Java. *Abangan* beliefs and practices are heavily influenced by pre-Islamic Hindu and Buddhist beliefs and practices and by Hindu and Buddhist mysticism. They sometimes lightheartedly refer to themselves as *Islam statistik*, 'statistical Muslims'. *Santris* are strict and orthodox Muslims of a generally conservative bent in Indonesia.

Abbasid

The name of the second Muslim dynasty which ruled from 750 until 1258. This period saw the gradual fragmentation of the universal community and the reduction in the authority of the *khalifa* until he was merely the titular head of the Sunni Muslim community, whose main function was to act as legitimizing authority for the numerous secular rulers who exercised effective political control in the provinces and in the capital, Baghdad. From 1251 until 1517, there was an Abbasid shadow *Khilafa* in Egypt, established in order to meet a perceived need for a continuing source of legitimacy.

ahadith

See *hadith*.

ahkam

Plural of *hukm*, decision or judgment. In Muslim law the term has two technical meanings: individual injunctions by God and the whole of His dispensation; and, in a more restricted sense, the body of positive legal rulings.

ahl al kitab

'People of the Book'; originally applied to Jews and Christians only, as the possessors of earlier revelations recorded in their scriptures. The term was later extended to the Sabeans and Zoroastrians. The genuineness of the earlier revelations and the continuity between them and that vouchsafed to the Prophet meant, in theory, that they were regarded as distinct from,

239

and better than, idolators and polytheists. In practice, the somewhat better treatment that this implied often occurred. However, their failure to recognize that they had deviated from the true path and to adopt Islam often resulted in a greater or lesser degree of persecution.

akhbari

One of the two schools of thought in Shi'a Islam which fought for supremacy in Iran during the seventeenth century. The *akhbaris* opposed the use of *ijtihad* and sought to base Shi'a jurisprudence on the use of *hadith* in place of the rationalist principles advocated by their opponents the *usulis*. They also rejected *ijma'* as a source of doctrine and law, and the principle of the permissibility of all actions unless there is a clear text forbidding such actions. It follows that the only *marja' al taqlid* (q.v.) for the *akhbaris* is the Hidden Imam (see *imam al zaman*).

'alim

See *ulama*.

'amil

Literally 'one who acts' or 'agent'. The term has acquired two technical meanings:

(a) a government agent or official, usually concerned with administration and finance, and in particular a tax collector;
(b) the active partner in a partnership arrangement in which one or more partners provides capital only and one partner uses the capital so provided to finance commercial, industrial, or other economic activity. See *mudaraba*.

amir al mu'minin

'Commander of the Believers' though often translated 'Commander of the Faithful'. The title was adopted by the second *khalifa*, 'Umar ibn al Khattab, on his election, although it had been used earlier to designate military commanders. From its adoption by 'Umar until the end of the Caliphate it was exclusively reserved for the holder of that office. Its use by a ruler thus implied a claim to the office, whether in a universal sense or in the sense of claiming to be an independent Muslim authority.

Glossary

ansar

'Helpers' or 'adherents'. The term is normally applied to those inhabitants of Madina who supported and assisted the Prophet after his move from Mecca to Medina in 622. In modern times, the term was adopted by the Sudanese Mahdi to describe his followers. The usage is still current.

'aql

Strictly, intellect, intelligence, or reason. For the Shi'a, however, 'aql has been elevated to a primary source of doctrine and law. Thus, the major elements of Shi'a doctrine are explained not only in terms of the revelation and divine command but also in terms of rational and logical deduction. In the law, legal decisions are valid only when they conform to the dictates of logical reasoning.

awqaf

See *waqf*.

bara'a

Strictly, release or exemption from a duty, from an accusation, and from responsibility, etc. The term has acquired a technical meaning in doctrine and law: in the absence of proof to the contrary, the natural presumption is freedom from obligation or liability. The application of this principle clearly provides the maximum possible freedom of action.

batin

The inward or esoteric meaning normally construed in contradistinction to the *zahir*, the outward, exoteric, or literal meaning. The two terms have been applied both in a number of straightforward antitheses and in the more mystical and philosophical aspects of Islam. The adjectival forms are *batini* and *zahiri* respectively.

bida'a, p. bida'

Innovation, i.e. a practice or belief for which there is no precedent in the *Qur'an* or the *Sunna*. The term is frequently applied to practices, concepts, and administrative arrangements which have been adopted from other social, political, and religious systems. The proper definition of what constitutes *bida'* is often problematic, since many such adaptations are fully consistent with the fundamental principles of Islam. Moreover, much of the practice outside the purely religious sphere is in fact innovation as defined above, but has been fully incorporated into the Islamic system.

al birr wa'l taqwa

A Qur'anic term signifying pious goodness, inclusive of acts of piety, combined with and contrasted to fear of God in the sense of being in awe of Him and wishful to please Him.

dar

Normally 'house', but the term is also used, particularly in the plural (*diyar*) to mean an area, region, or country. It is used widely with the technical meaning of a tribal area.

dar al harb

Literally, the house or country of war. Classical Muslim doctrine divides the world into *dar al harb*, i.e. non-Muslim territory, and *dar al islam*, i.e. Muslim territory. The concept became in due course the basis for the Muslim law of nations. *Dar al islam* originally comprised the entire Muslim community wherever it was geographically. Today, the distinction is normally between territories in which the political authority and the law is Muslim and territories where they are not.

dar al islam

Literally, the land of Islam. See *dar al harb*.

da'wa

Originally the invitation addressed to men by God and the Prophet to embrace Islam. Today, the word normally means the activities of missionaries seeking either to convert non-Muslims or to bring Muslims who have strayed back to the true path. Many missionary organizations also have an overt political purpose.

dawla

Government or the domain of politics. The concept comprises all that relates to administrative, political, juridical, financial, and social organization.

din

Religion, but in a wider sense than the normal meaning of the word. Two useful definitions are: 'the corpus of prescriptions which God has promulgated through the voice of His Apostle'; and 'the act of worship, the care to avoid bad and blameworthy deeds, to respect right and justice in social relationships, and to purify the soul and prepare it for the future life; in a word, all the laws whose aim is to bring man near to God'.

din wa dawla

The relationship between the temporal and spiritual. The term is often cited as evidence of the inseparability of 'Church' and 'state' in Islam. A modernist view is that *din* and *dawla* are not identical, but that Islam, which comprehends both, provides the link and is at one and the same time both *din* and *dawla*.

faqih, pl. fuqaha

One who practises *fiqh* (q.v.), a jurisconsult.

Fatimid

An Ismaili Shi'a dynasty in North Africa, and later Egypt, which ruled from 909 to 1171.

fatwa

Opinion of a jurist on a point of law or legal problem. A *fatwa* may deal with a weighty point of law, but may also deal with social issues, e.g. the legality or otherwise of abortion and birth control; with ritual matters, e.g. the permissibility of using stunning devices before the ritual slaughter of cattle; and political issues, e.g. the legitimacy of a ruler.

fiqh

Originally, 'understanding, knowledge, or intelligence', the term has become the technical term for jurisprudence, the science of Muslim law, which covers all aspects of religious, political, and civil life. In practical terms, *fiqh* is the process by which God's law is translated into detailed rules of law and conduct and the application of those rules in varying circumstances. Most Sunni Muslims identify the sources for this process of interpretation as the *Qur'an*, the practice of the Prophet (the *Sunna*), analogy (*qiyas*), and consensus (*ijma*), though some insist upon the right to use independent reasoning (*ijtihad*). See these terms for a fuller definition.

fi sabil Allah

Literally, 'in God's way', or following the true path laid down by God. The term frequently has undertones of fighting, either to defend the Muslim community or to expand it.

hadd, pl. hudud

Literally, 'limits'. The term has acquired a narrow technical meaning: punishments laid down in the *Qur'an* or the *Sunna* for specified crimes. The crimes are theft, armed robbery, illicit sexual relations, slanderous accusation of unchastity, apostasy, and drinking alcohol. In addition punishment for murder is often included although this is a loose usage (see *qisas*).

hadith, pl. ahadith

Tradition of the prophet, being an account of what the Prophet said and did, and of his tacit approval or disapproval of things said or done in his presence. Collectively, the *hadith* record the practice of the Prophet, the *Sunna*. A *hadith* normally consists of two parts: the record of the thing said or done, and a chain of transmitters through the generations from the time of the Prophet to the time of recording in writing. Modern scholarship has shown that many *hadith* are fabrications, but there seems no reason to doubt the genuineness of many others.

hadith qudsi, pl. ahadith qudsiyya

A special type of *hadith* in which the text is believed to contain God's message, though not necessarily God's exact words. As such, they are regarded by many Muslims as binding in the same way as a clear Qur'anic injunction is.

Hanafi

One of the four Sunni schools of theology and law, so named after its founder Abu Hanifi.

Hanbali

One of the four recognized schools of Sunni Islam and the prevalent school in Saudi Arabia. The Hanbalis are the most rigorous of the four schools in terms of the accepted sources of the law and doctrine. They recognize the *Qur'an* and the *Sunna* as legitimate sources, though they take a rather restrictive view of what constitutes a genuine *hadith*. For them, *'ijma'* means the consensus of the Prophet's Companions only and the use of *qiyas* is rigorously circumscribed. However, they insist on the use of *ijtihad*, have developed the concept of public interest as a source of the law and doctrine, and hold that only that which is clearly forbidden in the *Qur'an* and the *Sunna* is illegal. These basic principles collectively give rise to a system which is superficially rigid, authoritarian, and conservative in outlook, but which is in practice remarkably flexible and dynamic.

al harb al qudsi al difa'i

'Holy defensive war.' A principle developed by the Shi'a to deal with the problems inherent in the Shi'a doctrine that only the Imam (i.e. the Hidden Imam after the occultation of the Twelfth Imam) could declare *jihad* (q.v.). The principle empowered the leader of the Shi'a community to declare war in defence of the Shi'a community.

hiyal

In Muslim law, legal devices which were devised in order to circumvent the strict dictates of Muslim law. They have been described as legal devices to achieve results which could not be directly achieved if the letter and spirit of the law were observed. A good example is the use of various forms of double sale in order to get around the prohibition of interest.

ibadat

Strictly, 'acts of devotion' or 'religious observances'. A distinction is regularly drawn between *ibadat* and *mu'amilat*, transactions or conduct. The former comprises the duties and obligations clearly and unambiguously laid upon Muslims by God, including ritual practices. The latter comprises human interpretation of God's will and includes social, political, economic, and administrative regulations and practices. *Ibadat* are by definition immutable, but *mu'amilat* are deemed to be modifiable in the light of changing circumstances. The distinction has been enthusiastically espoused by liberal reformers as justification for change.

Ibadhi

The Ibadhis, or *ibadhiyya*, are a moderate sect of Islam, but are neither Sunni nor Shi'a. Most authorities regard them as an offshoot of the *khawarij* (q.v.), the first Muslim schismatics. The Ibadhis vehemently reject this view. They are moderate in doctrine and practice, and although there are differences over some of the finer points of theology and law, they are practically indistinguishable from the Sunnis. Indeed, they describe themselves as the fifth Sunni school. They reject the Sunni doctrine of the *khilafa*, but the Ibadhi *imam* does not share the infallibility and sinlessness of the Shi'a *imam*.

ihtiyat

Strictly, 'caution'. Though not unknown in Sunni Islam, *ihtiyat* is more a Shi'a concept. When there is a difference of opinion between *mujtahids* on the correct ruling on a particular issue, the rulings of the most eminent *mujtahids* should be examined and the strictest of those rulings adopted.

ijma'

Strictly, consensus. *Ijma'* is one of the recognized sources of the law in both Sunni and Shi'a doctrine, on the basis of a *hadith* to the effect that 'my people will never agree on error'. There has been considerable dissension over the proper identification of those qualified to participate in the consensus. For some, it is the entire Muslim community; for some, the first generation of Muslims only; for some the recognized medieval jurists; and for some it is the recognized scholars of a particular period. For the Shi'a *ijma'* means the consensus of opinion of the ulama of a particular time, but must include — or reflect — the opinion of the Prophet or one of the twelve Imams.

ijtihad

Independent reasoning from first principles. Where a legal problem was not susceptible to resolution by recourse to the traditional sources of the law, suitably qualified individuals were deemed capable of deriving a solution by the use of logic and reason, working from first principles. Most Sunni Muslims believe that the 'Gate of *ijtihad*' was closed in the eleventh century. However, the Hanbalis and the Shi'a have rejected this line of reasoning and the underlying rationale: that the exercise of *ijtihad* was no longer possible once the four schools codified their views on the grounds that there was no one suitably qualified to do so. All modern reform movements insist upon the right to exercise *ijtihad*, although the limits are as varied as the movements.

'ilm al kalam

Normally translated as theology, though this is an approximation. Two useful definitions, both by Muslim scholars, are:

'a science which enables a man to procure the victory of the dogmas and actions laid down by the Legislator of the religion and to refute all opinions contradicting them',
and

'the science which is concerned with firmly establishing religious beliefs by adducing proofs and with banishing doubts'.

imam

For Sunnis, the *imam* is the spiritual leader of the community. However, it is often used interchangeably with *khalifa* (q.v.), and in practice the distinction between spiritual and temporal leadership is blurred. For the Shi'a, the term means one of the twelve designated successors to the Prophet exercising both spiritual and temporal authority. The twelve Imams are sinless, infallible, and designated by God. Today, the term *imam* is regularly applied by both Sunnis and Shi'a to the person appointed to lead the Friday prayer and to preach a sermon during that prayer.

imam al zaman

Strictly, the Imam of the Age. The concept was developed in order to reconcile the Shi'a insistence that there is necessarily always an Imam and the Shi'a doctrine of the occultation, or disappearance, of the twelfth Imam. He, though in occultation, is still mysteriously present as *imam al zaman*. The term Hidden Imam is often used.

imama

The office of the *imam* (q.v.).

iman

Faith or true belief. To be valid, *iman* must comprise three elements: internal conviction, spoken expression, and the performance of the prescribed duties.

ishtira'

Legislative acts by the *umma* or by the state. Some modernists use the term, which they see as synonymous with *tashri'*, to cover legislative acts by the state in respect of matters which they believe are susceptible to continuous modification of the manner in which the general principles set out in the *Qur'an* and the *Sunna* were applied: policy formulation, the conduct of government, administrative matters, taxation, etc. The concept was a further development of the distinction between *ibadat* and *mu'amilat* (q.v.).

Ismailis

The Ismailis, or Seveners, are a Shi'a sect who broke away from the mainstream of the Shi'a over the designation of the Seventh Imam. Originally very extreme in doctrine and practice, but have now become relatively moderate. The Aga Khan is the leader of the main branch of the Ismailis.

istihsan

Literally, choosing for the better, the term is variously translated 'juristic preference' and 'favourable construction'. In dealing with legal issues which are not covered by a clear and incontrovertible authority in the Qur'an, the *hadith*, or *ijma'*, a jurist may avoid reaching a decision on the basis of a strict application of analogical reasoning (*qiyas*, q.v.) where this would result in an unnecessarily harsh or inequitable ruling. Instead, the jurist uses common sense to arrive at the most sensible and equitable decision, provided always he can justify his action by reference to the recognized sources.

istishab

A juristic principle to the effect that a given judicial situation previously existent is held to continue to exist unless and until it can be proved that it no longer exists or has been modified. Thus, for example, the wife of a missing man may not remarry, nor can his estate be distributed until proof of death is established. The principle can also apply to judicial decisions.

jahiliyya

The Age of Ignorance; the Dark Ages. The term is regularly used to mean the pre-Islamic period. However, the meaning has been extended, notably by Mawdudi and Sayyid Qutb, to include the corruptness of Muslim society.

Jamaat-i-Islami

A political party in Pakistan founded by Maududi. It seeks the creation of a genuine Islamic state and has a very conservative view of what this entails.

jihad

Strictly, exertion, though the term is normally translated 'holy war'. The greater *jihad* is exertion directed, individually or collectively, towards the attainment of spiritual and religious perfection. The lesser *jihad* is military action aimed at the expansion of Islam or its defence.

kafir, pl. *kuffar*

Infidel, unbeliever. Those who do not believe in or accept the message of Islam. However, the *ahl al kitab* (i.e. Christians, Jews, and Sabians) are a special category, in that their adherence to their own beliefs is tolerated. Idolators and polytheists do not enjoy any toleration. Nevertheless, the term has acquired pejorative undertones and the term is now generally regarded as an insult (and is frequently used as such).

kanun

A Turkish term derived from the Arabic *qanun* used to describe the regulatory legislation of the political authority of the state which was not deemed to be part of the revealed law. As such it lacks the full divine legitimacy and authority of the revealed law, although such legislation must be in accordance with the basic principles of Islam. See also *siyasa shara'iyya*.

kanun-name

Normally a decree by the Ottoman Sultan providing legal guidance on a particular topic. The term was occasionally extended to include regulations enacted by the vizier and by provincial governors. The fields covered included public law, state organization, taxation, penal law and commercial law, and regulations. See *kanun*.

khalifa

Strictly, a successor or one who comes after. In Sunni Islam the title was applied to the successors to the Prophet's temporal authority over the community. For some the *khalifa* also inherited the Prophet's spiritual authority, though not his prophetic function, but for many spiritual guidance rested with the community as a whole. The normal designation was *khalifat rasul Allah*, successor to the Messenger of God, but this was later modified to *khalifat Allah* (q.v.). A distinction was drawn between the first four *khalifas* and their successors; the latter, having adopted the dynastic principle instead of the earlier elective principle, were less worthy. The Shi'a reject the term and its implications and term the leader of the community the *Imam* (q.v.).

khalifat Allah

A later modification of the position of the *khalifa* in which he assumed the title and functions of vice-regent (or Representative) of God on earth. This change, which is etymologically dubious, implied some degree of divine legitimacy if not designation. Among some modernist schools of thought the term has been applied more widely to the community of believers as a collective vice-regent of God on earth.

khassa

Strictly, special or set apart. The term is used by the Shi'a to distinguish themselves from other Muslims, who are not, in Shi'a eyes, true Muslims.

khawarij

'Those who went out'. The first schismatic group in early Islam, who protested vehemently against proposals to bring to an end the civil war which followed the murder of the third *khalifa*. Loudly protesting that 'judgement belongs to God alone', they withdrew from the army led by Ali and established themselves as a separate group. The *Khawarij* insisted upon the right to depose an *imam* who has deviated, rejected the doctrine of justification by faith without works, and regarded anyone who has committed a mortal sin to be an apostate. The sect broke up into a number of separate groups who ranged from violent extremism to relative moderation.

Glossary

khilafa

The office of the *khalifa* (q.v.).

khums

One fifth of the spoils of war was reserved, on the basis of a verse in the *Qur'an*, for use by 'God and the Apostle, and the near of kin, and the orphans, and the needy, and the wayfarer'. (Q8:41). In Shi'a doctrine, the *khums* is a tax levied at the rate of 20 per cent on net income and profits from specified goods and activities. Half of the sum is regarded as the Imam's share and is paid to the *marja' al taqlid* (q.v.). The remaining half is to be disbursed on the charitable purposes noted above.

madhhab, pl. madhahib

The term used to denote the four Sunni schools of law and doctrine, i.e. the Hanbalis, the Malikis, the Hanafis, and the Shafi'is.

mahdi

The 'rightly guided one' who will bring justice and peace to the world before the end of the world and the Day of Judgement. In Shi'a doctrine, the *mahdi* will be the Hidden Imam who will return to rule the world in justice and peace and will convert all mankind to Shi'a Islam.

marja' al taqlid

Reference point for emulation. In Shi'a doctrine, the term originally meant a jurisprudent whose rulings and actions were to be accepted and followed without question by those less educated. Initially there could be any number of reference points, but in the eighteenth and nineteenth centuries it became customary for leading *mujtahids* to defer to the rulings of the person recognized as the most knowledgeable. This led to the notion that there could be a single *marja' al taqlid*.

maslaha

The public interest. A legal principle based on the maxim that necessity makes prohibited things permissible. This maxim legitimized juridical rulings which were strictly speaking contrary to established doctrine but which were clearly more equitable and more in the public interest than

251

a ruling made on purely doctrinal grounds. There is a clear analogy with *siyasa shara'iyya* (q.v.).

mu'amalat

See *ibadat*.

mudaraba

A partnership arrangement in which one or more partners provide capital but have no other function, and one or more partners puts the capital to productive use in commercial, industrial, or other economic activity. Profit and loss are shared in agreed proportions between the partners. The terms *qard*, *muqarida*, and *qirad* mean much the same.

mufasila

Separation, dissociation, or parting company with someone or something.

mufti

One qualified to issue legal rulings. See *fatwa*. In practice, a *mufti* is often the senior official jurisprudent in a Muslim state.

muhkam

A distinction is drawn between those verses in the *Qur'an* which are clear and unambiguous, *mukham*, and those which are unclear, ambiguous, or allegorical, *mutashabih*. The former is generally held to comprise those verses which contain clear and precise ordinances and statements from which can be inferred the fundamental principles of Islam, in particular the ethical and social teachings. The contents of the *mutashabih* verses require to be interpreted in the light of the principles, ordinances, and statements contained in the *muhkam* verses.

Mujaddid

Literally, a renewer. The term is applied to those who seek a regeneration of the authentic Islam as a response to perceived deviation from the commands of the *Qur'an* and the *Sunna*.

mujahid, pl. mujahidun or mujahidin

One who is actively engaged in *jihad* (q.v.). In practice the term normally connotes someone actively engaged in fighting in defence of Islam. Today it is often the Muslim equivalent of freedom fighter.

mujtahid

One qualified to exercise *ijtihad* (q.v.).

mulk

Royal power. Such power is strictly speaking reserved for God. However, the term acquired temporal and dynastic connotations and was used to describe the Muslim rulers after the *Rashidun* in a manner to suggest that they did not measure up to the standards required.

Mulla

A Persian term which strictly means a learned person or a scholar. It is sometimes used to refer to the lower ranks of the clerical hierarchy in Iran and sometimes to the entire hierarchy.

mu'min, pl. mu'minun or mu'minin

One who believes (in Islam). One who has *iman* (q.v.).

murabaha

Strictly, a means of making a profit. It is an arrangement to provide financing for trading purposes in which a bank buys a commodity and sells it on at an agreed mark up or profit. The system was devised to meet the requirements of classical doctrine and has since been extended to cover a variety of financial transactions, the mark up or profit being described as administrative costs, development charges, etc.

mu'tamid

Authorized agent, representative, etc. The term was used in Muslim Spain to denote provincial governors.

mutashabih

See *muhkam*.

al na'ib al 'amm

In Shi'a doctrine, the general representative or deputy of the Hidden Imam. The term initially referred to the Shi'a ulama collectively, but gave them authority in religious and judicial affairs only. It was later extended to cover political affairs, though not without opposition, and the notion of a single *na'ib* has gained some currency.

al nizam al islami

The Islamic order. A distinction is made between an Islamic order and an Islamic state. The former appears to be a state governed in accordance with the principles of Islam and the revealed law. The latter appears to mean the re-creation of political and social life as enjoyed under the Prophet and the first four *khalifas*.

qadi

Normally translated 'judge'. However, his function is to dispense justice in accordance with the revealed law. Since that law, though theoretically comprehensive, is not in practice comprehensive, the *qadi's* jurisdiction and competence were restricted. In modern times, his jurisdiction has been largely limited to matters of personal status and specialized matters such as inheritance and the administration of *waqf* property and income.

qard

See *mudaraba*.

qirad

See *mudaraba*.

qisas

Retaliation. The principle of an eye for an eye and a tooth for a tooth.

In cases of murder and bodily injury, the perpetrator is subject to an equal injury inflicted on him or her by the injured party or, in the case of murder, the next of kin. There are complex rules governing the manner in which such retaliation is carried out, and the injured party may choose to accept blood money instead.

qiyas

Analogical deduction or analogical reasoning, the fourth source of the law. When the solution to a problem cannot be derived directly from the *Qur'an*, the *Sunna*, or from accepted consensus, the jurist seeks to identify an accepted ruling to a problem which has sufficient similarity to allow the application of the terms, reasoning, and methodology of the accepted ruling to the new problem by a process of analogical reasoning. It is, in fact, a particular form of *ijtihad* (q.v.).

Qur'an

Muslims believe that God spoke to the Prophet Muhammad through the Archangel Gabriel. Muhammad then recited the revelation to his followers. The entire revelation, which took place over a number of years, was later recorded in writing. That record is known as the *Qur'an*, the term being used some seventy times in the *Qur'an* itself. Muslims naturally believe that the *Qur'an* is the Word of God, that it is the last and most perfect of a series of revelations transmitted by God through a series of prophets, and that it contains God's commands to man covering all aspects of man's behaviour. It is therefore the first and primary source of the law.

Rashidun

Properly, *al khulafa' al rashidun*, the rightly guided successors to the Prophet. The term means the first four *khalifas* who all knew the Prophet and were elected by the community. The period of their rule is regarded, like the period of the Prophet's rule, as an exemplar of Muslim society which all Muslims should seek to emulate and re-create.

riba

The taking of interest, usury. *Riba* is forbidden in Muslim law, but there has been considerable argument about the precise meaning, with definitions ranging from the taking of any interest to the imposition of excessive rates of interest.

ribh, pl. *arbah*

Legitimate profit.

Rustamid

An Ibadhi dynasty based on Tahert in Algeria which ruled from 776 to 908.

Safavid

The most famous and glorious of the native Persian dynasties which ruled the Persian Empire from 1502 to 1736. The first Safavid Shah made Shi'a Islam the state religion.

al salaf

Also *al salaf al salih*. 'The pious elders'. The term has come to mean the first generation of Muslims who are generally held by Sunnis to have a special understanding of Islam and its principles and its practices because of their close association with the Prophet.

salafiyya

A term frequently adopted by reformers and reformist movements which called for a return to the principles and practices of the *salaf*.

santri

See *abangan*.

Shafi'i

One of the four recognized Sunni schools of law and doctrine. Al Shafi'i, after whom the school is named is generally regarded as the architect of the classical structure of theology, law, and doctrine.

shari'a

The term normally used to refer to Muslim law, i.e. the divinely revealed law. However, there is considerable disagreement over the precise definition. For some, it consists only of legislation clearly laid down in the *Qur'an* and the *Sunna* together with the norms and principles set out therein. For most Muslims it consists of the corpus of detailed law set out in the codices of the recognized schools. Since the *shari'a* is immutable and eternally valid, the latter definition has led to a number of casuistic arguments to permit the making of new positive law to cover situations not covered in the *shari'a*.

Shi'a

Strictly *shi'at Ali*, the party of Ali, i.e. those who believed that Ali was the rightful successor to the Prophet. Although originally a purely political movement, Shi'a Islam developed a distinct theological and doctrinal belief system. Strictly, the term embraces a number of sects, but is habitually used to denote only one of them: that prevalent in Iran.

shura

Consultation. Classical theory held that a ruler should consult the leaders of the community who had a duty to give advice. Modernists have translated the concept into a form of quasi-democratic assembly, the Majlis al Shura, which may be appointed, elected, or a combination of the two.

siyar

The plural of *sira*, conduct or way of behaviour. The term has been used since the eighth century to denote the conduct of the Muslim state in its relations with other states and communities. It is thus both international relations and international law as normally understood in the West.

siyasa shara'iyya

Government in accordance with the revealed law. The principle argued that the political authority had the prerogative of supplementing the law by issuing administrative regulations and other measures, provided that such regulations and measures were clearly consistent with the basic principles of Islam. The political authority had a duty to protect the public interest in the process of giving effect to the general purposes of God for the Muslim society. He therefore had an overriding discretion to decide how best to achieve these two aims.

Glossary

sufi

The name given to Muslim mystics. The *sufi* seeks to attain knowledge of God by a process of inner purification, often combined with mediation, asceticism, and the fervent practice of worship. *Sufis* developed the concept of the *tariqa* (q.v.) as a system of communal worship, complete with special rites, initiation ceremonies, and a hierarchical membership.

sunna

Habitual practice or customary procedure. Initially, the term meant the habitual practice of Muslims in a particular area, but was later applied more restrictively to mean the practice of the Prophet, inclusive of sayings and actions, as recorded in the *hadith* (q.v.). The *Sunna* of the Prophet is one of the four sources of the law. For the Shi'a the *Sunna* means the sayings and actions of the Prophet and of the twelve Imams.

Sunni

'Orthodox' Muslims. Those who accept the legitimacy of the line of *khalifas* who succeeded the Prophet.

Sura

The name given to the individual chapters of the *Qur'an*.

tafsir

Commentary or interpretation, particularly of the *Qur'an*. Commentaries normally comprise a detailed examination of the text, together with an interpretation of the precise signification of the text.

Takfir wa Hijra

The name applied to an extremist offshoot of the Muslim Brotherhood in Egypt, who regard all society as un-Islamic and who believed that true Muslims (i.e. themselves) must separate themselves spiritually and socially from the society of unbelievers. They sought a strict re-creation of the Muslim community under the Prophet and the first four *khalifas* to be achieved by following the example of the prophet in the early Muslim period.

258

takhayyur

Also *takhyir*. An extension of *talfiq* (q.v.) which allowed a Muslim to chose between the rulings of all four Sunni schools on any point of doctrine, law, or ritual. Some modernists have taken it further and see *takhayyur* as a means of developing a unified synthesis between the four schools by means of a systematic comparison between them.

talfiq

The principle that a judge could choose, in any particular case, that interpretation of the law which best suited the circumstances, whether it came from his own school or another.

taqiyya

Strictly, caution, though often translated as religious dissimulation. It means a dispensation from the requirements of religion, but is permissible only when there is an overwhelming danger of unacceptable loss of property or life, and when there is no harm to religion (undefined). It is understandably more characteristic of the Shi'a and has often been invoked for less than justifiable reasons.

taqlid

Imitation or emulation. This principle requires jurists to adopt or follow the rulings, utterances, and actions of predecessors without question. The Shi'a hold that every layman is bound to follow the rulings and practice of a qualified religious scholar who becomes the *marja' al taqlid* (q.v.), the reference point for emulation. *Taqlid* between *mujtahids* was theoretically forbidden. Emulation of a dead person was not acceptable.

tariqa

Originally, the system of rituals and communal practices developed by the *sufis* (q.v.). The term has popularly come to mean the *sufi* orders or confraternities. Some *tariqas* play an important role in the provision of social welfare in addition to their purely religious role.

tashri'

See *ishtira'*.

tawhid

The oneness, unity, and uniqueness of God, epitomized in the first half of the profession of faith: there is no God but God. This apparently simple proposition has been much discussed by theologians and rendered more complex by consideration of such questions as whether the unity is internal or external, whether it means that God has no partner, whether it means that only God has real or absolute existence, etc.

ta'zir

Strictly, deterrence. The term describes those punishments for transgression of the law which were not prescribed in the *Qur'an* and were therefore left to the discretion of the judge. Hence, discretionary punishment, whose purpose was corrective, as distinct from the *hadd* (q.v.) punishments which were retributive.

ulama, sing. *'alim*

People of learning, scholars. More narrowly, the term is normally applied to those who are learned in Muslim theology, doctrine, law, etc.

Umayyad

The first Muslim dynasty, which ruled from 661 to 750 AD.

umma

The entire Muslim community.

usul al fiqh

The roots or sources of Muslim jurisprudence. For Sunni Muslims these are the *Qur'an*, the practice of the Prophet (the *Sunna*), consensus (*ijma'*), and analogy (*qiyas*). Some authorities also insist that independent reasoning (*ijtihad*) should be included. For Shi'a Muslims, the recognized sources are the *Qur'an*, the *Sunna* (inclusive of the practice of the twelve Imams), *ijma'* (with a somewhat different interpretation of the term), and reason (*'aql*).

'uzla

Retirement, separation, isolation, or segregation.

velayat-i-faqih

The Persian version of *wilayat al faqih* (q.v.).

Wafd Party

A major Egyptian political party established after the First World War. Its primary aims were the removal of British influence, both direct and indirect, in Egypt.

Wahhabis

The usual, though erroneous, Western name for the followers of the doctrines of Muhammad ibn Abdul Wahhab. They dislike the term and call themselves *muwahhidun* (unitarians). They are adherents of the Hanbali school of doctrine and law, but lay great stress on the oneness and uniqueness of God and eschew all innovations which can in any way be seen as derogating from this cardinal article of faith.

waqf pl. awqaf

A charitable trust. One accepted definition is: the detention of the corpus from the ownership of any person and the gift of its usufruct or income either presently or in the future to some charitable purpose. The income generated by *waqf* property may be applied to a specified charitable purpose from the establishment of the *waqf*. It may also be reserved for the benefit of a specified person or group of persons and their descendants in perpetuity, subject to the proviso that the income shall be devoted to a particular charitable purpose if and when the line of descent dies out. Declaration of property as *waqf* for a limited period of time is not permitted: it must be in perpetuity.

watan

Homeland, country, state.

wilayat al faqih

Strictly, the guardianship, or governance, of the jurisconsult. The term, as used by Ayatollah Khomeini, is a political philosophy. For a Muslim state to be a truly Muslim state, the government must act in accordance with God's will and His commands. Since the jurisconsults are best qualified to interpret that will and those commands, they are clearly those best qualified to be the political authority. Furthermore, if a single *faqih* is clearly pre-eminent and recognized as such by his peers, he becomes the sole and supreme political authority, irrespective of the constitutional structure.

zahir

See *batin*.

Zaidi

A moderate Shi'a sect which has been predominant in the Yemen for many centuries.

zakat

Strictly, 'alms-giving', 'charity' or voluntary donations. The law requires that everyone should devote a fixed proportion of specified assets to charity. The *Qur'an* defines the recipients as the poor, the needy, those entrusted with the collection and distribution of the alms, those who will become converts, the emancipation of slaves, travellers, debtors, and those who fight in God's cause. Originally, donors distributed *zakat* privately, but it became a form of compulsory tax payable to the Treasury who would then arrange distribution. *Zakat* was of course a minimum payment and devout Muslims were encouraged to make additional payments for charitable purposes. It is clear from the Arabic root from which the term derives that there was a large element of purification in the payment of *zakat*.

Zubayrid

A short-lived separatist state ruled by Abdullah ibn al Zubayr who revolted against the second Umayyad *khalifa* set up his own state in Iraq.

Biographical Notes on Major Historical Figures

Abduh, Muhammad (1849–1905)

Generally regarded as the father of Egyptian modernism. After a period of collaboration with Jamal al Din al Afghani (q.v.) during which he sought to encourage a reformist, liberal interpretation of Islam, he entered the Egyptian legal service where he rose to be Mufti of Egypt. Although in his official capacity as Mufti he was bound to rule in accordance with the prevailing school of law in Egypt, he took a much more eclectic approach in his private legal rulings and in his writings. His views are summarized in Chapter 7.

Abu Bakr (c.570–634)

The first *khalifa*. Little is known about his life before his conversion to Islam, but he rose to prominence as the leading member of the Muslim community after the Prophet and acted as the Prophet's chief adviser. His daughter A'isha was the Prophet's third and favourite wife. He was responsible for setting in train the rapid expansion of the Muslim domains. He is reputed to have lived a life of great simplicity both before and after his election as *khalifa*, rejecting wealth, pomp, and pretension.

al Afghani, Jamal al Din (1838/9–97)

A vigorous proponent of pan-Islam and anti-colonialism, who preached the necessity of revival and reform. His objective was a single and united Caliphate comprising all Muslim countries which could resist European attempts to interfere. Although well versed in Muslim theology and doctrine, he wrote little, apart from his contributions to newspapers and journals. With Muhammad Abduh he established a weekly journal, *al 'urwat al wuthqa* (the Indissoluble Bond) in 1884, in which he disseminated his political and pan-Islamic ideas.

Ali (c.598–660)

Ali ibn Abi Talib was the Prophet's cousin and son-in-law and the fourth *khalifa*, ruling from 656 until his death. Ali is important less for his exploits than for the fact that controversy over his position in the early community led to the major split between the Sunnis and the Shi'a. The latter believe that Ali was divinely appointed as the rightful successor to the prophet and that, therefore, the first three *khalifas* were usurpers.

Ansari, Shaikh Murtaza (1799–1864)

Shaikh Murtaza Ansari was famous for his memory, his innovative teaching methods, the speed with which he dealt with problems, and his upright character. His most important contribution to developments in the principles of jurisprudence was his four principles for dealing with cases in which doubt existed. (See Chapter 2 — Shi'a legal theory — for details). He became sole *marja' al taqlid* in 1850.

al Ash'ari, Abu al Hasan (873–935)

A moderate theologian, originally of the rationalist school of thought, who subsequently adopted the mainstream Sunni orthodox views. However, he retained a measure of rationality and developed a thesis which provided rational arguments in support of orthodox theology.

Averroes

See Ibn Rushd.

dan Fodio, Uthman (1754–1817)

Uthman dan Fodio was a member of a family of Fulai scholars in the independent Husa kingdom of Gobir. He led a revivalist movement in northern Nigeria and parts of the Sudan and by 1809 had established a large Muslim empire which later became the Muslim Sultanate of Sokoto in northern Nigeria.

al Dawani, Muhammad ibn As'ad Jalal al Din (1427–1501)

Jalal al Din al Dawani studied in Shiraz, and after holding a number of official positions became *qadi* of Fars. He wrote numerous commentaries and philosophic works, but his best-known work, known as *Akhlaq-i Jalali*, is a treatise on ethics, economics, and politics. (See Chapter 3 — Jalal al Din Dawani and Fadhl Allah Khunji — for details.)

Hasan al Banna (1906–49)

The founder and first General Guide of the Muslim Brotherhood. He began to develop his thesis that the ills afflicting the Muslim society could only be cured by a return to true Islam while studying at a teacher-training college in Cairo. He was not, however, a rigid traditionalist, but rather a reformer who saw the need to reconcile Islam and modern life. He also understood the need to cater for the material needs of his followers as well as their spiritual needs.

Ibn Khaldun (1332–1406)

Wali al Din Abdul Rahman ibn Muhammad Ibn Khaldun was a noted Muslim historian, sociologist, and philosopher. He was born in Tunis, where he completed his early studies, but then passed some twenty-three years in further studies and political adventurism in a number of Muslim states. Thereafter, he returned to the life of a scholar, initially in Tlemcen, but later in Cairo. His most famous work is his *Muqaddima* — an introduction to his universal history in which he developed his study of human civilization and social facts in a scientific manner. He also set out his theory of state formation and decay which remains valid today. (See Chapter 3 — Ibn Khaldun — for details.)

Ibn Rushd (1126–98)

Ibn Rushd was born in Cordova into an important Muslim family: both his father and his grandfather had been *qadis*. He was a scholar of Qur'anic sciences and of the natural sciences (physics, medicine, biology, and astronomy), and was also a philosopher and theologian. He is better known in the West as Averroes, and is justly famed for his medical and philosophic writing. Some see him as the last great Sunni speculative philosopher.

Ibn Taymiyya (1263–1328)

Taqi al Din Ahmad Ibn Taymiyya was a major theologian and jurisconsult of the Hanbali school who spent much of his life in prison or under house-arrest because of his uncompromising views. He sought to integrate and balance tradition, reason, and free will, and might be defined as a conservative reformer. (See Chapter 3 — Ibn Taymiyya — for details.)

Iqbal, Muhammad (1875–1938)

Muhammad Iqbal was a major influence on Muslim thought in the Indo-Pakistan subcontinent. After a traditional Islamic education, he pursued further education at Cambridge and Munich Universities, obtaining a PhD from the latter in 1907. He was a poet, a mystic, and a philosopher who sought to reconcile Muslim thought and Western philosophy and science.

He was also the intellectual founder of Pakistan. (See Chapter 6 — Muhammad Iqbal: the reconstruction of the theory — for details.)

Khan, Sir Sayyid Ahmad (1817–98)

Sir Sayyid Ahmad Khan was an educational reformer and the founder of Islamic modernism in British India. He was born in Delhi and entered the service of the East India Company following the death of his father in 1838. Following the Indian Mutiny in 1857, he sought to reconcile the British and the Indian Muslims. The essence of his theology and political philosophy was that the Work of God (i.e. Nature and its fixed laws) is identical with the Word of God (i.e. the *Qur'an*), a view which attracted fierce condemnation. (See Chapter 6 — Sir Sayyid Ahmad Khan: speculative rationalism — for details.)

Khunji, Fadhl Allah ibn Ruzbihan (1455–1521)

Fadhl Allah Khunji was a Persian religious and political scholar who was born in Shiraz, but who spent much of his life in the eastern provinces of the Uzbek empire. He wrote a number of treatises on a wide range of topics, but is perhaps best known for his *suluk al muluk* (The ways of kings), the main purpose of which was to explain to the ruler what his rights, duties, and functions were and to identify their bases. (See Chapter 3 — Jalal al Din Dawani and Fadhl Allah Khunji — for details.)

al Mahdi, Muhammad Ahmad ibn Abdullah (1844–85)

A Sudanese preacher who called for a return to early Islam in accordance with the *Qur'an* and the *Sunna*. In 1881 he announced that he had been divinely appointed the *mahdi*. By 1885 he and his followers were able to establish a short-lived Mahdist state. His descendants are still important political and religious figures in the Sudan.

Maududi, Abul A'la (1903–79)

Abul A'la Maududi was a journalist, a political activist, and a scholar of conservative bent. A prolific writer whose world view of Islam led him to reject both the concept of a secular and united independent India and the proposal for a separate Muslim Pakistan. Nevertheless, he paradoxically founded the Jamaat-i-Islami, which has become a conventional political party in Pakistan, and participated in the early ideological and constitutional debates. (See Chapter 6 — Abul A'la Maududi: conservative orthodoxy triumphant — for details.)

al Mawardi (*c.*972–1058)

Abu al Hasan Ali ibn Muhammad ibn Habib al Mawardi was a Sunni jurist, theorist on public administration, and moralist. He was born in Basra and, after a period of teaching in Basra and Baghdad, served as a *qadi* in Nishapur. He then returned to Baghdad where he acted as a juridical adviser at the court of the *khalifa*. His most celebrated book is the *kitab al ahkam al sultaniyya* (Book of the Principles of Government) in which he set out his theory of government, together with the rights and duties of the ruler, and a detailed exposition of the rules of delegated authority.

Mu'awiya (d. 680)

Mu'awiya ibn Abu Sufyan was born in the first decade of the seventh century and became a major influence in the merchant community in Mecca, under the tutelage of his father. He converted to Islam about 630 and became secretary to the Prophet. Following the conquest of Syria, in which he played an active part, he became governor of Damascus, and, in due course, governor of Syria. He led an ultimately successful revolt against Ali (q.v.) and as fifth *khalifa* was the founder of the Umayyad dynasty.

Muhammad ibn Abdul Wahhab (1703–92)

Muhammad ibn Abdul Wahhab was born in Central Arabia into a family of Hanbali teachers. He studied in Mecca and Medina and after some years of travel returned to his homeland, where he called upon the people to purify the faith of popular practices and return to a strict adherence to the *Qur'an* and the *Sunna*. Out of his teaching grew the movement popularly called the Wahhabi movement. Its followers dislike the term intensely, preferring to be known as the *muwahhidun* (often translated as unitarians).

Qutb, Sayyid (1906–66)

Sayyid Qutb was born in a small village in the Assiut district of Egypt, but his family moved while he was still a child to Helwan, a suburb of Cairo. He trained as a teacher, completing his studies in 1933, and after a spell as a lecturer he became an Inspector of Schools. While serving in this capacity he visited the US, an experience which seems to have made a great impression on him. Shortly after he returned to Egypt he joined the Muslim Brotherhood and soon became its leading ideologue. He was arrested in 1954 along with other Brotherhood leaders and tried for seeking to overthrow the state. He was sentenced to fifteen years' hard labour and remained in prison until 1964, when he was released, only to be re-arrested on charges of conspiring to assassinate the Egyptian President and overthrow the government. He was sentenced to death and the sentence was carried out in August 1966. Apart from his commentary on the *Qur'an*, he wrote a number of books, of which the best known are *Social Justice in Islam* and *Milestones*. (See Chapter 7 — Sayyid Qutb: radical ideologue and the politics of despair — for details.)

Ridha, Rashid (1865–1935)

Muhammad Rashid Ridha, a Syrian who went to Egypt to study, was a disciple of Muhammad Abduh, though he later came to follow a conservative orthodox line which emphasized the importance of basing a rejuvenated Islam on the faith and practice of the Prophet and his immediate Companions (the *salaf* or the pious elders). His followers adopted the name *salafiyya* for this reason. He founded a journal, *al manar* (The Lighthouse) in 1898, in which he published much of the writing of Muhammad Abduh (q.v.) and expounded his own increasingly conservative ideas. (See Chapter 7 — Rashid Ridha: pragmatic conservatism — for details.)

al Sarakhsi (d. 1090)

Shams al A'imma Abu Bakr Muhammad bin Ahmad al Sarakhsi was an important jurisprudent, though little is known of his life. He is principally known for his treatise on jurisprudence and for his commentary on Shaybani's (q.v.) treatise on international law.

Shah Wali Allah (1703–62)

One of the early Indian Muslim reformers who sought with some success to reintegrate the socio-economic and religio-ethical structure of Islam. At the age of sixteen, he succeeded his father as principal of a religious college in Delhi. In his forties he made the pilgrimage to Mecca and stayed on for some months to study. On his return to Delhi, he resumed his teaching activities and wrote voluminously. In both his theological and sociopolitical thinking he was a conciliator and compromiser. (See Chapter 6 — Shah Wali Allah: orthodoxy, reconciliation, and reform — for details.)

Shariati, Ali (1933–77)

Dr Ali Shariati studied at Mashad University and the Sorbonne, where he obtained a PhD in sociology and Islamic studies. He then returned to Iran where his socialist leanings drew the wrath of the Shah's government and he was imprisoned in 1973. In 1975 he was released and allowed to move to the UK, where he died in 1977.

al Shaybani (750–804)

Abu Abdullah Muhammad ibn al Hasan al Shaybani was born at al Wasit, though he spent his early years and much of his later life in Kufa as a teacher and jurist. His major contribution was his treatise on the Muslim law of nations, the first attempt to set out systematically the Muslim theory of international law and international relations. (See Chapter 4 — International Law in Islam — for details.)

Suggestions for Further Reading

I have chosen not to provide a bibliography for this book since this will hardly assist the general reader. Instead, I list below a number of books which anyone wishing to pursue a particular subject will find useful. The literature is vast and any listing as short as this one is bound to be very selective. Only a few of my favourite volumes have been noted, and the omission of a particular author or a particular book should not be taken as a mark of disapproval.

H.A.R. Gibb, *Islam: An Historical Survey*, Oxford: Oxford University Press, 1975, originally published in 1949 under the title *Mohammedanism*), is still one of the best conventional introductions to Islam. Fazlur Rahman, *Islam*, 2nd edn, Chicago: University of Chicago Press, 1979 is a good example of the modernist Muslim approach written by a leading Pakistani Muslim thinker and teacher. Fazlur Rahman, *Islam and Modernity*, Chicago: University of Chicago Press, 1982 is an interesting though sometimes provocative example of speculative modernism. Malise Ruthven, *Islam in the World*, Harmondsworth: Penguin Books, 1984 is a very readable survey written by a journalist who has specialized in Middle East Affairs. These books all touch on Shi'a Islam, but their coverage is necessarily limited. A valuable survey of Shi'a Islam is Moojan Momen, *An Introduction to Shi'i Islam*, New Haven and London: Yale University Press, 1985, and two useful expositions of Shi'a beliefs written by a leading Shi'a scholar are Muhammad Rida al-Muzaffar, *The Faith of Shi'a Islam*, trans. various, London: The Muhammadi Trust, 1982 and *The Beliefs of the Shi'ite School*, trans. S.M.S. Haidar, London: The Islamic Seminary, 1985. Roy Mottahedeh, *The Mantle of the Prophet*, New York: Simon and Schuster, 1985 provides a fascinating insight into religion and politics in Iran.

Noel J. Coulson, *A History of Islamic Law*, Edinburgh: Edinburgh University Press, 1978 is a concise but comprehensive introduction to Islamic law. Majid Khadduri and Herbert J. Liebesney (eds) *Law in the Middle East, Vol. I: Origin and Development of Islamic Law*, Washington, DC: Middle East Institute, 1955 usefully complements Coulson. Two useful if conservative interpretations of what Islamic law requires of Muslims are Abdur Rahman I Doi, *Shari'ah: The Islamic Law*, London: Ta Ha Publishers, 1984, and Yusuf al-Qaradawi, *The Lawful and the Prohibited in Islam*, trans. Kamal El-Helbawy, M. Moinuddin Siddiqui and Syed Shukri, London:

Shorouk International (UK) Ltd, 1985 (previously published by American Trust Publications, Indianapolis).

Most of the books already listed cover political theory and practice, and international law and international relations. A more extended treatment of politics in the Middle East will be found in Hamid Enayat, *Modern Islamic Political Thought*, London: Macmillan, 1982 and Albert Hourani, *Arabic Thought in the Liberal Age, 1798–1939*, London, New York, and Toronto: Oxford University Press, 1962. Political thought in the Indo-Pakistan subcontinent is well covered in E.I.J. Rosenthal, *Islam in the Modern National State*, Cambridge: Cambridge University Press, 1965, and Aziz Ahmad, *Islamic Modernism in India and Pakistan (1857–1964)*, Oxford: Oxford University Press, 1967. Useful case studies of specific countries will be found in James P. Piscatori (ed.) *Islam in the Political Process*, Cambridge: Cambridge University Press, 1983, and John L. Esposito (ed.) *Islam in Asia*, New York and Oxford: Oxford University Press, 1987. The theory of international relations and law is covered with magisterial authority in Majid Khadduri, *War and Peace in the Law of Islam*, Baltimore: The Johns Hopkins Press, 1955, and in Majid Khadduri, *The Islamic Law of Nations: Shaybani's Siyar*, Baltimore: The Johns Hopkins Press, 1966. James P. Piscatori, *Islam in a World of Nation-States*, Cambridge: Cambridge University Press, 1986 deals with Islam and nationalism and the nation-state, while Adeed Dawisha (ed.) *Islam in Foreign Policy*, Cambridge: Cambridge University Press, 1983 contains a number of useful case studies illustrating the practice.

Islamic economics is a difficult subject since it is still relatively new. However, Khurshid Ahmad (ed.) *Studies in Islamic Economics*, Leicester: The Islamic Foundation, 1980 is a useful compilation of monographs, and M.A. Mannen, *Islamic Economics: Theory and Practice*, new and revised edn, Sevenoaks: Hodder & Stoughton, 1986 is a detailed and comprehensive textbook. M. Rodinson, *Islam and Capitalism*, trans. Brian Pearce, Harmondsworth: Penguin Books, 1977 is a readable account of the historical experience written by a prominent French left-wing thinker.

John O. Voll, *Islam: Continuity and Change in the Modern World*, Boulder and Harlow: Westview Press and Longman, 1982 provides a comprehensive overview of the history of revivalist/fundamentalist movements. Richard P. Mitchell, *The Society of the Muslim Brothers*, London: Oxford University Press, 1969 remains a standard text on the subject, while Gilles Keppel, *The Prophet and the Pharaoh*, trans. Jon Rothschild, London: Al Saqi Books, 1985 is a valuable study of more recent Muslim extremism in Egypt. Among Sayyid Qutb's major works, two are particularly relevant: *Social Justice in Islam*, trans. John B Hardie, Washington, DC: American Council of Learned Societies, 1953 and *Milestones*, trans. S. Badrul Hasan, Karachi: International Islamic Publishers, 1981. The first is well done, but the second is a poor translation. Johannes J.G. Jansen, *The Neglected Duty*, London: Macmillan, 1986 includes a meticulous translation of the major work by Muhammad Abdul Salam Faraj. Much of Maududi's output is now available in translation. Perhaps the most useful is *Islamic Law and Constitution*, trans. and ed. Khurshid Ahmad, 8th edn, Lahore: Islamic Publications, 1983, but *A Short History of the Revivalist Movement in Islam*, trans. Al Ash'ari, 2nd revised edn, Lahore: Islamic Publications, 1972 is an interesting monograph. Finally, Khomeini's political philosophy will be found in *Islam and Revolution*, trans. Hamid Algar, London: KPI, 1985.

Index